D0018078

Reflections
for Ragamuffins

Reflections for Ragamuffins

DAILY DEVOTIONS FROM THE WRITINGS
OF BRENNAN MANNING

BRENNAN MANNING
EDITED BY ANN MCMATH WEINHEIMER

HarperSanFrancisco
A Division of HarperCollins*Publishers*

FIRST EDITION

Library of Congress Cataloging-in-Publication Data
Manning, Brennan.
       Reflections for Ragamuffins: daily devotions from the Writings of
       Brennan Manning / Brennan Manning. Ann McMath
       Weinheimer, editor.—1ˢᵗ ed.
Includes bibliographical references and index.
ISBN 0-06-065457-0 (pbk.)
1. Devotional calendars. I. Weinheimer, Ann McMath. II. Title.
BV4811.M297   1997
242'.2—dc21   97-46167

05 RRD H 20 19 18 17

For Paul Sheldon and a friendship
that comes along once in a lifetime.

Contents

A WORD BEFORE

Noah Webster defines *ragamuffin* as a "street urchin." The biblical definition of *ragamuffin* is much more profound, as a brief investigation of Scripture will show.

Ambling down the corridors of salvation-history, we notice that God has ever shown a special affection for the poor and lowly, the humble of heart. From the moment the theocracy was shaped on Mount Sinai, Yahweh led Israel to understand that he expected something more from his chosen people than the mere external observance of the Mosaic Law. As the years passed, the Israelites gradually became aware that it was the ragamuffins (the *anawim*—literally, "the little poor ones"—as they were called in Hebrew) who were the special objects of God's tenderness and compassion.

At first the term *ragamuffin* bore only a sociological or economic meaning. The ragamuffins were the homeless, the landless, the street urchins, the dispossessed, whom God would one day restore to prosperity. Later, through the influence of the prophet Isaiah, the term took on a spiritual sense of tremendous depth. Isaiah's ministry began with a vision of God "seated on a high and lofty throne surrounded by a choir of angels chanting 'holy, holy, holy is the Lord of hosts!'" The vision burned on his soul an indelible impression: God is *totaliter aliter*, Totally Other. Human feelings could not touch him, and human thought could not contain him. As Charles de Foucauld learned at the hour of his conversion, "God is so great that there is an infinite distance between God and all that is not God."

While the idea of mystery remains an embarrassment to many a modern mind, it is the heartbeat of the prophets and saints of every era. They know that God can and will do anything so long as men and women are humble enough to acknowledge their need of him.

The later prophets, taking their cue from Isaiah, called these simple, humble people the *anawim* or, in contemporary idiom, "ragamuffins." This is how the vocabulary of poverty changed from having an economic meaning to having a spiritual one. The basis of the transfer was the Isaian principle: God works his divine effects only when persons acknowledge human insufficiency (or, in AA language, human powerlessness). God's true friends felt themselves to be really poor before him. They sensed that the most fundamental act of religion was that they owed their life and being to Another. Dependence and loving surrender were the very breath of their life. The ragamuffins were the poor in spirit, those who were little in their own sight, those who were conscious of their nakedness and poverty before God and who thus cast themselves without reservation on his mercy.

This was the spirit that God looked for in his people; it is the only attitude that rings true to human creaturehood. It compounds a sense of personal powerlessness with unfailing confidence in the love of God and total surrender to the guidance of his will. The ragamuffins were indeed the remnant, the true Israel to whom the messianic promises had been made.

When at last the Son of God drew aside the curtain of eternity and stepped into human history at Bethlehem, those who came forward to meet him were the truly poor in spirit: Joseph, Zachariah and Elizabeth, Simeon and Anna, the shepherds and the Magi. These formed his court, the holy ragamuffin remnant promised by the prophets. But long before, God's gaze had rested with special affection on Mary, the young Jewish woman of Nazareth. No one was so truly poor in spirit, so keenly conscious of need for him, so perfectly surrendered to his will. That is why he chose her to be the mother of the Messiah—the least and lowliest in the long line of ragamuffins.

Of course, when Jesus began his prophetic ministry, he immediately identified the ragamuffin spirit with himself: "Learn from me, for I am gentle and humble of heart." And the first group called to the Kingdom? "Blessed are the ragamuffins; the reign of God is theirs."

Reflections for Ragamuffins is a series of meditations written over a span of twenty-two years—years of joy and suffering, fidelity and infidelity, intense commitment and serious relapses, muddling and struggling to be faithful to Jesus. I share these reflections with a specific purpose in mind: not to transmit inspiring thoughts, but to awaken, revive, and rekindle radical, ruthless trust in the God bodied forth in the carpenter from Nazareth.

I firmly believe that the splendor of a human heart that trusts it is unconditionally loved gives God more pleasure and causes him more delight than the most magnificent cathedral ever erected or the most thunderous organ ever played.

Ruthless trust in a ragamuffin today is a rare and precious thing because it often demands a degree of courage that borders on the heroic. When the shadow of Jesus' cross falls upon lives in the form of failure, sorrow, rejection, abandonment, unemployment, loneliness, depression, the loss of a loved one; when we are deaf to everything but the shriek of our own pain; when the world around us suddenly seems to be a hostile, menacing place, we may well cry out in anguish, "How could a loving God permit this to happen?" And the seed of distrust is sown, plunging us into a moment of choice: Will we turn away from God, or will we turn toward him even though the darkness hides him from our sight? To choose the light of God in the dark night of despair is an act of heroic courage.

I continue to confront this choice in the darkest, loneliest, and most desolate moments of my life. By inviting you to join me on this ragamuffin journey, I ask of you no more than I ask of myself: to trust in God's love no matter what happens to us.

BRENNAN MANNING, NEW ORLEANS
SEPTEMBER 24, 1997

GOD'S LOVE

————— 🈯 —————

God's love is based on nothing, and the fact that it is based on nothing makes us secure. Were it based on anything we do, and that "anything" were to collapse, then God's love would crumble as well. But with the God of Jesus no such thing can possibly happen. People who realize this can live freely and to the fullest. Remember Atlas, who carries the whole world? We have Christian Atlases who mistakenly carry the burden of trying to deserve God's love. Even the mere watching of this lifestyle is depressing. I'd like to say to Atlas: "Put that globe down and dance on it. That's why God made it." And to these weary Christian Atlases: "Lay down your load and build your life on God's love." We don't have to earn this love; neither do we have to support it. It is a free gift. Jesus calls out: "Come to me, all you Atlases who are weary and find life burdensome, and I will refresh you."

> The Lord appeared to us in the past, saying:
> "I have loved you with an everlasting love;
> I have drawn you with loving-kindness."
>
> JEREMIAH 31:3

THE INCARNATION OF COMPASSION

The numerous physical healings performed by Jesus to alleviate human suffering are only a hint of the anguish in the heart of God's Son for wounded humanity. His compassion surges from the bowels of his being and operates on a level that escapes human imitation. Jesus resonated with the depths of human sorrow. He became lost with the lost, hungry with the hungry, and thirsty with the thirsty. On the cross he journeyed to the far reaches of loneliness so that he could be lonely with those who are lonely and rob loneliness of its killing power by sharing it himself.

He did then and he does now. Jesus vibrates to the hope and fear, the celebrations and desolations of each of us. He is the incarnation of the compassion of the Father. The fifteenth-century mystic Meister Eckhart wrote, "You may call God love, you may call God goodness, but the best name for God is compassion." When we speak of Jesus Christ as Emmanuel, God with us, we are saying that the greatest lover in history knows what hurts us. Jesus reveals a God who is not indifferent to human agony, a God who fully embraces the human condition and plunges into the thick of our human struggle.

> Jesus called his disciples to him and said, "I have compassion for these people; they have already been with me three days and have nothing to eat. I do not want to send them away hungry, or they may collapse on the way."

MATTHEW 15:32

————[✠]————

Whenen God introduces creative tension into our lives by calling us to break camp, abandon the security and comfort of the status quo, and embark in perilous freedom on a new exodus, our insecurity and procrastination may focus only on the darker implications of the challenge and plunge us anew into unhealthy guilt. Stubbornly to stand still when the Lord is clearly challenging us to growth is hardheartedness, infidelity, and a dangerous lack of trust. But to start trekking across the desert impulsively without the guidance of the cloud and the fire is reckless folly. When God's call is not clarified and the inner voice remains indistinct, our restlessness and interior disquiet may be signaling a new exodus into greater openness, vulnerability, and compassion, a deeper purity of heart, a transformed mind and spirit. The landscape of the American church is littered with burned-out bodies and abortive ministries born of unhealthy guilt and fear of resisting God's will.

Who will acquit us from guilt? Who will free us from the bondage of projectionism, perfectionism, and moralism? Who will rewrite the script? Thanks be to God for Jesus Christ our Lord!

> When you see the ark of the covenant of the LORD
> your God, and the priests, who are Levites, carrying it,
> you are to move out from your positions and follow it.
> Then you will know which way to go, since you have
> never been this way before.

JOSHUA 3:3–4

BEING CHERISHED

————————— 🕆 —————————

Several years ago, Edward Farrell, a priest from Detroit,
went on a two-week summer vacation to Ireland to visit
relatives. His one living uncle was about to celebrate his
eightieth birthday. On the great day, Ed and his uncle got up
early. It was before dawn. They took a walk along the shores of
Lake Killarney and stopped to watch the sunrise. They stood
side by side for a full twenty minutes and then resumed walking. Ed glanced at his uncle and saw that his face had broken
into a broad smile. Ed said, "Uncle Seamus, you look very
happy." "I am." Ed asked, "How come?" And his uncle replied,
"The Father of Jesus is very fond of me."

If the question were put to you, "Do you honestly believe
that God *likes* you?"—not loves you because theologically he
must—how would you answer? God loves by necessity of his
nature; without the eternal, interior generation of love, he
would cease to be God. But if you could answer, "The Father is
very fond of me," there would come a relaxedness, a serenity,
and a compassionate attitude toward yourself that is a reflection
of God's own tenderness. In Isaiah 49:15, God says: "Does a
woman forget her baby at the breast, or fail to cherish the son of
her womb? Yet even if these forget, I will never forget you" (JB).

> "No one will be able to stand up against you all the
> days of your life. As I was with Moses, so I will be
> with you; I will never leave you nor forsake you."
>
> JOSHUA 1:5

————————[✥]————————

The heart of the Father was Jesus' hiding place, a strong protective space where God was near, where the desert intimacy was renewed, where trust, love, and self-awareness never died but were continually rekindled. In times of opposition, rejection, hatred, and danger he retreated to that hiding place where he was loved. In times of weakness and fear a strength and mighty perseverance were born there. In the face of mounting incomprehension and mistrust, the Father alone understood him. "No one knows who the Son is except the Father . . . " (Luke 10:22). The Pharisees plotted secretly to destroy him; fair-weather friends shifted their allegiance; one disciple denied him and another betrayed him; but nothing could remove Jesus from his Father's love. In the seclusion of desert places he rendezvoused with El Shaddai, and what those moments meant to him can scarcely be apprehended. But this much can be said: the primary, growing, definitive identity and consciousness of Jesus to be his Father's Son, Servant, and Beloved was profoundly reinforced. Nothing must interfere with proclaiming the Good News of eternal life and helping people to a way of life that would enable them to grow toward eternity—a way of peace and justice, with room for human dignity to be recognized and for love to blossom.

> Because of the LORD's great love we are not consumed,
> for his compassions never fail.
> They are new every morning;
> great is your faithfulness.

LAMENTATIONS 3:22–23

AT THE CENTER OF THE GOSPEL

————————— ✠ —————————

Jesus Christ is not only the center of the gospel but the whole gospel. The four evangelists never focus on another personality. Fringe people stay on the fringe, marginal men remain on the periphery. No one else is allowed to take center stage. Various individuals are introduced only to interrogate, respond, or react to Jesus. Nicodemus, the Samaritan woman, Peter, Thomas, Caiphas, Pilate, and a score of others are background to the person of Jesus. He dwarfs everyone else. This is as it should be, because the New Testament is a time of salvation. When the final curtain falls, Jesus will upstage all the famous, beautiful, and powerful people who have ever lived in the course of human history. Every person will be seen as responding to Jesus. As T. S. Eliot put it, "O my soul, be prepared to meet him who knows how to ask questions." This is the proper theological understanding of the New Testament and the eschatological Lordship of Jesus Christ.

> *Since we live by the Spirit, let us keep in step with the Spirit.*

GALATIANS 5:25

———————⊞———————

"The devil never rejoices more," said Francis of Assisi, "than when he robs a servant of God of his peace of heart." Peace and joy go a-begging when the heart of a Christian pants for one sign after another of God's merciful love. Nothing is taken for granted, and nothing is received with gratitude. The troubled eyes and furrowed brow of the anxious believer are the symptoms of a heart where trust has not found a home. The Lord himself must pass through all the shades of the emotional spectrum with us—from rage to tears to amusement. But the poignant truth remains: we do not trust him. We do not have the mind of Christ Jesus.

> *He said to them, "Why are you troubled, and why do doubts rise in your minds?"*

> LUKE 24:38

PRESENTING OURSELVES BEFORE GOD

————— 🕆 —————

The Lord hears the cry of the poor. When the armistice with self-hatred is signed and we embrace what we really are, the process of liberation begins. But so often we are afraid to do so because of the fear of rejection. Like Quasimodo, the hunchback of Notre Dame who thought he was hideous, we daub cosmetics and spiritual makeup on our misery and supposed ugliness to make ourselves appear presentable to God. This is not our true self. Authentic prayer calls us to rigorous honesty, to come out of hiding, to quit trying to seem impressive, to acknowledge our total dependence on God and the reality of our sinful situation. It is a moment of truth when defenses fall and the masks drop in an instinctive act of humility.

> For we are taking pains to do what is right, not only in
> the eyes of the Lord but also in the eyes of men.

2 CORINTHIANS 8:21

————————[✷]————————

Perhaps the main reason that we are such poor practitioners of the art of being human, why we so often teeter on a tightrope between self-hatred and despair, is that we don't pray. We pray so little, so rarely, and so poorly. For everything else we have adequate leisure time. Visits, get-togethers, movies, football games, concerts, an evening with friends, an invitation we can't decline—and these are good because it is natural and wholesome that we come together in community. But when God lays claim on our time, we balk. Do we really believe that he delights to talk with his children? If God had a face, what kind of face would he make at you right now?

Would his face say, "When are you going to shape up? I'm fed up with you and your hang-ups. My patience is exhausted. We're going to have a little reckoning"? If God said only one word to you, would the word be *Repent?* Or would he say, "Thank you. Do you know what a joy it is to live in your heart? Do you know that I have looked upon you and loved you for all eternity?" What would God say? What is the feedback you get from your Creator?

> *"Then you will call upon me and come and pray to me, and I will listen to you. You will seek me and find me when you seek me with all your heart."*

JEREMIAH 29:12–13

THE THRILL OF GOD'S CREATION

———— 🈁 ————

I have seen some beautiful things recently. Hitchhiking across the Italian Alps, I saw a snow-covered peak at dawn. In Florence, I stood for two hours before Michelangelo's *David* with my mouth open, unconscious of time until being abruptly told by a guard that the museum was closing and it was time to leave. Running along the Jersey shore, I saw a fiery sun falling into the gathering darkness. We first experience beauty usually in the things that surround us. Sometimes in sensible things, other times in the transparency of a look or a glance that reveals a soul full of light. Whenever we encounter the beautiful, our hearts awaken, stir, quicken, thrill, because there is an extraordinary, magic power in the least thing: a tiny plant burgeoning in spring, a shade of the sky at a given moment of the day, a calm, cold night brilliant with starshine—all things that ravish the heart. They're a small taste of Paradise Lost on an earth where so many things are torn and tearing. They are little oases in the vast wasteland of the world.

> *Lift your eyes and look to the heavens:*
> *Who created all these?*
> *He who brings out the starry host one by one,*
> *and calls them each by name.*
> *Because of his great power and mighty strength,*
> *not one of them is missing.*

ISAIAH 40:26

———————[⚛]———————

What is the quality of my faith commitment? Is there movement and development? Is it alive and growing? Faith is a real personal relationship with Jesus of Nazareth. Like any human love affair, it can never be static, exhausted, terminal, settled. When Scripture, Eucharist, and ministry become routine, they are moribund. When the Father's love is taken for granted, we paint him into a corner and rob him of the opportunity to love us in new and surprising ways. Then faith begins to shrivel and shrink. When I become so spiritually sophisticated that "Abba" is old hat, then the Father has been had, Jesus has been tamed, the Spirit has been domesticated, and the Pentecostal fire has been extinguished. Evangelical faith is the antithesis of cozy, comfortable piety. Faith means you want growing intimacy with Jesus Christ. Cost what it may, you want to want nothing else. The moment I conclude that I can now cope with the awesome love of God, I am dead. I could more easily contain the Gulf of Mexico in a shot glass than I can comprehend the wild, uncontainable love of God.

If our faith is going to be criticized, let it be for the right reasons. Not because we are too emotional but because we are not emotional enough. Not because our passions are so powerful but because they are so puny. Not because we are too affectionate but because we lack a deep, passionate, undivided love for the person of Jesus Christ.

> *I have fought the good fight, I have finished the race,*
> *I have kept the faith.*

2 TIMOTHY 4:7

A CALL TO ACTION

————[※]————

T he Christian who realizes the gravity of his situation knows that the decision brooks no delay. The Storyteller calls us not to fear but to action. Procrastination only prolongs self-hatred. We cling to cheap painted fragments of glass when the pearl of great price is being offered. When a disciple's very existence is threatened, when he stands on the threshold of moral ruin, when everything is at stake, the hour has struck for bold and resolute decision making. It is not just another itinerant salesperson at the door with superfluous bric-a-brac; it is the Christ of God offering an incredible opportunity, the chance of a lifetime. "I, the light, have come into the world, so that whoever believes in me need not stay in the dark anymore" (John 12:46 JB).

Share with God's people who are in need. Practice hospitality.

ROMANS 12:13

THE CALL ON JESUS' LIFE

———————[✠]———————

Jesus' growing intimacy with his Father and the awareness of his Father's holiness filled him with an all-consuming thirst for the Father. His interior life of trust and loving surrender was not simply a matter of personal prayer, private religious experience, and delighting in God's intimate presence while being oblivious to the real world in its struggle for redemption, justice, and peace. The inner life of Jesus Christ took expression in a special, vital quality of presence in the world in the most active situations.

There was a towering desire within him to reveal his Father in serving the poor, the captive, the blind, and all who are in need. Jesus was entirely devoured by his mission. It was the experience of the Father's holiness that created the imperative of preaching the reign of God's justice, peace, and forgiving love.

He did not have a fixed abode. "Foxes have holes and birds of the air have nests, but the Son of Man has no place to lay his head" (Luke 9:58). He never lingered long in one place. When the disciples looked for him, he responded, "Let us go somewhere else—to the nearby villages—so I can preach there also. That is why I have come" (Mark 1:38). Others might stay behind preoccupied with security, sensation, and power, but Jesus went on without stopping, always driven by the vision of the mission that impelled him.

> After this, Jesus traveled about from one town and village to another, proclaiming the good news of the kingdom of God. The Twelve were with him.

LUKE 8:1

WAS JESUS MERRY?

———————— 𝍏 ————————

D id Jesus smile? Did he actually laugh?
     The Gospels never mention his doing either.
They do testify that he wept twice—over Jerusalem
and Lazarus, his city and his friend. Is it likely, however, that
this sacred man, like us in all things but ungratefulness, could
have wept from sorrow but not laughed for joy? Could Jesus
have failed to smile when a child cuddled up in his arms or
when the headwaiter at Cana nearly fainted at the six hundred
gallons of vintage wine or when he saw Zacchaeus out on a
limb or when Peter put his foot in his mouth one more time?

I simply cannot believe that Jesus did not laugh when he
saw something funny or did not smile when he experienced in
his being the love of his Abba. He attracted not only a leading
Pharisee and a Roman centurion but also children and simple
folk like Mary Magdalene. Our human experience tells us that
Jesus could not have done that if he always wore the solemn
face of a mourner or the stern mask of a judge, if his face did not
often crease into a smile and his whole body erupt in merry
laughter.

> And when he finds it, he joyfully puts it on his shoul-
> ders and goes home. Then he calls his friends and
> neighbors together and says, "Rejoice with me; I have
> found my lost sheep."

LUKE 15:5–6

GIVING COMPASSION—
STARTING WITH OURSELVES

————————🕂————————

I n returning to ourselves, in contemplating the compassion of Jesus and realizing that "this means me," we come under the mercy and qualify for the name tag "blessed." In urging us to compassionate caring for others, Jesus invites us to have compassion for ourselves. The measure of our compassion for others lies in proportion to our capacity for self-acceptance and self-affirmation. When the compassion of Christ is interiorized and appropriated to self, the breakthrough into being for others occurs. In the reverse of a catch-22 situation, the way of compassionate caring for others brings healing to ourselves, and compassionate caring for ourselves brings healing to others. Solidarity with human suffering frees the one who receives and liberates the one who gives through the conscious awareness "I am the other."

> *Make every effort to live in peace with all men and to be holy; without holiness no one will see the Lord.*

HEBREWS 12:14

No Payment Possible

————[⚕]————

The sinners to whom Jesus directed his messianic mission were real sinners. They had done nothing to merit salvation. Yet they opened themselves to the gift that was offered them. The self-righteous, on the other hand, put their trust in what they had merited by their own efforts and closed their hearts to the message of salvation.

But the salvation that Jesus promised could not be earned. There could be no bargaining with God in a petty poker table atmosphere; "I have done this; therefore, you owe me that." Jesus utterly destroys the juridic notion that our works demand payment in return.

As you do not know the path of the wind,
or how the body is formed in a mother's womb,
so you cannot understand the work of God,
the Maker of all things.

ECCLESIASTES 11:5

———— 🕀 ————

For most of us the generic confession of sinfulness comes easily: All human beings are sinners; I am human; therefore, I am a sinner. A hasty examination of conscience reveals minor infractions of the law, or what Roman Catholic locution calls "venial sins." This vague admission of wrongdoing is necessary in order to qualify for membership in the community of the saved. But saved from what?

Our blindness to the sinfulness of someone like Mother Teresa, for instance, exposes our superficial understanding of the mystery of iniquity lurking within every human being. Her heroic works of charity shielded us from the truth of her inner poverty as well as from our own. For if we emulate her sacrificial love in some small fashion, we are lulled into a false sense of security that persuades us that we have no need of repentance today. When the little saint humbly confessed her brokenness and her desperate need for God, either we were uncomprehending or we secretly suspected her of false modesty.

. . . In other words, we see ourselves as basically nice, benevolent people with minor hang-ups and neuroses that are the common lot of humanity. We rationalize and minimize our terrifying capacity to make peace with evil and thereby reject all that is not nice about us.

> "It is not by strength that one prevails;
> those who oppose the LORD will be shattered.
> He will thunder against them from heaven;
> the LORD will judge the ends of the earth.
> He will give strength to his king
> and exalt the horn of his anointed."

I SAMUEL 2:9–10

FREEDOM IN SECURITY

————⟨⟩————

The Lord passed through the world, a figure of light and truth, sometimes tender, sometimes violent, always just, loving, effective, but not insecure. "If freedom is in thought, word, and action," wrote Kahlil Gibran, "he was the freest of all men." A word, a gesture, a few syllables traced in sand, a command like "Come, follow me!" and destinies were changed, spirits reborn, hearts filled with joy. Jesus walked on the water almost inadvertently; he chatted with Samaritans, prostitutes, children. He spoke to them of truth and mercy and forgiveness with never a shadow of insecurity darkening his countenance.

One who trusts in the Lord knows that by clinging to a miserable sense of security the possibility of transparency is utterly defeated. Just as the sunrise of faith requires the sunset of our former unbelief, our false ideas, our erroneous and circumscribed convictions, so the dawn of trust requires the abandoning of our craving for material and spiritual reassurances. Security in the Lord Jesus implies that we neither calculate nor count the cost any longer.

> But I have stilled and quieted my soul;
> like a weaned child with its mother,
> like a weaned child is my soul within me.

PSALM 131:2

———————— 🔲 ————————

The axis of the Christian moral revolution is love, and it is the only sign given by Jesus by which the disciple would be recognized. The danger lurks in our subtle attempts to minimize, rationalize, and justify our moderation in this regard. Turning the other cheek, walking the extra mile, offering no resistance to injury, being reconciled with one's brother, and forgiving seventy times seven times are not arbitrary whims of the Son of Man. He did not preface the Sermon on the Mount with, "It would be nice if. . . ." His "new" commandment structures the new covenant in his blood. So central is the precept of fraternal love that Paul called it the fulfillment of the Law.

> *"A new command I give you: Love one another. As I have loved you, so you must love one another."*

JOHN 13:34

HUNGER—BODY AND SPIRIT

————— ✠ —————

"Then John's disciples came and asked him, 'How is it that we and the Pharisees fast, but your disciples do not fast?'

"Jesus answered, 'How can the guests of the bridegroom mourn while he is with them? The time will come when the bridegroom will be taken from them; then they will fast'" (Matt. 9:14–15).

The Italian psychologist Psichiari once remarked, "The best preparation for prayer is a handful of dates and a glass of water." Physical fasting from food is the joining of the body to the spirit's hunger for God. Even after a one-day fast I find that I more readily enter the ardent longing for God expressed in Psalm 63: "O God, you are my God, earnestly I seek you; my soul thirsts for you, my body longs for you, in a dry and weary land where there is no water."

> *Gather to me my consecrated ones,*
> *who made a covenant with me by sacrifice.*

PSALM 50:5

20 ✠ REFLECTIONS FOR RAGAMUFFINS

———————[✚]———————

In spite of our reluctance and resistance, the essence and novelty of the new covenant is that the very law of God's being is love. Pagan philosophers like Plato and Aristotle had arrived through human reasoning at the existence of God, speaking of him in vague, impersonal terms as the Uncaused Cause and the Immovable Mover. The prophets of Israel had revealed the God of Abraham, Isaac, and Jacob in a more intimate and passionate manner. But only Jesus revealed that God is a Father of incomparable tenderness, that if we take all the goodness, wisdom, and compassion of the best mothers and fathers who have ever lived, they would only be a faint shadow of the love and mercy in the heart of the redeeming God.

> *And so we know and rely on the love God has for us.*
> *God is love. Whoever lives in love lives in God, and*
> *God in him.*

1 JOHN 4:16

TRUE POVERTY
———— 🔆 ————

J esus, my Brother and Lord, I pray as I write these words for the grace to be truly poor before you, to recognize and accept my weakness and humanness, to forgo the indecent luxury of self-hatred, to celebrate your mercy and trust in your power when I'm at my weakest, to rely on your love no matter what I may do, to seek no escapes from my innate poverty, to accept loneliness when it comes instead of seeking substitutes, to live peacefully without clarity or assurance, to stop grandstanding and trying to get attention, to do the truth quietly without display, to let the dishonesties in my life fade away, to belong no more to myself, not to desert my post when I give the appearance of staying at it, to cling to my humanity, to accept the limitations and full responsibility of being a human being— really human and really poor in Christ our Lord.

> The LORD is good to those whose hope is in him,
> to the one who seeks him;
> it is good to wait quietly
> for the salvation of the LORD.

LAMENTATIONS 3:25–26

———————※———————

T his scenario has been playing in my mind: A young female disciple of Jesus wanted to develop a spirit of compassion for all human beings. But when she went to the supermarket to gather her groceries, she found her compassion sorely tested by an ugly assistant manager who would subject her to unwelcome caresses.

One dreary, rainy day she could tolerate it no longer and began to shout angrily at the manager. To her mortification she saw Jesus, who was reaching for a jar of peanut butter on the shelf and quietly observing her behavior. Shamefaced, she came and stood before the Lord, expecting to be rebuked for her anger.

"What you should do," Jesus kindly counseled her, "is to fill your heart with as much loving-kindness as you can muster. Then whack him over the head with your umbrella."

Nowhere in Scripture does Jesus indicate that being compassionate means being a doormat. There is no trace of restraint when Jesus roars, "The devil is your father and you prefer to do what your father wants" (see John 8:44). We hear utter frustration in the words "How much longer must I put up with you?" (see Matt. 17:17), unmitigated rage in "Get behind me Satan!" (see Matt. 16:23), and blazing wrath in "Stop turning my Father's house into a marketplace" (see John 2:16).

The wisdom to discern when it is appropriate to turn the other cheek and when it is time to raise the umbrella comes only from listening to the heartbeat of the Great Rabbi.

Be self-controlled and alert.

1 PETER 5:8

THE STARTING PLACE FOR BEING

The Sermon on the Mount is a portrait of the heart of Jesus Christ. The Beatitudes offer a deep insight into his preferences, his prejudices, and his total personality. In giving us what John Powell calls the Be-Attitudes, Jesus said that these are the attitudes that will enable you *to be* like him. He talked about *being* pure of heart. He talked about *being* compassionate. He talked about the attitudes that are deep down inside us, and he said, "If you really want to be like me, this is how you ought to think." And right atop the list is "be poor in spirit."

To be poor in spirit means to cling to your impoverished humanity and to have nothing to brag about before God. Paul writes, "What do you have that you haven't received; and if you have received it, why do you go about boasting as if you hadn't received it?"

Offer hospitality to one another without grumbling.

1 PETER 4:19

———[※]———

Seventeen centuries after religious leaders had made the Sabbath a day of legalism, the hair-splitting pharisaical interpretation of the Sabbath washed ashore in New England. In the Code of Connecticut we read: "No one shall run on the Sabbath Day, or walk in his garden, or elsewhere, except reverently to and from meeting. No one shall travel, cook victuals, make beds, sweep house, cut hair, or shave on the Sabbath. If any man shall kiss his wife, or wife her husband on the Lord's Day, the party in fault shall be punished at the discretion of the court of magistrates."

Paradoxically, what intrudes between God and human beings is our fastidious morality and pseudopiety. It is not the prostitutes and tax collectors who find it most difficult to repent; it is the devout who feel they have no need to repent, secure in not having broken rules on the Sabbath.

> *See! The winter is past;*
> *the rains are over and gone.*
> *Flowers appear on the earth;*
> *the season of singing has come,*
> *the cooing of doves*
> *is heard in our land.*
>
> SONG OF SONGS 2:11–12

THE RULE-RIDDEN SABBATH

————[❋]————

Unfortunately, after the Babylonian exile the primary spiritual meaning of the Sabbath had become obscured. Under spiritually bankrupt leadership, a subtle shift in focus took place. The Pharisees, who carried religion like a shield of self-justification and a sword of judgment, installed the cold demands of rule-ridden perfectionism because that approach gave them status and control while reassuring believers that they were marching in lockstep on the road to salvation. The Pharisees falsified the image of God into an eternal, small-minded bookkeeper whose favor could be won only by the scrupulous observance of laws and regulations. Religion became a tool to intimidate and enslave rather than liberate and empower. Jewish believers were instructed to focus their attention on the secondary aspect of the Sabbath—abstention from work.

The joyous celebration of creation and covenant stressed by the prophets disappeared. The Sabbath became a day of legalism. The means had become the end. (Herein lies the genius of legalistic religion—making primary matters secondary and secondary matters primary.) Concurrently, what emerged was a farrago of prohibitions and prescriptions that transformed the Sabbath into a heavy burden leading to nervous scrupulosity—the kind of Sabbath Jesus of Nazareth inveighed against so vehemently.

For this is what the LORD says:

" You were sold for nothing,
and without money you will be redeemed."

ISAIAH 52:3

———[✠]———

Closely related to the quality of my faith is the intensity of my hope. The word of Jesus carries the implicit theme that the world is out to do us good. When you stop and think about it, that's an extraordinary idea. In most of our lives we have the impression that the world has done us considerable harm and comparatively little good. Yet, if the Abba of Jesus loves us, if he pursues us as a tremendous Lover who is dying (in his Son) to be with us, then we are committed to the notion that his world, the work of his hands, is out to do us good. And that means taking the risk of letting others do good to us. It means going into the wedding feast and celebrating with the firm conviction that we are not going to be chumped, cheated, or disastrously surprised.

> "No weapon forged against you will prevail,
> and you will refute every tongue that accuses you.
> This is the heritage of the servants of the LORD,
> and this is their vindication from me,"
> declares the LORD.

ISAIAH 54:17

A RIGHT RESPONSE

————— 🔅 —————

In first-century Palestine, the people of Judea and Galilee fudged and hedged on the proclamation of the reign of God. Jesus announced that the old era was done, that a new age had dawned, and the only appropriate response was to be captivated with joy and wonder.

His listeners did not say, "Yes, Rabbi, we believe you," or "No, Rabbi, we think you are a fool." Rather, they said, "What about the sap-suckin' Romans?" or "When are you going to produce an apocalyptic sign?" or "Why aren't you and your disciples within the Jewish Law?" or "Whose side do you take in the various legal controversies?" . . .

Since the day that Jesus first appeared on the scene, we have developed vast theological systems, organized worldwide churches, filled libraries with brilliant christological scholarship, engaged in earthshaking controversies, and embarked on crusades, reforms, and renewals. Yet there are still precious few of us with sufficient folly to make the mad exchange of everything for Christ; only a remnant with the confidence to risk everything on the gospel of grace; only a minority who stagger about with the delirious joy of the man who found the buried treasure.

Shout aloud and sing for joy, people of Zion, for great
is the Holy One of Israel among you.

ISAIAH 12:6

PARADOXES

When I get honest, I admit I am a bundle of paradoxes. I believe and I doubt, I hope and I get discouraged, I love and I hate, I feel bad about feeling good, I feel guilty about not feeling guilty. I am trusting and suspicious. I am honest and I still play games. Aristotle said I am a rational animal; I say I am an angel with an incredible capacity for beer.

To live by grace means to acknowledge my whole life's story, the light side and the dark. In admitting my shadow side, I learn who I am and what God's grace means. As Thomas Merton put it, "A saint is not someone who is good but who experiences the goodness of God."

> *"For them I sanctify myself, that they too may be truly sanctified."*
>
> JOHN 17:19

NEEDING PROOF

————[✠]————

Trust that is at the mercy of the response it receives is a bogus trust. All is uncertainty and anxiety. All is precarious. In trembling insecurity the believer pleads for and even demands tangible reassurances from the Lord that his affection be returned. If he does not received them, he is disheartened, frustrated, maybe even convinced that it's all over or that it never really existed.

If he does receive them, he is reassured but only for a time. He presses for further proofs—each one less convincing than the one that went before. In the end, the need to trust dies of pure frustration. What the sincere Christian has not learned is that tangible reassurances, however valuable they may be, cannot create trust, sustain it, or provide any certainty of its presence. Jesus Christ calls us to hand over our autonomous self in complete confidence. Only when that decision is ratified and the craving for reassurances is stifled are transparency, certainty, and peace achieved.

But as for me, I will always have hope;
I will praise you more and more.
My mouth will tell of your righteousness,
of your salvation all day long,
though I know not its measure.

PSALM 71:14–15

———— 路 ————

E very time the Gospels mention that Jesus was moved with the deepest emotions or felt sorry for people, it led to his doing something—physical or inner healing, deliverance or exorcism, feeding the hungry crowds or praying for others. The Good Samaritan was commended precisely because he acted. The priest and Levite, paragons of Jewish virtue, flunked the test because they didn't do anything. "Which of these three, in your opinion, was neighbor to the man who fell in with the robbers?" The answer came, "The one who treated him with compassion." Jesus said to them, "Then go and do the same."

> *If anyone has material possessions and sees his brother*
> *in need but has no pity on him, how can the love of*
> *God be in him? Dear children, let us not love with*
> *words or tongue but with actions and in truth.*

1 JOHN 3:17–18

PUT THE MASK DOWN

———————[※]———————

I believe Jesus calls all of us to let go of the desire to appear good, to give up the appearance of being good, so that we can listen to the word within us and move in the mystery of who we are. The preoccupation with projecting the perfect image, of being a model Christian and edifying others with our virtues, leads to self-consciousness, sticky pedestal behavior, and bondage to human respect. As my spiritual director Larry Hein said, paraphrasing the Tao Te Ching, "Give up trying to look like a saint. It'll be a lot better for everybody."

Your attitude should be the same as that of Christ
Jesus:
Who, being in very nature God,
did not consider equality with God something to be
grasped,
but made himself nothing,
taking the very nature of a servant,
being made in human likeness.

PHILIPPIANS 2:5–7

———————[✲]———————

Jesus says simply, "Make your home in me, as I make mine in you" (John 15:4 JB). Home is not a heavenly mansion in the afterlife but a safe place right in the midst of our anxious world. . . .

Home is that sacred space—external or internal— where we don't have to be afraid, where we are confident of hospitality and love. In our society we have not only many homeless people sleeping on the streets, in shelters, or in welfare hotels, but also vagabonds who are in flight, who never come home to themselves. They seek a safe place through alcohol or drugs, or security in success, competence, friends, pleasure, notoriety, knowledge, or even a little religion. They have become strangers to themselves, people who have an address but are never at home, who never hear the voice of love or experience the freedom of God's children.

To those of us in flight, who are afraid to turn around lest we run into ourselves, Jesus says: "You have a home . . . I am your home . . . claim me as your home . . . you will find it to be the intimate place where I have found my home . . . it is right where you are . . . in your innermost being . . . in your heart."

Jesus replied, "If anyone loves me, he will obey my teaching. My Father will love him, and we will come to him and make our home with him."

JOHN 14:23

FALTERING STEPS

———————————[✜]———————————

When I get sprayed by the storms of life and find my faith has faltered, my courage has gone south, I often turn to Matthew 14:22–33. Jesus sees the disciples caught up in a squall. It is between three and six A.M. He comes walking toward them on the water. They are terrified. "It's a ghost," they cry out in fear. He says, "Courage! It is I! Do not be afraid."

Peter, nothing if not brash, decides to test the voice. "Lord, if it is you, tell me to come to you across the water." The tentative faith of that fearful "if" quickly deteriorates into sheer terror as Peter begins to walk to Jesus.

I find comfort (perhaps perverse pleasure) in knowing that the rock on which Jesus would build the Church sank like a stone.

> To this you were called, because Christ suffered for
> you, leaving you an example, that you should follow in
> his steps.
>
> 1 PETER 2:21

———————[✠]———————

I mpressions form images, which become fixed ideas, which give birth to prejudices. Anthony DeMello said, "If you are prejudiced, you will see that person from the eye of that prejudice. In other words, you will cease to see this person as a person." The Pharisee within spends most of his time reacting to labels, his own and others'.

The story is told of a man who went to the priest and said, "Father, I want you to say a mass for my dog."

The priest was indignant. "What do you mean, say a mass for your dog?"

"It was my pet dog," said the man. "I loved that dog, and I'd like you to offer a mass for him."

"We don't offer masses for dogs here," the priest said. "You might try the denomination down the street. Ask them if they have a service for you."

As the man was leaving, he said to the priest, "I really loved that dog. I was planning to offer a million-dollar stipend for the mass."

And the priest said, "Wait a minute. You never told me your dog was Catholic."

> *I charge you, in the sight of God and Christ Jesus and the elect angels, to keep these instructions without partiality, and to do nothing out of favoritism.*

1 TIMOTHY 5:21

JESUS' FEELINGS

——————[✦]——————

We have spread so many ashes over the historical Jesus that we scarcely feel the glow of his presence anymore. He is a man in a way that we have forgotten men can be: truthful, blunt, emotional, nonmanipulative, sensitive, compassionate—his inner child so liberated that he did not feel it unmanly to cry. He met people head-on and refused to cut any deal at the price of his integrity.

The Gospel portrait of the beloved Child of Abba is that of a man exquisitely attuned to his emotions and uninhibited in expressing them. The Son of Man did not scorn or reject feelings as fickle and unreliable. They were sensitive emotional antennae to which he listened carefully and through which he perceived the will of his Father for congruent speech and action.

As he approached Jerusalem and saw the city, he wept over it.

LUKE 19:41

————————⊞————————

The betrayals and infidelities in my life are too numerous to count. I still cling to the illusion that I must be morally impeccable, other people must be sinless, and the one I love must be without human weakness. But whenever I allow anything but tenderness and compassion to dictate my response to life—be it self-righteous anger, moralizing, defensiveness, the pressing need to change others, carping criticism, frustration at others' blindness, a sense of spiritual superiority, a gnawing hunger of vindication—I am alienated from my true self. My identity as Abba's child becomes ambiguous, tentative, and confused.

Our way of being in the world is the way of tenderness. Everything else is illusion, misperception, falsehood.

> *Be kind and compassionate to one another, forgiving*
> *each other, just as in Christ God forgave you.*

EPHESIANS 4:32

INTERIOR STILLNESS

It is much like the story of the harried executive who went to the desert father and complained about his frustration in prayer, his flawed virtue, and his failed relationships. The hermit listened closely to his visitor's rehearsal of the struggle and disappointments in trying to lead a Christian life. He then went into the dark recesses of his cave and came out with a basin and a pitcher of water.

"Now watch the water as I pour it into the basin," he said. The water splashed on the bottom and against the sides of the container. It was agitated and turbulent. At first the stirred-up water swirled around the inside of the basin; then it gradually began to settle, until finally the small fast ripples evolved into larger swells that oscillated back and forth. Eventually, the surface became so smooth that the visitor could see his face reflected in the placid water. "That is the way it is when you live constantly in the midst of others," said the hermit. "You do not see yourself as you really are because of all the confusion and disturbance. You fail to recognize the divine presence in your life, and the consciousness of your belovedness slowly fades."

It takes time for the water to settle. Coming to interior stillness requires waiting. Any attempt to hasten the process only stirs up the water anew.

> "Be still, and know that I am God;
> I will be exalted among the nations,
> I will be exalted in the earth."

PSALM 46:10

———————|☒|———————

The prayer of the poor in spirit can simply be a single word: *Abba*. Yet that word can signify dynamic interaction. Imagine a little boy trying to help his father with some household work or making his mother a gift. The help may be nothing more than getting in the way, and the gift may be totally useless, but the love behind it is simple and pure, and the loving response it evokes is virtually uncontrollable. I am sure it is this way between our Abba and us. At the deepest, simplest levels, we just want each other to be happy, to be pleased. Our sincere desire counts far more than any specific success or failure. Thus when we try to pray and cannot, or when we fail in a sincere attempt to be compassionate, God touches us tenderly in return.

> *In all their distress he too was distressed,*
> *and the angel of his presence saved them.*
> *In his love and mercy he redeemed them;*
> *he lifted them up and carried them*
> *all the days of old.*

> ISAIAH 63:9

THE FATHER'S CHARACTER

————— 🕀 —————

The Father's love is revealed in the Son's. The Son has been given to us that we might give up fear. There is no fear in love. The Father sent the Son that we might have life—life in all its fullness (see John 10:10). Is not the Son the Father's unsurpassable sign of love and graciousness? Did he not come to show us the Father's compassionate care for us? . . . The Father is not justice and the Son love. The Father is justice *and* love; the Son is love *and* justice.

Abba is not our enemy. If we think that, we are wrong.

Abba is not intent on trying and tempting and testing us. If we think that, we are wrong.

Abba does not prefer and promote suffering and pain. If we think that, we are wrong.

Jesus brings good news about the Father, not bad news.

"When [a man] looks at me, he sees the one who sent me."

JOHN 12:45

T he Gospel portrait of Jesus is that of a person who cherished life and especially other people as loving gifts from the Father's hand. The peripheral figures whom Jesus encountered in his ministry reacted in various ways to his person and his message, but few responded with gloom or sadness. (And they were those such as the rich young ruler who rejected his message.) The living presence of Jesus awakened joy and set people free. Joy was in fact the most characteristic result of all his ministry to ragamuffins.

> *"I am coming to you now, but I say these things while*
> *I am still in the world, so that they may have the full*
> *measure of my joy within them."*

JOHN 17:13

No Place for Pretense

Jesus cuts to the heart of the matter as he sets the child on his knee. The child is unselfconscious, incapable of pretense. I am reminded of the night little John Dyer, three years old, knocked on our door, flanked by his parents. I looked down and said, "Hi, John. I am delighted to see you." He looked neither right nor left. His face was set like flint. He narrowed his eyes with the apocalyptic glint of an aimed gun. "Where's the cookies?" he demanded.

The Kingdom belongs to people who aren't trying to look good or impress anybody, even themselves. They are not plotting how they can call attention to themselves, worrying about how their actions will be interpreted, or wondering if they will get gold stars for their behavior. Twenty centuries later, Jesus speaks pointedly to the preening ascetic trapped in the fatal narcissism of spiritual perfectionism, to those of us caught up in boasting about our victories in the vineyard, to those of us fretting and flapping about our human weaknesses and character defects. The child doesn't have to struggle to get himself in a good position for having a relationship with God.

> When Jesus saw Nathanael approaching, he said of him, "Here is a true Israelite, in whom there is nothing false."

> JOHN 1:47

———— [※] ————

The apostle Paul grasped the full meaning of Jesus' teaching on becoming worry free. Serving as a coat rack during the stoning of Stephen and as a ringleader in the slaughter of Christians, Paul might well have become pathological had he dwelled on his pre-Christian past. But he writes, "All I can say is that I forget the past and I strain ahead for what is still to come" (see Phil. 3:12–14).

Whatever past achievements might bring us honor, whatever past disgraces might make us blush, all have been crucified with Christ and exist no more.

But worry is not limited to the past. When the mind directs its gaze to the unknown future, it can spin fearful scenarios that also keep us in a chronic state of worry.

This worrying about the future prohibits our being aware of the living present. Spiritual traditions continually point out this problem. One of Jesus' most memorable teachings contains this contrast: "Do not worry about your life, what you *will* eat or what you *will* drink, or about your body, what you *will* wear. *Look* (present tense) at the birds of the air" (see Matt. 6:25–34). He ends this teaching with a piece of dark humor that has helped many people rein in the runaway mind: "Let the day's own trouble be sufficient for the day."

Attending to the present moment, watching it emerge and contributing to its creation, is one of the premier skills of the spiritual life.

> *Come, O house of Jacob,*
> *let us walk in the light of the* LORD

ISAIAH 2:5

LEARNING TRUST THROUGH TRIALS

———————⊠———————

The basic premise of biblical trust is that the God and Father of Jesus Christ wants us to live, to grow, to unfold, and to experience fullness of life. Trust is an attitude acquired gradually through many crises and trials. Through the agonizing trial with his son Isaac, Abraham learned that God wants us to live and not to die, to grow and not to wither. He discovered that the God who called him to hope against hope is reliable. Perhaps this is the essence of trust: to be convinced of the reliability of God.

Trust is purified in the crucible of trial. From the depths of a purified heart, trust clings to the belief that whatever happens in our lives is designed to form Christ within us. Unwavering confidence in the love of God inspires trust to thank God for the spiritual darkness that envelops us, for the loss of income, for the arthritis that is so painful, to pray with Charles de Foucauld: "Abba, I abandon myself into your hands. Do with me what you will. Whatever you may do, I thank you. I am ready for all. I accept all. Let only your will be done in me and all your people. I wish no more than this, O Lord. Into your hands I commend my spirit. I offer it to you with all the love of my heart, for I love you, Lord, and I give myself, surrender myself into your hands, without reserve, with boundless confidence, for you are my Father."

Against all hope, Abraham in hope believed and so became the father of many nations, just as it had been said to him, "So shall your offspring be."

ROMANS 4:18

TRUST—AT THE HEART
OF THE COMING KINGDOM

————————[※]————————

J esus found himself surrounded every day by people who were bent over double, by victims of running sores and withered limbs, by the mute and the deaf. The net effect of all this human misery on him was not depressing. The only charge he leveled against anyone—always the onlookers, never the victim—was lack of trust in God.

The predominant question for every Jew was how to bring on the reign of Israel's God. Jesus proposed a single way— the way of trust. Jesus did not *ask* his disciples to trust in God; he *told* them to trust in God. Trusting in God was not some feature out at the edges of Jesus' teaching; it was its heart and center. This and only this would hasten the reign of God.

We presume, however, that trust will ease confusion, dull the pain, redeem the times. The cloud of witnesses in Hebrews 11 testifies that this is not so. Our trust does not bring final clarity on this earth. It does not still the chaos or dull the pain or provide a crutch. When all else is unclear, the heart of trust says, "Into your hands I commend my spirit."

> *Then Esther sent this reply to Mordecai: "Go, gather together all the Jews who are in Susa, and fast for me. Do not eat or drink for three days, night or day. I and my maids will fast as you do. When this is done, I will go to the king, even though it is against the law. And if I perish, I perish."*

ESTHER 4:15–16

INSIDE AND OUT

———————[✠]———————

The rich in spirit devote considerable time to thinking about what they don't have; the poor to enjoying and celebrating what they do have. In the last century the atheist philosopher Friedrich Nietzsche reproached a group of Christians with words to this effect: "Yuk, you make me sick!" When their spokesman asked why, Nietzsche replied, "Because you redeemed don't look like you're redeemed!" The rich are often as downcast, guilt ridden, anxious, and dissatisfied as their unbelieving neighbors. The poor cry, "It is right to give him thanks and praise."

Blessed are the poor in spirit,
for theirs is the kingdom of heaven.

MATTHEW 5:3

———— 🕂 ————

The gentleness of Jesus with sinners flowed from his ability to read their hearts and to detect the sincerity and goodness there. Behind men's grumpiest poses and most puzzling defense mechanisms, behind their arrogance and airs, behind their silence, sneers, and curses, Jesus saw little children who hadn't been loved enough and who had ceased growing because someone had ceased believing in them. His extraordinary sensitivity and compassion caused Jesus (and later the apostles) to speak of the faithful as children no matter how tall, rich, clever, and successful they might be.

> But the LORD said to Samuel, "Do not consider his appearance or his height, for I have rejected him. The LORD does not look at the things man looks at. Man looks at the outward appearance, but the LORD looks at the heart."

1 SAMUEL 16:7

TENDER JUDGMENT

———— [✳] ————

The ultimate reason why we may forgive instead of condemn is because God himself does not condemn but forgives. Because he has freely chosen to put tenderness before law, we are authorized to do the same. In the imagery of the parables, God is constantly presented as the father rushing out to meet his son, the absurdly generous farmer who gives the latecomers the same wage as the day-long laborer, the judge hearing the prayer of the importunate widow. In the man Jesus the invisible God becomes visible and audible. . . . Jesus Christ taught prophetically, in the power of the Spirit, that Christian giving and forgiving should copy God's giving and forgiving. Acceptance is absolute, without inquiry into the past, without special conditions, so that the liberated sinner can live again, accept himself, forgive himself, love himself.

> . . . because of the tender mercy of our God,
> by which the rising sun will come to us from heaven
> to shine on those living in darkness
> and in the shadow of death,
> to guide our feet into the path of peace.

> LUKE 1:78–79

————————⊞————————

A gainst all the canons of prudence and discretion, Jesus announced the dawn of a new age, the inbreak of a higher righteousness, that he had come to save not the just but the sinners. And the sinner is accepted prior to any statement of sorrow. First comes grace (given tenderness), then metanoia. Real sinners deserving real punishment are gratuitously pardoned: they need only accept tenderness already present. Forgiveness is granted; they need only the wisdom to accept it and repent. These are the poor in spirit whom Jesus declares blessed. They know how to accept a gift. "Come on, all you who are wiped out, confused, bewildered, lost, beat up, scarred, scared, threatened, depressed, and I'll enlighten your mind with wisdom and fill your heart with tenderness that I have received from my Father." This is unconditional pardon. The sinner need only live confidently in the wisdom of accepted tenderness.

> *The LORD is gracious and compassionate,*
> *slow to anger and rich in love.*

> PSALM 145:8

BECAUSE HE LIVES

———— ✠ ————

After Jesus came down the Mount of Transfiguration, he told his disciples that he was going up to Jerusalem, that he would be executed, and that he would triumph over death. Jesus was not the least bit confident that he would be spared suffering. What he was confident of was vindication. Our hope, our acceptance of the invitation to the banquet, is not based on the idea that we are going to be free of pain and suffering. Rather, it is based on the firm conviction that we will triumph over suffering.

Do you believe that you, too, will live? Because that is the meaning of Christian hope. It is not Pollyanna optimism or wishful thinking. It is not something that yields to discouragement, defeat, and frustration. On the contrary, Christian hope stands firm and serene, confident even in the face of terminal cancer. However serious we believe Good Friday is, we are confident that Easter Day lies ahead of us. What if we do die? Jesus died, too, and if Jesus died we believe that now he lives and that we shall live, too.

> *Jesus said to her, "I am the resurrection and the life.*
> *He who believes in me will live, even though he dies."*

JOHN 11:25

THE VULNERABLE ONE

————— 🕀 —————

On the cross the open arms of the Crucified reached out to feel the pain and suffering of the world. The Son of compassion wanted to absorb the guilt, rejection, shame, and failure of his brothers and sisters. He came to us not with the crushing impact of his glory, but in the way of weakness, vulnerability, and need. Jesus was a naked, humiliated, exposed God on the cross who allowed us to get close to him.

The world does not understand such vulnerability.

> *He was oppressed and afflicted,*
> *yet he did not open his mouth;*
> *he was led like a lamb to the slaughter,*
> *and as a sheep before her shearers is silent,*
> *so he did not open his mouth.*

ISAIAH 53:7

TRUE FASTING

——————[✠]——————

F asting is the cry of the whole body-person, a yearning for the justice of God to be revealed. Therefore the Pharisees and John's disciples fasted. Jesus says: "You don't need to fast now. What you were hungry for, what you longed for, is here."

But why didn't they recognize him? Well-intentioned men, assiduous in prayer and personal discipline, they missed the hour of visitation. Why? Father Frank Miles, S.J., a veteran spiritual director, notes that in all his years of guiding people to the Lord, the greatest obstacle in the life of prayer is *expectations*. "Lord, I have fasted, denied myself, lost three pounds, and gone through the hammers of hell. Now I expect you to come in sweetness and joy, and abundantly compensate for all that arduous fasting." Is this the criterion of good prayer? If so, the prayer of Jesus in the Garden of Gethsemane was a bummer.

I don't expect a God who comes in failure, in loneliness, in poverty. Yet God comes to me where I live and loves me where I am. When I remain where I am, with everything that is moving inside me, salvation comes. Isn't that true in your own experience? The Lord saying, "I don't want your profound thoughts, the magnanimous acts of love that slide so easily off your tongue, your burnt offerings and holocausts; I want your heart."

> *"When you fast, do not look somber as the hypocrites do, for they disfigure their faces to show men they are fasting. I tell you the truth, they have received their reward in full."*

MATTHEW 6:16

———[✠]———

A t this moment in my own personal legend, martyrdom does not seem to require marching to the lions for Christ or bringing him to Zaire or Nicaragua as a missionary. The call I hear deep within me is to reveal his forgiving love to those who have trespassed against me. It costs a lot to pray, "Thy will be done"—death to the old man, overcoming grudges and long-standing resentments, transcending bitter memories and justifiable hostilities, reaching out in reconciliation to those who have turned me down, ripped me off, and screwed me up.

Maybe this is why the only four times that "thy will be done" occurs in the New Testament are in the context of martyrdom. The older I get, the more I realize the truth of the adage, "It's easier to die for Christ than to live for him."

> *We always carry around in our body the death of*
> *Jesus, so that the life of Jesus may also be revealed in*
> *our body.*

2 CORINTHIANS 4:10

J ESUS' E NNOBLED S OUL

——————[✺]——————

The Greek and Latin fathers of the Church posed the question: Could the beauty of Jesus have endured while he suffered all that was foretold of the Suffering Servant in the prophecy of Isaiah—a Man of Sorrow murdered for us, bloodied, despised, disfigured, a worm and not a man, who knew the nadir of an agony such as no man has ever dreamed? Was the Crucifixion really beautiful? For those who saw only the external tragedy, Jesus naked and nailed, flanked by two criminals, blood streaming from every wound and pore of his body, it was a horrible spectacle indeed. And for that reason, with the advent of Constantine, crucifixion was abolished as brutal and inhuman. But there is more to the death of Jesus than just that. There is the luminous, transcendent, interior beauty of his soul, and we must never forget it. The body of Jesus was racked, broken, bathed in blood, but his soul was ennobled by a dignity, suffused with a love that illuminated, transformed, and transfigured his suffering and death. This was the mightiest act of love ever to rise from a human soul. Surely the Crucifixion was a brutal, dehumanizing atrocity exteriorly, but it was beautiful because of the sentiments in Jesus' soul—unwavering obedience to the glory of his Father and illimitable love for men.

> It was just before the Passover Feast. Jesus knew that
> the time had come for him to leave this world and go to
> the Father. Having loved his own who were in the
> world, he now showed them the full extent of his love.

JOHN 13:1

———— 🕱 ————

The garbage in most of our lives is the relentless anxiety and agitation created by the fear that we will not get enough of the world's goodies to feel safe, secure, and turned on. The agony in the Garden centers on Jesus' prayerful struggle against the pressures of anxiety. . . . At this moment he represents the serious mind of the pilgrim Church. In the empathetic identification with Jesus, the Spirit infuses power to transcend fear and anxiety and to share in the Lord's intimate trust of the Father. Theologian Alex LeFrank notes, "The prayerful struggle against the pressures of anxiety remains at the heart of the contemplation of Christ crucified" (*Freedom for Service*). As Jesus wrestles with fidelity to his mission, adherence to his decision, and the lure to back away from his self-awareness, the Christian experiences the fellowship of his suffering and knows the power of his resurrection over security, sensation, and power.

> *"But seek first his kingdom and his righteousness, and all these things will be given to you as well."*

MATTHEW 6:33

✠ *UNCEASING FAITHFULNESS*

———————[✠]———————

J esus' trust in his Father is not a single decision that leaves him infallibly certain of his mission and quits-and-free of the Tempter. His brush with death in the desert is the first of a series of challenges to his self-awareness and inner identity as Son-Servant-Beloved of the Father. The enduring temptation of his ministry is to fulfill his mission in a way opposed to the Father, to begin with a flashy demonstration of power by turning stones into bread and to end with a sensational exhibition of might by coming down from the cross. The alluring attractiveness of cultivating security, sensation, and power with life in the Spirit is Satan's worldly way. Jesus utterly rejects it. In the final foolishness of love he freely accepts death on the cross. It is the ultimate act of trust in the Father, the climax of a life lived in God. Jesus knows who he is. On the deepest level of his existence, Jesus reaffirms his self-awareness as Son-Servant-Beloved of the Father and fulfills his mission as servant of righteousness over sin. The mission that absorbed him from the moment of his baptism has brought him to this. The death on the cross gives final, definitive, and everlasting form to Jesus' religious identity and to his intimate, loving trust in his Father. He is faithful to the end.

> *Righteousness will be his belt and faithfulness the sash around his waist.*

ISAIAH 11:5

————🕀————

How would Peter have developed if he had had to depend on my patience, understanding, and compassion? Instead of a shrug, sneer, slap, or curse, Jesus responded by naming him the leader of his Church and by entrusting him with supreme authority to preach the Good News in the power of the Holy Spirit! What a reversal of the normal pattern of human behavior, and what a subversion of the universally accepted law of retaliation! Rollo May maintains that it is so highly significant as to be almost a rule that moral courage finds its source in the identification of one's own sensitivities with the pain and degradation and suffering of one's fellow human beings. In this way he explains the indomitable spirit of Aleksandr Solzhenitsyn. In the man Jesus, the mind of God becomes transparent. There is nothing of self to be seen, only the unconditional love of God. Jesus lays bare the ground of man's being in his encounter with Peter in the courtyard.

> *"Greater love has no one than this, that he lay down*
> *his life for his friends."*

JOHN 15:13

DYING DAILY TO SELF

————— 🎴 —————

I once addressed a large gathering at the Indianapolis Convention Center. After I delivered a forty-minute sermon entitled "The Victorious Limp," the assembled community of eleven thousand rose to its feet and erupted in thunderous applause.

Instantly, my shadow self—the self that hungers for honor, recognition, power, glory, and human respect—experienced a rush of gratification.

In that fleeting moment of euphoria, God took pity on his poor, proud son and graced me in an extraordinary way. Standing at the podium, I was given a vision of myself lying in a coffin. I had run out of time.

As I stared at my lifeless body I remembered a story about a bishop who lay dying in his bed—fully clothed in all his episcopal vestments! I began to laugh, slowly, then uproariously, at myself for wearing my miter to the convention center.

During the penitential season of Lent (six weeks of self-denial, fasting, and intense prayer in preparation for the celebration of Easter), remember that Jesus says do these things in such a way that only your Abba sees and knows what you are up to. This is a season of hidden secret acts of loving-kindness. Lent is a frontal assault on the false self, a time of dying daily to self in order to rise to newness of life with Christ.

> *For you have delivered me from death*
> *and my feet from stumbling,*
> *that I may walk before God*
> *in the light of life.*

PSALM 56:13

No Place for Self-Indulgence

———— ✠ ————

The gradual transformation from an attitude of self-hatred to a spirit of self-acceptance is what occurs in the process of trying to be honest. Paradoxically, the human spirit soars in the daily endeavor to make choices and decisions that are expressive of the truth of who we are in Christ Jesus, not who we think we should be or whom somebody else wants us to be. Self-mastery over every form of sin, selfishness, emotional dishonesty, and degraded love is the less-traveled road to Christian freedom. "You cannot belong to Christ Jesus unless you crucify all self-indulgent desires and passions" (see Gal. 5:24). The perfect joy of Saint Francis, for instance, may be at the outset an unrealistic expectation, but each small victory over self-indulgence yields its own measure of elation. The beginning of Brother Leo's peptic ulcer probably can be traced to the day that Francis explained to him the meaning of perfect joy: "Above all the graces and gifts of the Holy Spirit which Christ gives to his friends is that of conquering himself and willingly enduring sufferings, insults, humiliations, and hardships for the love of Christ." Leaving levity in its place, there is no growth without pain, no integrity without self-denial, and neither is particularly attractive apart from the personal love of Jesus Christ.

> *Humble yourselves, therefore, under God's mighty*
> *hand, that he may lift you up in due time.*

1 PETER 5:6

CHOOSING THE CROSS

———— ⊡ ————

F or the apostle Paul, hostility to the cross is the foremost characteristic of the world. To the Galatians Paul writes that what stamps Christians most deeply is the fact that through Jesus' cross the world is crucified to him and he to the world. To the Corinthians Paul says we manifest the life of Jesus only if we carry his death about with us. What Paul says to them applies to every Christian. We are disciples only as long as we stand in the shadow of the cross.

The Master said, "He who does not take up his cross and follow me is not worthy of me." Dietrich Bonhoeffer, the German Lutheran martyr, caught the meaning of this when he wrote: "When Jesus calls a man, he bids him come and die." We have no reason or right to choose another way than the way God chose in Jesus Christ. The cross is both the symbol of our salvation and the pattern of our lives.

> *May I never boast except in the cross of our Lord Jesus Christ, through which the world has been crucified to me, and I to the world.*
>
> GALATIANS 6:14

———————[✚]———————

Reckless confidence for me is the unshakable conviction that Jesus and the Father love me in a way that
defies imagination. It means to accept without reservation all that the Abba of Jesus has ordained for my life, to
have the attitude of Jesus when he prayed in the Garden, "Not
my will but yours be done," to make my own the prayer of Dag
Hammarskjöld, "For all that has been, thanks. For all that shall
be, yes."

Perhaps the only honest measure of the recklessness of
my confidence is my readiness for martyrdom. Not only my
willingness to die for him and the sake of the gospel, but to live
for him one day at a time.

> *We have confidence in the Lord that you are doing*
> *and will continue to do the things we command.*

2 THESSALONIANS 3:4

THE HEART OF GOD

On a recent five-day silent retreat, I spent the entire time in John's Gospel. Whenever a sentence caused my heart to stir, I wrote it out longhand in a journal. The first of many entries was also the last: "The disciple Jesus loved was reclining next to Jesus. . . . He leaned back on Jesus' breast" (John 13:23, 25 JB). We must not hurry past this scene in search of deeper revelation or we will miss a magnificent insight. John lays his head on the heart of God, on the breast of the man whom the Council of Nicea defined as "being co-equal and consubstantial to the Father . . . God from God, Light from Light, True God from True God." This passage should not be reduced to a historical memory. It can become a personal encounter, radically affecting our understanding of who God is and what our relationship with Jesus is meant to be. God allows a young Jew, reclining in the rags of his twenty-odd years, to listen to his heartbeat!

> May the Lord direct your hearts into God's love and Christ's perseverance.
>
> 2 THESSALONIANS 3:5

———— ⊞ ————

For those who feel that their lives are a grave disappointment to God, it requires enormous trust and reckless, raging confidence to accept the love of Christ, which knows no shadow of alteration or change. When Jesus said, "Come to me, all you who labor and are heavy burdened," he assumed we would grow weary, discouraged, and disheartened along the way. These words are a touching testimony to the genuine humanness of Jesus. He had no romantic notion of the cost of discipleship. He knew that physical pain, the loss of loved ones, failure, loneliness, rejection, abandonment, and betrayal would sap our spirits, that the day would come when faith would no longer offer any assurance, any drive or comfort, that prayer would lack any sense of reality or progress, that one day we would echo the cry of Teresa of Avila, "Lord, if this is the way you treat your friends, it is no wonder you have so few."

> *All this is evidence that God's judgment is right, and as a result you will be counted worthy of the kingdom of God, for which you are suffering.*

2 THESSALONIANS 1:5

OUR COMPANION

————[※]————

J esus' intimacy with Abba God is translated into an intimate relationship with his disciples. He draws near to us and speaks in words of intense familiarity. "My little children, I shall not be with you much longer. . . . I will not leave you orphans. I will come back to you. I am going to prepare a place for you. I shall return to take you with me." The Jesus who speaks here is not just a teacher or a model for us to imitate. He offers himself to each of us as a companion for the journey, as a friend who is patient with us, kind, never rude, and quick to forgive, and whose love keeps no score of wrongs. This is a beautiful dimension of discipleship, and the New Testament lays great stress on it: "Here I stand, knocking at the door. If anyone hears me calling and opens the door, I will enter his house and dine with him. . . . Anyone who loves me will be true to my Word, and my Father will love him and we will come to him and make our dwelling place with him. . . . And know that I am with you always, even till the end of the world. . . . No longer do I call you servants; I have called you friends."

> "And surely I am with you always, to the very end of
> the age."

MATTHEW 28:20

———— 🈁 ————

Selfless service. This gift embodies and enfleshes the mind of Christ. It is the most effective way of transcending the consciousness that continually focuses attention on self. In his Passion, Jesus moves completely out of himself. He is the man for others. He forgets himself. He is concerned about his apostles (John 18:8). He moves out to Pilate, trying to reach him. He comforts the women on the way to the cross. He pardons the good thief. He provides for the care of Mary and John as they stand at the foot of the cross. The charismatic gift mediated here is the power to move out of oneself through selfless service.

> *When Jesus heard what had happened, he withdrew*
> *by boat privately to a solitary place. Hearing of this,*
> *the crowds followed him on foot from the towns. When*
> *Jesus landed and saw a large crowd, he had compas-*
> *sion on them and healed their sick.*

MATTHEW 14:13–14

PEACE

————————⊞————————

The way to peace begins with accepting the truth of myself—the whole truth. Any bit of me that I refuse to accept becomes the enemy. My struggle to cope with certain people has a simple explanation: they represent to me precisely those elements that I have refused to acknowledge and accept in myself.

To accept the truth of my own brokenness is unbearable, if not impossible, without turning to Christ. If my vision of myself is not purified by the mercy and compassion of Jesus, I have to get dishonest, camouflage my warts, and present to you a self that is mostly admirable, fault free, and superficially happy.

For Meister Eckhart the equation "in Christ = in peace" is always valid. When I accept the truth of myself, shipwrecked and saved, and give it over to the person of Jesus, I am in peace even if I don't *feel* at peace. The peace that comes from God and surpasses all understanding (Phil. 4:7) was wrought by Christ on the cross and does not depend on my shifting feelings and moods.

The peace that comes through accepting the whole truth about myself is rooted in Christ "who has reconciled all things in himself, making peace through the blood of his cross." The "Shalom" of Jesus is not a mere greeting but an authoritative declaration from the Son of God, a crucified word that produces the peace it proclaims.

> Search me, O God, and know my heart:
> test me and know my anxious thoughts.
> See if there is any offensive way in me,
> and lead me in the way everlasting.
>
> PSALM 139:23–24

————[❂]————

An old Hasidic rabbi, Levi Yitzhak of Berdichev in the Ukraine, used to say that he discovered the meaning of love from a drunken peasant. The rabbi was visiting the owner of a tavern in the Polish countryside. As he walked in, he saw two peasants at a table. Both were gloriously in their cups. Arms around each other, they were protesting how much each loved the other. Suddenly Ivan said to Peter, "Peter, tell me what hurts me." Bleary eyed, Peter looked at Ivan. "How do I know what hurts you?" Ivan's answer was swift: "If you don't know what hurts me, how can you say you love me?"

Do you know what made Jesus so loving a person, the greatest lover in history? He knew what hurt us. He knew then and he knows now—the loves and hates, hopes and fears, the joys and sadnesses of each of us. This is not pious poetry. The risen Jesus is not a vague figure in outer space. His resurrection did not remove him from us; it simply made it possible for him to touch not only Naim but New Orleans, not only Magdalene but me. Christian living makes no sense unless we believe that at this moment, Jesus knows what hurts us. Not only knows but, knowing, seeks us out—whatever our kind of poverty or pain, however we weep, wherever we feel unloved.

> *Worship the LORD with gladness;*
> *come before him with joyful songs.*
> *Know that the LORD is God.*
> *It is he who made us, and we are his;*
> *we are his people, the sheep of his pasture.*

PSALM 100:2–3

THE CERTAINTY OF FAITH

—————— [※] ——————

Undoubtedly in each of our lives there were periods of intense fervor when we could almost touch the goodness of God. Bible studies, prayer meetings, retreats, and devotional time were precious securities to many of us. It was pleasant to think about God, a comfort to speak to him, a joy to be in his presence. Perhaps all this has changed. We may feel we have lost Christ and fear that he will never return. Now it is difficult to connect two thoughts about him. Prayer has become artificial. Words spoken to him ring hollow in our empty soul. Worse, oppressive feelings of guilt sharpen the sense of loss. Night closes in around us. We have failed him. It is all our fault.

It is a comfort to know that this is a path that many have tracked before us. Moreover, it is reassuring to learn that the longed-for growth in faith is not far away. God's love and mercy have not abandoned us. Clouds may shroud us in darkness, but above the sun shines bright. God's mercy never fails. The Christian who surrenders in trust to this truth finds Jesus Christ in a new way. It marks the beginning of a deeper life of faith where joy and peace flourish even in the darkness, because they are rooted, not in superficial human feelings, but deep down in the dark certainty of faith that Jesus is the same yesterday, today, and forever.

> *Now faith is being sure of what we hope for and certain of what we do not see.*

HEBREWS 11:1

THE FALSE SELF

───────[✠]───────

The false self buys into outside experiences to furnish a personal source of meaning. The pursuit of money, power, glamour, sexual prowess, recognition, and status enhances one's self-importance and creates the illusion of success. The impostor is what he *does*.

For many years I hid from my true self through my performance in ministry. I constructed an identity through sermons, books, and storytelling. I rationalized that if the majority of Christians thought well of me, there was nothing wrong with me. The more I invested in ministerial success, the more real the impostor became.

The impostor prompts us to attach importance to what has no importance, clothing with a false glitter, what is least substantial and turning us away from what is real. The false self causes us to live in a world of delusion.

The impostor is a liar.

Our false self stubbornly blinds each of us to the light and the truth of our own emptiness and hollowness. We cannot acknowledge the darkness within. On the contrary, the impostor proclaims his darkness as the most luminous light, varnishing truth and distorting reality. This brings to mind the apostle John's words: "If we claim to be without sin, we deceive ourselves and the truth is not in us" (1 John 1:8).

> *What will he do to you,*
> *and what more besides, O deceitful tongue?*

PSALM 120:3

PRIORITIES

————-[☩]————-

T he conversation of most middle-class Americans, we are told, revolves around consumption: what to buy, what was just bought, where to eat, what to eat, the price of the neighbor's house, what's on sale this week, our clothes or someone else's, the best car on the market this year, where to spend a vacation. Apparently we can't stop eating, shopping, or consuming. Success is measured not in terms of love, wisdom, and maturity but by the size of one's pile of possessions.

What was it biblical scholar Ernst Kasemann said? "A man counts as a lover of the cross only insofar as it enables him to come to terms with . . . the powers and enticements of the world." What is outrageous about the disciple of Jesus is that he can afford to be indifferent. Dead to the world but gloriously alive in Christ, he can say with Paul, "I know how to be stuffed full, and I know how to be destitute." Such an attitude is anathema to Madison Avenue. The world will respect us if we court it, and it will respect us even more if we reject it in disdain or anger; but it will hate us if we simply take no notice of its priorities or what it thinks of us. In John's Gospel the Jews are said to be incapable of believing because "they receive glory from one another." There is a radical incompatibility between human respect and faith in Jesus Christ.

> "Do not store up for yourselves treasures on earth,
> where moth and rust destroy, and where thieves break
> in and steal."

MATTHEW 6:19

The Christ of the New Testament is not the God of the philosophers, speaking with detachment about the Supreme Being. We do not expect to find the Supreme Being with spit on his face. It jars us to discover that the invitation Jesus issues is: "Don't weep for me; join me. The life I have planned for you is a Christian life, much like the life I led." As my friend Dominique Voillaume once said to me on a wintry morning in Dijon, France, "*La vie est dure*," life is hard. It is hard to be a Christian, but it is too dull to be anything else. When Jesus comes into our lives with his scandalous cross in the form of mental anguish, physical suffering, and wounds of the spirit that will not close, we pray for the courage to "stand fast a little" against the insidious realism of the world, the flesh, and the devil.

> On that day they will say to Jerusalem,
> "Do not fear, O Zion;
> do not let your hands hang limp.
> The LORD your God is with you,
> he is mighty to save.
> He will take great delight in you,
> he will quiet you with his love,
> he will rejoice over you with singing."

ZEPHANIAH 3:16–17

THE CAREFUL CHOICE

———————🔣———————

A terrible thing has happened to Caiphas. Religion has left the realm of respect for person, immediate concern for the individual, for communion. For Caiphas, sacredness has become institutions, structures, abstractions. Caiphas is dedicated to the "people." Therefore, individual, flesh-and-blood men, real people, are expendable. Caiphas is dedicated to the "nation." But the nation does not bleed like Jesus. Caiphas is dedicated to the "Temple," a mere building, impersonal brick and mortar. Caiphas becomes impersonal himself, no longer a warm human being but a robot, as fixed and rigid as his own unchanging world.

The choice usually presented to Christians is not between Jesus and Barabbas. No one wants to appear an obvious murderer. The choice we have to be careful about is between Jesus and Caiphas. And Caiphas can fool us. He is a very "religious" man.

> *With his mouth the godless destroys his neighbor,*
> *but through knowledge the righteous escape.*

PROVERBS 11:9

THE FOLLY OF THE CROSS

————— ✠ —————

The Greeks envisioned the messiah figure as a philosopher greater than Plato. He would lead men to contemplate the order and harmony of the universe. But a messiah who would rattle this comfortable, cultured piety by reversing its values and going to death on a cross, victim of the irrational dregs of humanity—he would indeed be a stupidity to the Greeks.

Yet Paul preached the folly of the cross—the crucified Christ who is the power and wisdom of God—and he enjoyed incredible success. The preaching of the cross called the Spirit to life. Jews and Greeks alike laid aside their prejudices to be swept up into the power and wisdom of the cross.

> *For since in the wisdom of God the world through its wisdom did not know him, God was pleased through the foolishness of what was preached to save those who believe.*

I CORINTHIANS 1:21

DOWNWARD MOBILITY

———————✠———————

J esus remains Lord by being a servant.

The beloved disciple presents a mind-bending image of God, blowing away all previous conceptions of who the Messiah is and what discipleship is all about. What a scandalous reversal of the world's values! To prefer to be the servant rather than the lord of the household is the path of downward mobility in an upwardly mobile culture. To taunt the idols of prestige, honor, and recognition, to refuse to take oneself seriously or to take seriously others who take themselves seriously, and to freely embrace the servant lifestyle—these are the attitudes that bear the stamp of authentic discipleship.

The stark realism of John's portrait of Christ leaves no room for romanticized idealism or sloppy sentimentality. Servanthood is not an emotion or mood or feeling; it is a decision to live like Jesus. It has nothing to do with what we feel; it has everything to do with what we *do*—humble service. To listen obediently to Jesus— "If I, then, the Lord and Master, have washed your feet, you should wash each other's feet"—is to hear the heartbeat of the Rabbi John knew and loved.

When being is divorced from doing, pious thoughts become an adequate substitute for washing dirty feet.

> *So he got up from the meal, took off his outer clothing,*
> *and wrapped a towel around his waist. After that, he*
> *poured water into a basin and began to wash his disci-*
> *ples' feet, drying them with the towel that was*
> *wrapped around him.*

JOHN 13:4–5

MIRACLE IN CHICAGO

————— 🔯 —————

Let me share an example of ministering to the Lord in the moment of *his* adversity. This happened in Chicago's South Side on Holy Thursday night. I wrote in my journal: "The adoration of the Lord Jesus in the Eucharist began with a heaviness within me. It's freezing outside; the chapel is cold; my mind is opaque; but foremost is the nagging doubt about my own sincerity." Earlier in the day I sensed a tug in the direction of nonacceptance, when I read, "Where the Spirit of the Lord is, there is freedom." Do I really want to be free? Do I honestly desire a Kingdom lifestyle? What are the real tendencies and desires of my heart? Do I long more than anything else to be God's man? To serve rather than be served? To pray when I could play? Be slow to speak, Brennan, be cautious to answer. . . . I felt confusion and discouragement tiding within me.

Then a beautiful thing happened. I realized that the only reason I was at prayer was because I wanted to be with my friend. The doubt and uncertainty vanished. I knew I wanted to comfort Jesus in his loneliness and fear in the Garden. I wanted to watch not an hour but the whole night with him. The only words that formed on my lips were those of the little boy Willie-Juan in the fairy tale I had written the year past. Over and over I whispered, "I love you, my friend."

> *Test me, O LORD, and try me,*
> *examine my heart and my mind;*
> *for your love is ever before me,*
> *and I walk continually in your truth.*

PSALM 26:2–3

THE VALUE IN SUFFERING

————[✲]————

I t is more important to be a mature Christian than to be a great butcher or baker or candlestick maker; and if the only chance to achieve the first is to fail in the second, the failure will have proved worthwhile. Isn't it worthwhile if it teaches a man to be gentle with the failure of others, to be patient, to live in the wisdom of accepted tenderness and pass that tenderness on to others? Successful, he might have been wrapped up in his own success and insensitive to the anguish of others; he might never have come to understand the human heart; he might have come to think of success as his due. Later, if his little world collapsed through death or disaster, he would have no inner resources.

It is helpful to remember that the value of Jesus' suffering lay not in the pain itself (for in itself it has no value), but in the love that inspired it. Cyril of Jerusalem writes: "Never forget that what gives value to a sacrifice is not the renouncement it demands but the quality of love which inspired the renouncement." That is how we must approach Calvary. The human soul of Jesus ravished the heart of his heavenly Father with the wild generosity and unflagging obedience of his love.

> *Therefore, since Christ suffered in his body, arm yourselves also with the same attitude, because he who has suffered in his body is done with sin.*

I PETER 4:1

FORGIVENESS IN AN UNFORGIVING WORLD

———— ✠ ————

Scripture points to an intimate connection between compassion and forgiveness. According to Jesus, a distinctive sign of Abba's child is the willingness to forgive our enemies: "Love your enemies, and do good . . . and you will be sons of the Most High, for he himself is kind to the ungrateful and the wicked" (Luke 6:35 JB). In the Lord's Prayer we acknowledge the primary characteristic of Abba's children when we pray, "Forgive us our trespasses as we forgive those who trespass against us." Jesus presents his Abba as the model for our forgiveness: the king in Matthew 18 who forgives a fantastic sum, an unpayable debt, the God who forgives without limit (the meaning of seventy times seven).

God calls his children to a countercultural lifestyle of forgiveness in a world that demands an eye for an eye—and worse. But if loving God is the first commandment, and loving our neighbor proves our love for God, and if it is easy to love those who love us, then loving our enemies must be the filial badge that identifies Abba's children.

> Bear with each other and forgive whatever grievances
> you may have against one another. Forgive as the Lord
> forgave you.

COLOSSIANS 3:13

THE ABBA EXPERIENCE

———————[✠]———————

The greatest gift I have ever received from Jesus Christ has been the Abba experience. "No one knows the Son except the Father, just as no one knows the Father except the Son and those to whom the Son chooses to reveal him" (Matt. 11:27 JB). My dignity as Abba's child is my most coherent sense of self. When I seek to fashion a self-image from the adulation of others and the inner voice whispers, "You've arrived; you're a player in the Kingdom enterprise," there is no truth in that self-concept. When I sink into despondency and the inner voice whispers, "You are no good, a fraud, a hypocrite, and a dilettante," there is no truth in any image shaped from that message. As Gerald May has noted, . . . "How we view ourselves at any given moment may have very little to do with who we really are."

> *"Ah, Sovereign* LORD,*" I said, "I do not know how to speak; I am only a child."*

> JEREMIAH 1:6

———————❖———————

S ilence is not simply the absence of noise or the shutdown of communication with the outside world, but rather a process of coming to stillness. Silent solitude forges true speech. I'm not speaking of physical isolation; solitude here means being alone with the Alone, experiencing the transcendent Other, and growing in awareness of one's identity as the beloved. It is impossible to know another person intimately without spending time together. Silence makes this solitude a reality. It has been said, "Silence is solitude practiced in action."

> *Men listened to me expectantly,*
> *waiting in silence for my counsel.*
>
> JOB 29:21

RESISTANCE TO PRAYER

———— 桊 ————

Have you ever felt baffled by your internal resistance to prayer? By the existential dread of silence, solitude, and being alone with God? By the way you drag yourself out of bed for morning praise or . . . endure nightly prayer with stoic resignation, knowing that "this too shall pass"?

Beware the impostor!

The false self specializes in treacherous disguise. He is the lazy part of self, resisting the effort, asceticism, and discipline that intimacy with God requires. He inspires rationalizations, such as, "My work is my prayer; I'm too busy; prayer should be spontaneous so I just pray when I am moved by the Spirit." The false self's lame excuses allow us to maintain the status quo.

> But not all the Israelites accepted the good news. For
> Isaiah says, "Lord, who has believed our message?"

ROMANS 10:16

———————[✠]———————

For a long time, Catherine of Siena enjoyed a glorious prayer life. She had a highly conscious awareness of the divine indwelling. She loved to spend days alone, locked up in her little room, enjoying the presence of the beautiful God who dwelled in her heart. This was peace, joy, security. God, her God, was always with her. Life would always be a vision of peace.

So she thought, until one day when her comfortable existence exploded. She lost the familiar feeling of secure possession. The Christ of her heart was gone. She lost the sense of his presence, felt dead to his influence. Now even the memory of him seemed unreal. He had vanished into thin air. Now sin was the only thing that mattered. Impure images filled her thoughts and desires, and her body tingled in response. She felt as though she had been plunged into a pool of filth and that she had lost forever her clean, joyous life with Christ.

This loss became the moment of grace. In the same room where she had been so fiercely tempted, Catherine found Christ again. "Lord," she complained, "where were you when these foul images filled my mind?" The answer of Jesus opened up a new depth of faith: "Catherine, all during these temptations I have remained with you, right in your heart. Otherwise, you could not have overcome them."

> O people of Zion, who live in Jerusalem, you will weep
> no more. How gracious he will be when you cry for
> help! As soon as he hears, he will answer you.

ISAIAH 30:19

THE HIDDEN GOD

———————[✠]———————

A t the very moment when Jesus revealed to Catherine of Siena that he had been with her during her ordeal of severe temptation, she lost forever her former understanding of what it meant to experience the presence of God. His word taught her that his presence in the soul is something deeper and holier than she could imagine or feel. In this life, he must always be the hidden God. Human feelings cannot touch him; human thought cannot measure him. Experience cannot heighten the certainty of his presence any more than fear of his absence can lessen it. This word made Catherine realize as never before that nothing but sin could take Christ from her. Noise, irritating people, or temptation; success or failure; warm feelings or aridity; nothing but sin could separate her from Christ. He would always be there, in the quiet darkness of her soul, just as he had promised. She had lost the presence of God, only to find it again in the deep darkness of a richer faith. She had learned to celebrate the darkness.

> *Although the Lord gives you the bread of adversity and the water of affliction, your teachers will be hidden no more; with your own eyes you will see them.*

ISAIAH 30:20

———————[✠]———————

A t this moment, many ordinary men and women just like you and me are being invited to enter into the rhythm of loss and gain. In each of our lives, there no doubt have been periods of fervor when we could almost touch the goodness of God. We have enjoyed various religious exercises, precious securities for many of us, in which it was a joy to be in his presence. Perhaps all this has changed now: like Catherine of Siena we seem to have lost Christ, and we fear he might never return.

But the gain is never far away. God's love and mercy are too great and too lasting to depend on the rise and fall of his frail creatures. Clouds may shroud our soul in darkness, but above them the sun shines brightly; God's mercy never fails. Those who grasp the real meaning of this truth find Christ in a new way. This experience marks the beginning of a richer life in which joy and peace flourish even in the darkness, because they are rooted not in superficial human feelings, but deep down in the dark certainty of faith that Jesus is always the same.

Happiness and sadness may play havoc with our emotions, but once we learn that God dwells in darkness beneath the shifting surfaces of our souls, we know that that is where we must go to find him. There we will pray in peace and silence, attentive to the God who never changes.

> Whether you turn to the right or to the left, your ears
> will hear a voice behind you, saying, "This is the way;
> walk in it."

ISAIAH 30:21

VENERATION OF THE CROSS

Forty minutes of prime time in solitary prayer, usually divided into two twenty-minute periods, before a symbol of the crucified Christ is the most effective discipline I have found for making conscious contact with the living God and his liberating love. Lamentably, Christian piety has prettified the passionate God of Golgotha; Christian art has banalized unspeakable outrage into dignified jewelry; Christian worship has sentimentalized monstrous scandal into sacred pageant. We have corrupted our sense of reality by sentimentalizing it. Pious imagination, romantic preaching, and lifeless or raucous worship overshadow the real Jesus. The Christian should tremble and the whole community quake during the veneration of the cross on Good Friday.

> *He was despised and rejected by men,*
> *a man of sorrows, and familiar with suffering.*
> *Like one from whom men hide their faces*
> *he was despised, and we esteemed him not.*

ISAIAH 53:3

——————✠——————

I believe that the night in the Upper Room was the defining moment of John's life. Some sixty years after Christ's resurrection, the apostle—like an old gold miner panning the stream of his memories—recalled all that had transpired during his three-year association with Jesus. He made pointed reference to that holy night when it all came together, and he affirmed his identity with these words: "Peter turned and saw the disciple Jesus loved following them—the one who had leaned on his breast at the supper" (John 21:20 JB).

If John were to be asked, "What is your primary identity, your most coherent sense of yourself?" he would not reply, "I am a disciple, an apostle, an evangelist," but "I am the one Jesus loves.". . .

To read John 13:23–25 without faith is to read it without profit. To risk the passionate life, we must be "affected by" Jesus as John was; we must engage his experience with our lives rather than with our memories. Until I lay my head on Jesus' breast, listen to his heartbeat, and personally appropriate the Christ-experience of John's eyewitness, I have only a *derivative* spirituality. My cunning impostor will borrow John's moment of intimacy and attempt to convey it as if it were my own.

Whoever loves his brother lives in the light, and there
is nothing in him to make him stumble.

1 JOHN 2:10

JUDGING OTHERS

꽃

Isn't it true that each of us lives in a world of his own—the world of our minds? What a thickly populated world that can be! And what an unkind one! So often we are narrow, cold, haughty, unforgiving, and so judgmental! How readily we push Jesus Christ off his judgment seat and take our place there to pronounce on others though we have neither the knowledge nor the authority to judge anyone! None of us has ever seen a motive. Therefore, we do not suspect, we cannot suspect, what inspired the action of another. Thus, we are told not to judge. "If you want to avoid judgment, stop passing judgment" (see Matt. 7:1). But if we are reckless enough to judge another, it is well to remember that "your verdict on others will be the verdict passed on you. The measure with which you measure will be used to measure you" (see Matt. 7:2–3).

> You, then, why do you judge your brother? Or why do you look down on your brother? For we will all stand before God's judgment seat.
>
> ROMANS 14:10

THE PURSUIT OF TRUTH

The first step in the pursuit of truth is not the moral resolution to avoid the habit of petty lying—however unattractive a character disfigurement that may be. It is not the decision to stop deceiving others: it is the decision to stop deceiving ourselves. Unless we have the same relentless passion for the truth that Jesus exhibited in the Temple, we are undermining our faith, betraying the Lord, and deceiving ourselves. Self-deception is the enemy of wholeness because it prevents us from seeing ourselves as we really are. It covers up our lack of growth in the Spirit of the truthful One and keeps us from coming to terms with our real personalities.

> *How long will this continue in the hearts of these lying prophets, who prophesy the delusions of their own minds?*
>
> JEREMIAH 23:26

COMPLACENCY

———— 🀫 ————

By extinguishing the spirit that burns in [John's] Gospel, we scarcely feel the glow anymore. We have gotten so used to the ultimate Christian fact—Jesus naked, stripped, and crucified—that we no longer see it for what it actually is: an injunction to strip ourselves of earthly cares and worldly wisdom, all desire for human praise, greediness for any kind of comfort, spiritual consolations included; a summons to be stripped of those fine pretenses by which we manage to build up a fine picture of ourselves for the admiration of our friends; [a call] to let go of those pretenses that would make us believe that we really aren't worldly in the Johannine sense—the kind of worldliness that prefers the more attractive duty to the less attractive, that give more attention to the people we want to stand well with. Even the last rag we cling to—the self-flattery that suggests that we are being rather humble when we disclaim any resemblance to Jesus Christ—even that rag has to go when we are face-to-face with the crucified Son of Man.

> *They will throw their silver into the streets, and their gold will be an unclean thing. Their silver and gold will not be able to save them in the day of the LORD's wrath. They will not satisfy their hunger or fill their stomachs with it, for it has made them stumble into sin.*

EZEKIEL 7:19

———————[※]———————

As we stand on Calvary on Good Friday, one truth we learn is not to apply to the heart of Jesus the measure of our own stingy little hearts, so mean, so narrow, and so hard. If we make him as fussy, unforgiving, and vindictive as we are at our worst, we shall never comprehend how good, how patient and compassionate, how gentle and extravagant Jesus of Nazareth really is.

Jesus said, "He who sees me sees the Father." From our brother Jesus, who alone knows the Father, we learn that there is welcoming love, unconditional acceptance, a relentless and eternal affection that so far exceeds our human experience that even the Passion and death of Jesus is only a *hint* of it. Think on that for a moment: the torn, broken, lacerated, spit-covered, blood-drenched body of Jesus is only a hint of the Father's love. The very substance of our faith is the unwavering confidence that beyond this hint lies love beyond measure.

> *This is love: not that we loved God, but that he loved*
> *us and sent his Son as an atoning sacrifice for our sins.*

I JOHN 4:10

LIBERATION

------⟨✼⟩------

The crucified Christ reminds us that despair and disillusionment are not terminal but signs of impending resurrection. What lives beyond the cross is the liberating power of love, freeing us from the ego centeredness that says, "All I am is what I think I am and nothing more." One Good Friday morning . . . as I prayed in faith I heard him say, "Little brother, I witnessed a Peter who claimed that he did not know me, a James who wanted power in return for service, a Philip who failed to see the Father in me, and scores of disciples who were convinced I was finished on Calvary. The New Testament has many examples of men and women who started out well and then faltered along the way.

"Yet on Easter Day I appeared to Peter; James is not remembered for his ambition but for the sacrifice of his life for the kingdom; Philip did see the Father in me when I pointed the way; and the disciples who despaired had enough courage to recognize me as the stranger who walked the road to Emmaus. My point, little brother, is this: I expect more failure from you than you expect from yourself."

> May the LORD answer you when you are in distress;
> may the name of the God of Jacob protect you.

PSALM 20:1

————[✠]————

The meaning of Easter is more than hope beyond the grave, more than the infallible guarantee that the resurrection of Jesus Christ is the pledge of my own. His Easter victory means first his sovereignty over the living as well as the dead. The risen Christ is Lord of my life right now, meaning he is God above all the gods of the unreal world out there—security, power, wealth, beauty, or whatever else makes false claims on my life. Easter means for me empowerment to freedom, the freedom to be a living fulfillment of the First Commandment, "I am the Lord your God. . . . You shall have no other gods before me."

> This is why it says:
> "When he ascended on high,
> he led captives in his train
> and gave gifts to men."
>
> EPHESIANS 4:8

No Sad Christians!

————————🔆————————

During the fifty days of the Easter season culminating on Pentecost, Ignatius of Loyola encourages disciples to pray daily for the charisma of "intense gladness." Clearly, he does not mean a giddy cocktail-party gaiety or a brave attempt to smile through the tears, but a deep-seated joy in the resurrection triumph of Jesus Christ. . . .

If this prayer is heard, I shall have found a source of joy that is unassailable, for whatever happens, the Lord is always risen. Contingencies cannot suffocate this deep joy. Whether the day is stormy or fair, whether I am sick or healthy, whether I feel like a dirt ball or a butterfly, whatever comes cannot alter the fact that the Lord is risen.

> *Then will all your people be righteous*
> *and they will possess the land forever.*
> *They are the shoot I have planted,*
> *the work of my hands,*
> *for the display of my splendor.*
>
> ISAIAH 60:19

————[⚓]————

My brother or sister, the cross of Jesus not only illumines the enigma of suffering, it is a mighty source of light on every dilemma a human being can face. Let us see how it applies to an immediate, practical, and very touchy problem in the world and the church today. Jesus' death on Calvary illustrates better than anything else his lived principle of *not resisting evil*. The fact that evil can be overcome in this fashion is comprehended by very few Christians. And these few, this little band of disciples, are convinced that Jesus presented in his words and in his behavior not only a good way of doing things, not only an ideal to be carried out whenever it is convenient, but the only way of doing what he did. Redemption has come to us in the form of a cross. Suffering love is God's strategy for overcoming evil. His only strategy. God saves through suffering. Charles de Foucauld said, "Not by his words or his works, not even by his miracles, but by his Cross." He overcame evil by surrendering to it in love and obedience.

> *"My prayer is not that you take them out of the world*
> *but that you protect them from the evil one."*

JOHN 17:15

OUR DESTINY

———————[❖]———————

Perhaps the real question is: May the Christian—indeed must the Christian—face the possibility that there are occasions in which there is no Christian way to survive? Do we believe in the invincible power of redemptive suffering? Are there enough women and men of deep faith who are willing to work, suffer, and die in spiritual resistance to the inhuman attitudes that are now in control?

Happily, the cross is not the final word that God has spoken to his people. Our Christian lives look beyond Calvary to resurrection, and it is the human nature of the risen Christ, shot through and through with the radiance of divinity, that shows like a radiant mirror all that we are summoned to. The destiny of Christ our brother is our destiny. If we have suffered with him, we shall be glorified with him. The pattern is always the same. We reach life only through death, we come to light only through darkness, the grain of wheat must fall into the ground and die. Jonah must be buried in the whale's belly.

When you pass through the waters,
I will be with you;
and when you pass through the rivers,
they will not sweep over you.
When you walk through the fire,
you will not be burned;
the flames will not set you ablaze.

ISAIAH 43:2

──────⟨❄⟩──────

E very Easter brings to mind that beautiful story found in Nikolai Arseniew's book, *Mysticism in the East*. Comrade Lunachatsky was lecturing in Moscow's largest assembly hall shortly after the Bolshevik Revolution. His theme was "Religion: Opium of the People." All the Christian mysteries are but myths, he said, supplanted by the light of science. Marxist science is the light that more than substitutes for the legends of Christianity. Lunachatsky spoke at great length. When he finished, he was so pleased with himself that he asked if anyone in the audience of some seven thousand had anything to add. A twenty-six-year-old Russian Orthodox priest, just ordained, stepped forward. First he apologized to the commissar for his ignorance and awkwardness. The commissar looked at him scornfully: "I'll give you two minutes, no more." "I won't take very long," the priest assured him. He mounted the platform, turned to the audience, and in a loud voice declared, "Christ is risen!" As one man, that vast audience roared in response, "He is truly risen!"

May that response find an echo in your heart and mine because the resurrection of Jesus Christ from the dead is the source, the reason, the basis for the inarticulate joy of our Christian lives.

> *And the ransomed of the LORD will return.*
> *They will enter Zion with singing;*
> *everlasting joy will crown their heads.*
> *Gladness and joy will overtake them,*
> *and sorrow and sighing will flee away.*

ISAIAH 35:10

THE LORD OF LAUGHTER

————[✳]————

Christ is risen, alleluia. He is the Lord of the dance, the dance of the living. He is the Lord of laughter; our laughter is the echo of his risen life within us. He is the risen Lord of glory, who in sovereign authority can say: "Blessed are you who laugh now, because you can bring the joy of Easter to others. But blessed are you only if you can laugh at yourselves, if you don't take yourselves too seriously, if human living doesn't revolve around you and your needs. Only if you can take delight in all of my Father's creation—in sun and surf, in snow and star, in blue marlin and in robin redbreast, in Cezanne, Olivia Newton-John, and veal scaloppini, in the love of a man or woman, and in the presence of the living God within you. Only if your laughter means that you have let go in reckless confidence all that shackles you to yesterday, imprisons you in your small self today, and frightens you with the uncertainty of tomorrow. Blessed are you who laugh, because you are free!"

> Go, eat your food with gladness, and drink your wine
> with a joyful heart, for it is now that God favors what
> you do.

ECCLESIASTES 9:7

————[✠]————

The cross of Jesus will ever remain a scandal and foolishness to discriminating disciples who seek a triumphal
savior and a prosperity gospel. Their number is legion.
They are enemies of the cross of Christ. Jesus would have no
other name by which he could be called were it not the name
of the crucified. . . . His ministry was a seeming failure; his life
appeared to have made no difference; he was a naked, murdered, ineffectual, losing God. But in that weakness and vulnerability, the world would come to know the love of the Abba
of the Compassionate One.

> *But with loud shouts they insistently demanded that he*
> *be crucified, and their shouts prevailed.*

LUKE 23:23

SHARING HIS TRIUMPH

While Jesus was still trammeled by the human limitations of mortal flesh, he could not become, in the bold words of Paul, "the messianic Son of God in power." He could not be glorified until he had been crucified. The whole purpose of his redemptive suffering, death, and resurrection was to share with us the fruits of his Easter triumph. In the glorification of Jesus there was a "handing over of power," as Edward Schillebeecx said, in which the Father bestowed his kingly might on Christ whom he made to be *Kyrios*. "Sitting at the right hand of God," the Lord Jesus (Christians came to be known as the people who call upon the Kyrios, the Lord) pours out the Holy Spirit to form the holy People of God, a community of prophets and lovers who would surrender to the mystery of the fire of the Spirit that burns within, who would live in ever greater fidelity to the shattering, omnipresent Word, who would enter into the center of all that is, into the very heart and mystery of God, into the center of that flame that consumes and purifies and sets all aglow with peace, joy, boldness, and extravagant love—which is what it means to claim the name "Christian," follower of Jesus Christ.

> *But thanks be to God, who always leads us in triumphal procession in Christ and through us spreads everywhere the fragrance of the knowledge of him.*

2 CORINTHIANS 2:14

———————[✿]———————

Bizarre as it sounds, the ministry of praising God's goodness, wisdom, and love during times of pain and heart-
ache is a beautiful expression of faith in action, a living
expression of trust that "God makes *all* things work together for
the good of those who have been called according to his
decree." In his moving little book, *Our Heavenly Father*, Dr.
Robert Frost writes, "There is nothing more precious to God
than our praise during affliction. Not praise for what the devil
has done, but praise for the redeeming power of our loving
heavenly Father. What he does not protect us from, He will
perfect us through. There is indeed a special blessing for those
who do not become offended at God during adversity.
Furthermore, we become a special blessing to Him!"

> *Why are you downcast, O my soul?*
> *Why so disturbed within me?*
> *Put your hope in God,*
> *for I will yet praise him,*
> *my Savior and my God.*

PSALM 43:5

EVANGELIZATION

———————❧———————

The fundamental mission of the church is preaching the Good News of Jesus Christ. But there has been a loss of faith in the power of the Word. We feel it won't be effective if we say it as it is. It will turn people off; let's rebuild the temporal order first.

But there is a startling discontinuity between human reasoning and what God's Word says the priority is. War, loneliness, world hunger, abortion—these are rooted in man's rebellion. Man must submit in faith to Jesus Christ and repent. Putting a Band-Aid here and there on this or that moral problem is not the answer. Evangelization hits the core: man must submit in faith to Jesus Christ and repent. He must renounce his autonomy and self-sufficiency. Personal appropriation of the death and resurrection of Christ is the one foundation for Christian community and world peace. Failure to act on the gospel imperative to evangelize has resulted in holding to the form of Christianity while denying its power. Beautiful liturgies; mass; regional, national, and international meetings; crusades against immorality are good and have their places, but none of them is an adequate substitute for dying to self.

> But you, keep your head in all situations, endure hardship, do the work of an evangelist, discharge all the duties of your ministry.
>
> 2 TIMOTHY 4:5

A LIFE OF INTEGRITY

———————[✠]———————

One day Jesus announced that he had not come to call the virtuous, but the sinners. Then he proceeded to break bread with a notorious public sinner, Zacchaeus.

Jesus reinforced his words with deeds. He was not intimidated by authority figures. He seemed unfazed by the crowds' complaints that he was violating the Law by going to a sinner's house. Jesus broke the law of traditions when the love of persons demanded it.

Begrudgingly, the Pharisees were forced to acknowledge Jesus' integrity: "Master, we know that you are an honest man, that you are not afraid of anyone, because a man's rank means nothing to you, and that you teach the way of God in all honesty" (Mark 12:14 JB). Although it was a ploy to trap him, this admission tells us something of the impact Jesus had on his listeners. A life of integrity has prophetic clout even with cynics.

Yes, indeed, this man was truly a Rabbi unlike any other in Palestine. He may never have studied under a great teacher; he had no degree. He was a layman, an uneducated Galilean peasant, but his Word thundered with authority: he was the Great Rabbi because his being and his doing, like his humanity and his divinity, were one.

> Then Jesus said to the crowds and to his disciples:
> "The teachers of the law and the Pharisees sit in
> Moses' seat. So you must obey them and do everything
> they tell you. But do not do what they do, for they do
> not practice what they preach."

MATTHEW 23:1-3

RECKLESS LOVE

———————[✠]———————

The focus of Mary Magdalene's attention throughout the Passion was not suffering but the suffering Christ "who loved her and delivered himself up for her." We must not allow these words to be interpreted as allegory. The love of Jesus Christ on the cross was a burning reality for Magdalene, and her life is utterly incomprehensible except in terms of it. If you approach Mary of Magdala to speak of the Christian life, charismatic spirituality, or the gifts of the Holy Spirit, you speak of Jesus Christ nailed to the cross or you do not speak at all.

Do not burden her with your insights into apophatic mysticism; do not insult her with your gift of tongues. She has only one question: "Do you know him?" In the realm of Christian discipleship it is conceivable that the Church has never had a greater lover of Jesus Christ than Mary Magdalene. It is insolent to infer a chummy ménage à trois if the center of your life is not the crucified Lord.

> "Therefore, I tell you, her many sins have been for-
> given—for she loved much. But he who has been for-
> given little loves little."

LUKE 7:47

WHO IS HE?

――――[✝]――――

The challenge, so keenly put in the New Testament, "Who do you say that I am?" is addressed to each of us. Who is the Jesus of your own interiority? Describe the Christ that you have personally encountered on the grounds of your own self.

Only a superficial stereotyped answer can be forthcoming if we have not developed a personal relationship with Jesus. We can only repeat and reproduce pious turns of speech that others have spoken or wave a catechism under children's noses if we have not gained some partial insight, some small perception, of the inexhaustible richness of the mystery of who is Jesus Christ.

> *We proclaim to you what we have seen and heard, so that you also may have fellowship with us. And our fellowship is with the Father and with his Son, Jesus Christ.*

1 JOHN 1:3

ONE'S LIFE COMMITMENT

———— 🔯 ————

On Calvary Jesus seals his election as Messiah, holds firmly to it despite the loneliness and desolation that are exerting tremendous pressure against his self-awareness as Son-Servant-Beloved. The Christian participates in the Pasch of the Lord by sharing in the suffering and dying that result from remaining steadfast to his own commitment. The power of darkness (security, sensation, and power) attempts to seduce him to turn back, to renege on his commitment, to renounce his obedience to Christ by a kind of physical or moral self-annihilation. The cross confronts the Christian with the cost of discipleship, reminds him there is no cheap Pentecost, and carries within it the living power to enable him to endure the inevitable humiliations, rejections, sacrifices, and loneliness that the journey to higher Christian consciousness imposes.

> Therefore, my dear brothers, stand firm. Let nothing move you. Always give yourselves fully to the work of the Lord, because you know that your labor in the Lord is not in vain.

1 CORINTHIANS 15:58

A JOYFUL HEART

———— 🔣 ————

Thanksgiving is the song of the saved sinner. Steeped in Calvary-awareness of the merciful love of the redeeming God, the Christian's life becomes one of humble, joyful thanksgiving. Through no merit of his own, but by divine mercy, he has been called out of darkness into wondrous light. "For it is by grace you have been saved, through faith—and this not from yourselves, it is the gift of God" (Eph. 2:8). Unnecessary emotional suffering—depression, anxiety, guilt, fear, and sadness—is vanquished by the transforming power of the love of Jesus Christ. The cross is a confrontation with the overwhelming goodness of God and the mystery of his love. God is pleased when we work; he is delighted when we sing. And the saved sinner sings, "It is right to give him thanks and praise."

> *From them will come songs of thanksgiving*
> *and the sound of rejoicing.*
> *I will add to their numbers,*
> *and they will not be decreased;*
> *I will bring them honor,*
> *and they will not be disdained.*

JEREMIAH 30:19

THE GREATEST SIN

———— 🖾 ————

Paul Claudel, the poet, said that the greatest sin is to lose the sense of sin. The man without a lively sense of the horror of sin does not know Jesus Christ crucified. The knowledge that sin exists and that man is a sinner comes only from the cross. The Christian can delude himself into believing that sin is simply an aberration or a lack of maturity, that preoccupation with security, sensation, and power is caused by oppressive social structures and personality hang-ups, that he is sinful but not a sinner—a mere victim of circumstances, compulsions, environment, addictions, upbringing, and so forth. The Passion nails these lies, illusions, and rationalizations to the cross of truth. Even the last perversion of truth he clings to—the self-flattery that suggests he is being rather humble when he disclaims any resemblance to Jesus Christ—has to go.

> *They will spread out their hands in it,*
> *as a swimmer spreads out his hands to swim.*
> *God will bring down their pride*
> *despite the cleverness of their hands.*

ISAIAH 25:11

The power and wisdom of God is singularly manifested in the death and resurrection of Jesus Christ. Is it really surprising that from Jesus' greatest act of love, his greatest power would flow? The life of the Christian is not the imitation of a dead hero. The Christian lives in Christ and Christ lives in the Christian through the Holy Spirit. He is empowered to lead a new life where sin has no place. If he does not, he frustrates the power of the Paschal mystery by his refusal of faith in the power. "How often are Christians unwilling to believe that they have been transformed and that the impossible has become possible?" asks Scripture scholar John McKenzie.

> Do not conform any longer to the pattern of this world,
> but be transformed by the renewing of your mind.
> Then you will be able to test and approve what God's
> will is—his good, pleasing and perfect will.

ROMANS 12:2

FINDING THE FATHER

———————— ⌘ ————————

F urther along in his ministry, Jesus would say, "The Father and I are one," indicating an intimacy of life and love that defy description. To Philip he would say, "He who sees me sees the Father." And again, "It is the Father living in me who is doing this work." Jesus is the human face of God, with all the attitudes, attributes, and characteristics of the Father.

So many Christians I know stop at Jesus. They remain on the Way without going where the Way leads them—to the Father. They want to be brothers and sisters without being sons and daughters. In them, the lament of Jesus in John 17 is fulfilled: "Father of all goodness, the world has not known you" (v. 25 PHILLIPS).

As the Father loved him, so Jesus would love us and invite us to do the same. "Love one another as I have loved you."

"I and the Father are one."

JOHN 10:30

————————✠————————

For Paul, "in Christ" was far more than a conventional way of signing a letter. It was the meaning of time, the focal point of history: it contained the explanation of the universe. God made the world, Paul said, and all that is in it, for Christ. The Father loves the world only in Christ, and the world returns the Father's love only through Christ. He is the center of reality and the reason for its existence. Paul writes in Colossians 1:16, in Christ "all things were created: things in heaven and on earth . . . all things were created by him and for him."

If you ask yourself, "Why am I walking around this planet, why do I exist?" Paul says, "You must answer: for the sake of Christ." If the angels were to ask, they must point to the Nazarene Carpenter and make the same answer, "We exist for the sake of Christ." If the whole cosmos were suddenly to become articulate, then from north to south, and east to west, it would cry out in chorus, "We exist for the sake of Christ." The name of Christ would issue from the seas and the deserts. It would be tapped out by the patterning rain. It would be written in the skies by the lightning. The storms would roar the name "Jesus Christ," and the mountains would echo it back. The sun's fierce nuclear furnace would blaze out: "The whole universe is full of Christ. He is the way, the truth, the life, the parable of the Father unraveling the riddle of existence."

For God was pleased to have all his fullness dwell in him.

COLOSSIANS 1:18

SCIENCE

———————✠———————

No believer who is open to all that is true, just, lovely, gracious, and practical (Phil. 4:8) disdains the contributions of science. The valuable insights of contemporary psychology amply redeem the ragged regimen of modern studies and experimentation. The plethora of periodicals, books, and research programs has added significantly to our understanding of human behavior and has provided a key to unlocking the inner chambers of the mind. . . . Today when the Church is exquisitely attuned to the inner movements of God in the natural order, it is presumptuous to criticize the naturalism of the scientific perspective. However, the disciple of Jesus Christ is bound to recognize the weakness and inadequacy of any system of attaining higher Christian consciousness that is merely human.

To find the precise point of entry where the maturity of the psychologist can find place in the transcendent mystery of Christian life does not require a long and laborious search. The inspired Word of God lights the way. And the gospel points to the cross of Jesus Christ.

Can anyone teach knowledge to God,
since he judges even the highest?

JOB 21:22

THE PRESENT POWER
OF HIS RESURRECTION

-----------[※]-----------

I f the central saving act of Christian faith is relegated to the future, with the fervent hope that Christ's resurrection is the pledge of our own, and that one day we shall reign with him in glory, then the risen One is pushed safely out of the present. Limiting the resurrection either to the past or to the future makes the present risenness of Jesus largely irrelevant, safeguards us from interference with the ordinary rounds and daily routine of our lives, and preempts communion *now* with Jesus as a living person.

In other words, the resurrection needs to be experienced as present risenness. If we take seriously the word of the risen Christ, "Know that I am with you always; yes, to the end of time," we should expect that he will be actively present in our lives. If our faith is alive and luminous, we will be alert to moments, events, and occasions when the power of resurrection is brought to bear on our lives. Self-absorbed and inattentive, we fail to notice the subtle ways in which Jesus is snagging our attention.

> *Give thanks to the LORD, for he is good;*
> *his love endures forever.*

I CHRONICLES 16:34

THE END OF DEATH

————————[❈]————————

The Easter man has his eyes fixed on Jesus, "the author and perfecter of our faith" (Heb. 12:2), who claimed that death was finished, that he had the answer to the problem of death, and that, to prove it, he would rise from the dead. "Destroy this temple," was Jesus' answer, "and in three days I will raise it up." They retorted, "This temple took forty-six years to build, and you are going to raise it up in three days?" Actually, he was talking about the temple of his body. Clearly, the Pharisees thought he was out of his mind, but he was gathering a large following. So they decided to put him to death and sealed his tomb with a stone. Only the tomb wouldn't stay closed, and the man came back to haunt his murderers and every man who has ever lived after him. The Easter man knows that it is more than remotely possible that he was right, that he did have the answer to the problem of death, that his followers could cry out securely, invincibly, triumphantly, "O death, where is your victory, death where is your sting?" Death, you are a phantom, the bogeyman of little children! The only reason my Father allows you to exist is to usher me into the one experience deserving of the name Life.

> He who has an ear, let him hear what the Spirit says
> to the churches. He who overcomes will not be hurt at
> all by the second death.

REVELATION 2:11

———————[✠]———————

The living presence of Jesus is his resurrection, and I should be experiencing its power. As Paul wrote to the Philippians: "I wish to know Christ and the power flowing from his resurrection" (see Phil. 3:10). In some way, Jesus rises in the faith of the community, and the resurrection is present to us. Clearly, then, Easter is not just another day in the weary round of time. It is the day of days, the feast of feasts, the center of the gospel and our whole Christian religion. Every time we celebrate Eucharist, we renew the Pesach of Jesus—his breakthrough from death to life. Around the table that ancient Hebrew cry of joy and wonder becomes our own: "Alleluia, Alleluia, Alleluia! Christ is risen; death could not hold him. Now he lives no more to die."

> *For none of us lives to himself alone and none of us dies to himself alone. If we live, we live to the Lord; and if we die, we die to the Lord. So, whether we live or die, we belong to the Lord.*

ROMANS 14:7–8

RECKLESS CONFIDENCE

------------------------🎴------------------------

I want to make a bold, unqualified, and unequivocal statement: The key events of the Lent-Easter cycle—the death of Jesus Christ on the cross on Good Friday and his glorious breakthrough to new life on Easter morning—are not merely a summoning, but an empowering to a life of *reckless confidence* regarding our past, our present, and our future. It is confidence and nothing but confidence, immense, unshakable, reckless, raging confidence that leads to love, to life, to freedom, to Jesus.

The great German theologian Karl Rahner writes in his book *Foundations*: "A person is always a Christian in order to become one, and this is also true of what we are calling a personal relationship to Jesus Christ in faith, confidence and love." A new possibility exists. We can be more than we are at any one moment.

In Mark 11:22–24, Jesus says, "Have faith in God. . . . I tell you the truth, if anyone says to this mountain, 'Go, throw yourself into the sea,' and does not doubt in his heart but believes that what he says will happen, it will be done for him. Therefore I tell you, whatever you ask for in prayer, believe that you have received it, and it will be yours."

Do you see how far Jesus calls us to push our confidence? Believe that you have it already!

> *We have come to share in Christ if we hold firmly till*
> *the end the confidence we had at first.*

HEBREWS 3:14

———— ⚜ ————

Modern theology's preoccupation with the resurrection of Jesus Christ is not apologetic. His Easter triumph is no longer simply viewed as the proof par excellence that establishes the truth of Christianity. All New Testament scholars agree that the resurrection actually occurred and that the force of the gospel flows from it. For example, the teaching of the Sermon on the Mount is powerful because the risen Jesus stands by it, and thereby gives it its final and present meaning.

If Jesus did not rise, we can safely praise the Sermon on the Mount as a magnificent ethic. If he did, praise does not matter. The sermon becomes a portrait of our ultimate destiny. Faith means that those who believe in the resurrection receive the gospel message, and it reshapes them in the image and likeness of God. The meaning of the resurrection is inseparable from the teaching of Jesus. The gospel reshapes the hearer through the power of the resurrection. The gospel claims there is a hidden power in the world—the living presence of the risen Christ. It liberates man from the slavery that obscures the image and likeness of God in men.

> *"Blessed are those who hunger and thirst for*
> *   righteousness,*
> *for they will be filled."*

MATTHEW 5:6

CELEBRATING THE EUCHARIST

W hat of our eucharistic celebrations? Are they beautiful in the eyes of the Father? Answer no if the songs, words, and gestures are rubrical niceties and liturgical novelties sapped of any interiority. Then, in the words of Paul, even though you are filled with all knowledge and a faith that could move mountains, your Eucharist is sounding brass and tinkling cymbal. But answer yes if word, music, and movement are the outward expression of the inner attitude of your soul, if they are the overflow of the wild generosity of your love, if your heart is fused with Christ's as he renews in an unbloody way the drama of Calvary. The beauty of the eucharistic liturgy, like that of Calvary, is essentially interior.

> *"I am the vine; you are the branches. If a man*
> *remains in me and I in him, he will bear much fruit;*
> *apart from me you can do nothing."*

JOHN 15:5

—————❋—————

Jesus says to us: "Either you give life to others in your relationships with them, or you drain them of it." Life can be
taken out of others in rivulets and drops, in the small daily
failures of inattention, that bitterest fruit of self-absorption, as
surely as by the terrible strokes to their hearts.

Writes Frederick Buechner: "Sin sprouts, as banana
trees on the Nile, whenever the effect of your relationships
with others is to diminish rather than enlarge them. There is
no neutral corner in your human encounters, no antiseptic
arena in which 'nobody else is hurt' or 'nobody else knows
about it.' You either make people a little better, or leave them a
little worse. You define your faith and moral posture in the ordinary stuff of your daily routine. The Kingdom belongs to those,
as artless as children, who love others simply and directly, without thinking about anything but them. The inheritors of the
Promise are those unsung folks who lend others a hand when
they're falling. That's the only work that matters in the end."

Hear what the LORD *says to you, O house of Israel.*

JEREMIAH 10:1

LION AND LAMB

———— ⊞ ————

This is not pious piffle. The risen Jesus is not The Man Upstairs (as some macho males like to say), a celestial gas, or the invisible honorary president of outer space. His resurrection was not an escape into the Great Beyond while the band played, "Up, Up, and Away." His breakthrough into new life on Easter morning unfettered him from the space-time limitations of existence in the flesh and empowered him to touch not only Nepal but also New Orleans, not only Matthew and Magdalene but also me. The Lion of Judah in his present risenness pursues, tracks, and stalks us here and now. When we cry out with Jeremiah, "Enough already! Leave me alone in my melancholy," the Shepherd replies, "I will not leave you alone. You are mine. I know each of my sheep by name. You belong to me. If you think I am finished with you, if you think I am a small god that you can keep at a safe distance, I will pounce upon you like a roaring lion, tear you to pieces, rip you to shreds, and break every bone in your body. Then I will mend you, cradle you in my arms, and kiss you tenderly.". . .

The Lion who will kill all that separates us from him; the Lamb who was killed to mend that separation—both are symbols and synonyms for Jesus. Relentlessness and tenderness; indivisible aspects of the Divine Reality.

> *A bruised reed he will not break,*
> *and a smoldering wick he will not snuff out,*
> *till he leads justice to victory.*

MATTHEW 12:20

RESURRECTION JOY

―――――✠―――――

Compassion, the ability to suffer with the hurt of another, is an essential Christian quality. Equally important is the capacity to rejoice in the happiness of another. Intense gladness is anchored in the joy that Christ now experiences at the right hand of his Father. Every tear has been wiped away. There is no more mourning or sadness in the life of the risen Jesus. . . .

In the early Church, each Sunday was known as the feast of "little Easter." In our own culture the Christian Sabbath is a summons to the joy and optimism of resurrection Sunday.

> And the disciples were filled with joy and with the
> Holy Spirit.

ACTS 13:52

THE GOLDEN RULE

E arly on in Sunday school or catechism class, we learned the Golden Rule: "Always treat others as you would like them to treat you." Yet our melancholy marriages, dysfunctional families, splintered churches, and loveless neighborhoods indicate that we have not learned well.

"Learning by heart" is another matter entirely. The rhythm of relentless tenderness in the Rabbi's heart makes loving terribly personal, terribly immediate, and terribly urgent. He says, "I give you a new commandment; it is *my* commandment; it is *all* I command you: Love one another as I have loved you." Only compassion and forgiveness count. Love is the key to everything. Living and loving are one.

> *"So in everything, do to others what you would have them do to you, for this sums up the Law and the Prophets."*

MATTHEW 7:12

THE SMILING CHRIST

The smiling Christ heals and liberates. With newly discovered delight in ourselves, we go out to our brothers and sisters as we are, where they are, and minister the smiling Christ to them. Not far away from us, there is someone who is afraid and needs our courage; someone who is lonely and needs our presence. There is someone hurt needing our healing; unloved, needing our touching; old, needing to feel that we care; weak, needing the support of our shared weakness. One of the most healing words I ever spoke as a confessor was to an old priest with a drinking problem. "Just a few years ago," I said, "I was a hopeless alcoholic in the gutter in Fort Lauderdale." "You?" he cried. "O thank God!" When we bring a smile to the face of someone in pain, we have brought Christ to him.

May God be gracious to us and bless us
and make his face shine upon us,
Selah.

PSALM 67:1

THE CRUCIAL QUESTION

————[✠]————

"**W**hat think you of Christ, whose son is he?" is the crucial question of the gospel. To provide the answer is the purpose of the New Testament: "That you may know God and the One he has sent, Jesus Christ."

Jesus demanded faith in himself. He reproached the disciples in the storm-tossed boat, "O you of little faith." And he demanded hope in himself: "Come to me, all you who labor and find life wearisome, and I will refresh you." And in emphatic terms, he demanded love of himself, "He who loves his mother or father more than me is not worthy of me."

> "Whoever has my commands and obeys them, he is
> the one who loves me. He who loves me will be loved
> by my Father, and I too will love him and show myself
> to him."

JOHN 14:21

———————[※]———————

As a fringe benefit, practicing silent solitude enables us to sleep less and to feel more energetic. The energy expended in the exhausting pursuit of illusory happiness is now available to be focused on the things that really matter—love, friendship, and intimacy with God.

Being alone with the Alone moves us from what John Henry Newman called rational or notional knowledge to real knowledge. The first means that I know something in a remote, abstract way that never intrudes on my consciousness; the second means I may not *know* it but I act on it anyway. In solitary silence we listen with great attentiveness to the voice that calls us the beloved. God speaks to the deepest strata of our souls, into our self-hatred and shame, our narcissism, and takes us through the night into the daylight of his truth.

> *Seek the LORD while he may be found;*
> *call on him while he is near.*

ISAIAH 55:6

THE POWER THAT OVERCOMES

———————————[✠]———————————

Easter Day vindicated the way of Jesus and validated the authority of his lordship. The Master told us never to underestimate the power of our culture. Our world, full of incredible foolishness, will insist that we are the fools. Yet Easter convinces us of God's wisdom and his power to transform our world. Our faith in the risen Jesus is the power that overcomes ourselves, our culture, and our world.

In the words of Paul in Romans 12:2, "Do not conform any longer to the pattern of this world, but be transformed by the renewing of your mind. Then you will be able to test and approve what God's will is—his good, pleasing and perfect will."

As a result, he does not live the rest of his earthly life
for evil human desires, but rather for the will of God.

I PETER 4:2

————— ✠ —————

In the winter of 1968–69, I lived in a cave in the mountains of the Zaragosa Desert in Spain. . . .

On the night of December 13, during what began as a long and lonely hour of prayer, I heard in faith Jesus Christ say, "For love of you I left my Father's side. I came to you who ran from me, fled me, who did not want to hear my name. For love of you I was covered with spit, punched, beaten, and affixed to the wood of the cross."

These words are burned on my life. Whether I am in a state of grace or disgrace, elation or depression, that night of fire quietly burns on. I looked at the crucifix for a long time, figuratively saw the blood streaming from every pore of his body, and heard the cry of his wounds: "This isn't a joke. It is not a laughing matter to me that I have loved you." The longer I looked, the more I realized that no man has ever loved me and no one ever could love me as he did. I went out of the cave, stood on the precipice, and shouted into the darkness, "Jesus, are you crazy? Are you out of your mind to have loved me so much?" I learned that night what a wise old man had told me years earlier: "Only the one who has experienced it can know what the love of Jesus Christ is. Once you have experienced it, nothing else in the world will seem more beautiful or desirable."

He has taken me to the banquet hall,
and his banner over me is love.

SONG OF SONGS 2:4

SELF-JUSTIFICATION

———————[✳]———————

More often than I like to admit, I still get bamboozled into trying to make myself acceptable to God. It seems I cannot forgo this crazy enterprise of getting myself into a position where I can see myself in a good light.

Anyone caught up in the same oppression of self-justification understands what I am saying. In our own way we are as absurd as the character in the Agatha Christie novel who cannot imagine heaven as being anything but an occasion to make herself useful—little imagining that everybody else in heaven is struggling to endure the unceasing persecution of her devoted service. Will we ever be free of the Pelagian fantasy that we save ourselves?

> *How can I repay the LORD*
> *for all his goodness to me?*
> *I will lift up the cup of salvation*
> *and call on the name of the LORD.*
> *I will fulfill my vows to the LORD*
> *in the presence of all his people.*

PSALM 116:12–14

————— ⊞ —————

Creation is a response to the vast delight of God. Man is basically good. His human nature, fallen but redeemed, is freed from the slavery of sin and capable of the heights of holiness. The body, risen with Christ in baptism, is a sacred vessel, a shrine of the imperishable Spirit. (We could do with a good deal less of the pessimism about man found in certain Christian circles. As Dr. Robert Frost has stated: "The Lord once brought me up short with the challenge: 'Why do you persist in seeing your children in the hands of the devil, rather than in the hands of their faithful Shepherd?' I then realized that in my mind I had been imagining that all the evils of our present age were ultimately more powerful than the timeless love of God.")

Pain, inconvenience, sin—these are the *problems* of being, the alarming, embarrassing, even tragic things that God is apparently willing to put up with in order to have beings at all. But whatever they are, they are not the *root* of being. That root is *joy*.

> You will go out in joy
> and be led forth in peace;
> the mountains and hills
> will burst into song before you,
> and all the trees of the field
> will clap their hands.

ISAIAH 55:12

NOBLESSE OBLIGE!

———————— ❧ ————————

The new law then is a law of liberty. It is characterized by freedom. "It is for freedom that Christ has set us free" (Gal. 5:1).

The apostle Paul has already made it clear that freedom from law does not mean freedom to sin. If we have received a call to liberty from law, we are not called to make such liberty a license for lust. Paul is simply following the teaching of Jesus that the good tree will bear good fruit (see Luke 6:43). It amounts to a practical translation of the philosophical principle, "action follows being." Just as a child acts differently toward his father than an outsider would, so a friend of God acts like a friend of God. Christian action follows Christian being. We must live out in our lives what we are. This is the primary law of our existence. Noblesse oblige! The child of a king must not live like a peasant.

> Then I heard what sounded like a great multitude, like the roar of rushing waters and like loud peals of thunder, shouting:
>
> Hallelujah!
> For our Lord God Almighty reigns.
> Let us rejoice and be glad
> and give him glory!
> For the wedding of the Lamb has come,
> and his bride has made herself ready.
>
> REVELATION 19:6–7

———————[❋]———————

L ife teaches us how difficult it is to receive anything from someone who has all the answers, who is completely cool, utterly unafraid, invulnerable, needing nothing and no one, always on top of life and in control of every situation. We feel unnecessary, unneeded, and reluctant to receive. So Jesus comes in the way of weakness, giving us the chance to love him and making us feel that we have something to give him. Isaiah prophesied that he would be "like a lamb led to the slaughter or a sheep before the shearers" (53:7 NAB). Jesus, who understands the human heart, allowed the image of a dumb, helpless animal to be applied to himself.

> *We all, like sheep, have gone astray,*
> *each of us has turned to his own way;*
> *and the LORD has laid on him*
> *the iniquity of us all.*

> ISAIAH 53:6

HIS PASSION

————[✠]————

Through his Passion and death, Jesus carried away the essential sickness of the human heart and broke forever the deadly grip of hypocrisy on our souls. He has robbed our loneliness of its fatal power by traveling himself to the far reaches of loneliness. . . . He has understood our ignorance, weakness, and foolishness and granted pardon to us all ("Forgive them, Father, they do not know what they are doing"). He has made his pierced heart a safe place for every defeated cynic, hopeless sinner, and self-loathing derelict across the bands of time. God reconciled *all* things, everything in heaven and *everything* on earth, when he made peace by his death on the cross (Col. 1:20).

The cross reveals that Jesus has conquered sin and death and that nothing, *absolutely nothing*, can separate us from the love of Christ. Neither the impostor nor the Pharisee, neither the lack of awareness nor the lack of passion, neither the negative judgments of others nor the debased perception of ourselves, neither our scandalous past nor our uncertain future, neither the power struggles in the church nor the tensions in our marriage, not fear, guilt, shame, self-hatred, or even death can tear us away from the love of God, made visible in Jesus the Lord.

Listening to the faint heartbeat of the dying Rabbi is a powerful stimulus to the recovery of passion.

> *I will give them singleness of heart and action, so that they will always fear me for their own good and the good of their children after them.*

JEREMIAH 32:39

————— 🔆 —————

My own experience, as well as that of many other evangelists, verifies that you can tell it like it is, that the majority of people are turned off, but that the Word will not return empty. Father John Bertolucci went to a wedding reception and ended up evangelizing to six hundred people. In Marrero, Louisiana, during a parish renewal, I was asked to speak to three hundred high school girls. For them it was a command performance. Most didn't want to be there. They came to the church giddy, chattering, laughing, and starving for lunch at noon. I planned to speak for one hour on the theme "Jesus Christ Crucified, the Power of God, and the Wisdom of God." I never finished. After forty minutes the sobbing was so loud I had to stop. I invited the girls to come forward and venerate the cross as we do on Good Friday. The movement from their seats to the sanctuary represented a movement away from the darkness in their lives to the light who is Jesus Christ, a conversion, a turning from self-centeredness to the Man who loved them and delivered himself up for them. . . . Preaching Christ crucified without any histrionics or theatrics calls the Spirit to life.

And who through the Spirit of holiness was declared
with power to be the Son of God by his resurrection
from the dead: Jesus Christ our Lord.

ROMANS 1:4

THE ONE BESIDE US

———— ✠ ————

Standing on a London street corner, G. K. Chesterton was approached by a newspaper reporter. "Sir, I understand that you recently became a Christian. May I ask you one question?"

"Certainly," replied Chesterton.

"If the risen Christ suddenly appeared at this very moment and stood behind you, what would you do?"

Chesterton looked the reporter squarely in the eye and said, "He is."

Is this a mere figure of speech, wishful thinking, a piece of pious rhetoric? No, this truth is the most real fact about our life; it is our life. The Jesus who walked the roads of Judea and Galilee is the One who stands beside us. The Christ of history is the Christ of faith.

> "Then go quickly and tell his disciples: 'He has risen
> from the dead and is going ahead of you into Galilee.
> There you will see him.' Now I have told you."

MATTHEW 28:7

———— ✠ ————

E xperientially, the inner healing of the heart is seldom a
sudden catharsis or an instant liberation from bitterness,
anger, resentment, and hatred. More often it is a growing
into oneness with the Crucified who has achieved our peace
through his blood on the cross. This may take considerable
time because the memories are still so vivid and the hurt is still
so deep. But it *will* happen. The crucified Christ is not merely a
heroic example to the Church: he is the power and wisdom of
God, a living force in his present risenness, transforming our
lives and enabling us to extend the hand of reconciliation to
our enemies.

> *I will give them an undivided heart and put a new*
> *spirit in them; I will remove from them their heart of*
> *stone and give them a heart of flesh.*

EZEKIEL 11:19

THE DEMANDS OF FORGIVENESS

———————— ✠ ————————

The summons to live as forgiven and forgiving children is radically inclusive. It is addressed not only to the wife whose husband forgot their wedding anniversary but also to parents whose child was slaughtered by a drunken driver, to the victims of slanderous accusations, and to the poor living in filthy boxes who see the rich drive by in Mercedes. . . .

The demands of forgiveness are so daunting that they seem humanly impossible. The exigencies of forgiveness are simply beyond the capacity of ungraced human will. Only reckless confidence in a Source greater than ourselves can empower us to forgive the wounds inflicted by others. In boundary moments such as these there is only one place to go—Calvary.

Stay there for a long time and watch as Abba's Only-Begotten dies utterly alone in bloody disgrace. Watch as he breathes forgiveness on his torturers at the moment of their greatest cruelty and mercilessness. On that lonely hill outside the city wall of old Jerusalem, you will experience the healing power of the dying Lord.

> *"For if you forgive men when they sin against you,*
> *your heavenly Father will also forgive you."*

MATTHEW 6:14

———————[✠]———————

"Jesus, in [whose] body lives the fullness of divinity" (Col. 2:9 JB), singularly understands the tenderness and compassion of the Father's heart. Eternally begotten from the Father, he is Abba's Child. Why did Jesus love sinners, ragamuffins, and the rabble who knew nothing of the Law? Because his Abba loved them. He did nothing on his own, but only what his Abba told him. Through meal sharing, preaching, teaching, and healing, Jesus acted out his understanding of the Father's indiscriminate love—a love that causes his sun to rise on bad men as well as good, and his rain to fall on honest and dishonest men alike (See Matt. 5:45).

> *When he saw the crowds, he had compassion on them,*
> *because they were harassed and helpless, like sheep*
> *without a shepherd.*

MATTHEW 9:36

WHAT ARE YOU AFRAID OF?

————————❋————————

The question that the gospel of grace puts to us is simply this: Who shall separate you from the love of Christ? What are you afraid of?

Are you afraid that your weakness could separate you from the love of Christ? It can't.

Are you afraid that your inadequacies could separate you from the love of Christ? They can't. . . .

Difficult marriage, loneliness, anxiety over the children's future? They can't.

Negative self-image? It can't.

Economic hardship, racial hatred, street crime? They can't.

Rejection by loved ones or the suffering of loved ones? They can't.

Persecution by authorities, going to jail? They can't. . . .

The gospel of grace calls out: Nothing can ever separate you from the love of God made visible in Christ Jesus our Lord.

You must be convinced of this, trust it, and never forget to remember. Everything else will pass away. . . . Faith will become vision, hope will become possession, but the love of Jesus Christ that is stronger than death endures forever.

> Who shall separate us from the love of Christ? Shall
> trouble or hardship or persecution or famine or naked-
> ness or danger or sword?
>
> ROMANS 8:35

FRIENDS

———— 🉐 ————

W hat caught my eye this morning was a verse in John 21. Jesus calls out, "Friends, come and have breakfast." Breakfast on the beach along the Sea of Tiberias consists of fish and chips grilled to messianic perfection, and seasoned with such gentleness that the absence of catsup and tartar sauce passes unnoticed. When one might have expected the impact of unbearable glory, the risen Jesus is attentive to a basic human need—the morning meal. This man, living and breathing with a bar of sunlight in his hair, is the long dream of Israel come true. This man, real as the distant mountains, is none other than God himself. And he calls these weathervane men who cannot be trusted "friends."

A friend is someone who stays with you in the bad weather of life, guards you when you are off your guard, restrains your impetuosity, delights in your wholeness, forgives your failures, does not forsake you when others let you down, and shares whatever he is having for breakfast—moon pie, cold pizza, or fish and chips.

The friendship of Jesus enables us to see others as he saw the apostles: flawed but good, wounded healers, children of the Father. We discover that we are compatible and comfortable with a wide spectrum of people and begin to pray, as Thomas Merton did, "I thank God that I am like the rest of men."

> "I no longer call you servants, because a servant does
> not know his master's business. Instead, I have called
> you friends, for everything that I learned from my
> Father I have made known to you."

JOHN 15:15

LEGALISTIC CHRISTIANITY

————— [※] —————

This is the God of the gospel of grace. A God who, out of love for us, sent the only Son he ever had wrapped in our skin. He learned how to walk, stumbled and fell, cried for his milk, sweated blood in the night, was lashed with a whip and showered with spit, was fixed to a cross, and died whispering forgiveness on us all.

The God of the legalistic Christian, on the other hand, is often unpredictable, erratic, and capable of all manner of prejudices. When we view God this way, we feel compelled to engage in some sort of magic to appease him. Sunday worship becomes a superstitious insurance policy against his whims. This God expects people to be perfect and to be in perpetual control of their feelings and thoughts. When broken people with this concept of God fail—as inevitably they must—they usually expect punishment. So, they persevere in religious practices as they struggle to maintain a hollow image of a perfect self. The struggle itself is exhausting. The legalists can never live up to the expectations they project on God.

> He replied, "Isaiah was right when he prophesied
> about you hypocrites; as it is written:
>
> 'These people honor me with their lips,
> but their hearts are far from me.
> They worship me in vain;
> their teachings are but rules taught by men.'"

MARK 7:6–7

———— [※] ————

The mystery of the Lord's ascension contains an important lesson for the security-prone conscience. Jesus said to his disciples, "I tell you the truth: It is for your good that I am going away" (John 16:7). Why? How could Jesus' departure profit the apostles? Primarily because if he failed to go "the Paraclete will never come to you, whereas if I go, I will send him to you." Secondarily because while he was still visible on earth, there was always the danger that the apostles would be so wedded to the sight of his human flesh that they would leave the certainty of faith and lean upon the tangible evidence of the senses. To see Jesus in the flesh was good, but "blessed are those who have not seen and yet have believed" (John 20:29).

> *"But I tell you the truth: It is for your good that I am going away. Unless I go away, the Counselor will not come to you; but if I go, I will send him to you."*

JOHN 16:7

THE POWER OF PENTECOST

——— 🞧 ———

Jesus Christ crucified is the power of God and the wisdom of
God (1 Cor. 1:24). The power of Pentecost flows from the
cross. Pentecost is not the feast of the Holy Spirit, but the
feast of the resurrection power and glory of Jesus Christ com-
municated to others. Jesus was not constituted the messianic
Son of God in power until he had died in the flesh. So it is with
us. The power of the risen Lord transmitted to the Church
through the Pentecostal Spirit (who propels the journey into
higher consciousness) cannot be received except through participation in the death of Jesus.

The death-resurrection process was initiated in sacramental baptism (Rom. 6:3–4), but if we are to continue to
drink of the life-giving water of the Spirit, we must draw near
to the body of our crucified God from whom the saving waters
flow (John 19:34). We must continually be formed into the
pattern of his death (Phil. 3:10). If there are few Spirit-filled,
power-laden, transparent Christians, it is because so few have
plunged into the Pasch of Jesus and died to sin, selfishness,
dishonesty, and degraded love.

> He himself bore our sins in his body on the tree, so
> that we might die to sins and live for righteousness; by
> his wounds you have been healed.

1 PETER 2:24

———————————❋———————————

Because of the mysterious substitution of Christ for the Christian, each encounter with a brother or sister is a real encounter with the risen Lord, an opportunity to respond creatively to the gospel, and mature in the wisdom of accepted tenderness. Time has been given to us to cause love to grow, and the success of our lives will be measured by how delicately and sensitively we have loved. There is no escaping the gospel logic that all our thoughts, words, and deeds addressed to others are in a real way addressed to Christ himself.

No one has ever seen God; but if we love one another,
God lives in us and his love is made complete in us.

I JOHN 4:12

A GOD WHO LOVES SINNERS

———— 图 ————

The God of Judaism forgives the person who has changed his ways, done penance, and shown that he is leading a better life. Under the old covenant there is no forgiveness for those who remain sinners: the sinner faces judgment. But the God of Jesus does not judge us, for he loves even those who are evil. In a word, the Father of Jesus loves sinners. He is the only God man has ever heard of who behaves this way. Unreal gods, the inventions of men, despise sinners. But the Father of Jesus loves all, no matter what they do. And this, of course, is almost too incredible for us to accept.

> *Rend your heart*
> *and not your garments.*
> *Return to the LORD your God,*
> *for he is gracious and compassionate,*
> *slow to anger and abounding in love,*
> *and he relents from sending calamity.*

JOEL 2:13

THE SERVICE OF ACTION

————🕆————

During World War II, an American Marine, badly wounded on Saipan, was bleeding to death. A Navy corpsman rushed to his aid. At the risk of his own life, he played the Good Samaritan, pouring oil and wine on the wounds of his bleeding brother. The Marine was not particularly gracious or grateful. When the battle subsided, the regiment commander, who had watched the scene from the safety of a bunker, approached the corpsman and said, "Kid, I wouldn't have done that for a million dollars!" The corpsman's glorious answer—"Neither would I."

He learned his lesson well. Maybe he didn't know that what he was doing for the unknown soldier, he was doing for Jesus Christ. What matters is—he *acted*.

> *What good is it, my brothers, if a man claims to have faith but has no deeds? Can such faith save him? Suppose a brother or sister is without clothes and daily food. If one of you says to him, "Go, I wish you well; keep warm and well fed," but does nothing about his physical needs, what good is it? In the same way, faith by itself, if it is not accompanied by action, is dead.*

JAMES 2:14–17

LOVING IN DEED

———— ※ ————

When Jesus said he was hungry and thirsty and naked in those around us, he was referring to more than mere corporeal needs. Surrounded by people who are hungry and thirsty and naked in their souls, they come to us hungry for understanding, thirsting for affirmation, naked with loneliness, and wanting to be covered with the mantle of our genuine concern. So often I refuse to give it to them. I'm not really interested in their hopes, fears, dreams, joys, aspirations, and disappointments. Yet I claim that I am dedicated to God, that I live for Jesus Christ, that I am dedicated to my religion. What kind of religion is this? Jesus thundered, "None of those who cry out, 'Lord, Lord,' will enter the Kingdom of God but only the one who does the will of my Father in heaven" (see Matt. 7:21). And surely it is the will of the Father that we spend our days loving in deed as Jesus did.

> *Everyone who believes that Jesus is the Christ is born of God, and everyone who loves the father loves his child as well. This is how we know that we love the children of God: by loving God and carrying out his commands.*

1 JOHN 5:1–2

———— 图 ————

Last year at the end of a parish week of renewal in Louisiana, a man approached me outside the rectory, muttered, "I've prayed about this," slipped an envelope into my pocket, and hurried away. I was overdue at a reception in the parish hall, so I jogged over, completely forgetting about the envelope. Preparing for bed later that night, I cleaned out my pockets, opened the envelope, and looked at a check for six thousand dollars for God's poor.

The next day I sent the money off to a poor man with a large family in desperate financial straits. Know what happened? Within five days I received nine letters from the man overflowing with gratitude and describing in detail how the money was being used to help his family and others. That experience gave me a beautiful insight into what a poor man is like.

When he receives a gift, he experiences and expresses genuine gratitude. Having nothing, he appreciates even a slight gift. I have been given the utterly undeserved gift of salvation in Jesus Christ. Through no merit of mine, but by his mercy, I've been given a bona fide invitation to drink new wine forever at the wedding feast in the Kingdom of God.

> *And I confer on you a kingdom, just as my Father conferred one on me, so that you may eat and drink at my table in my kingdom and sit on thrones, judging the twelve tribes of Israel.*

LUKE 22:29–30

THE REALITY OF HOPE

———————[✠]———————

One spiritual writer has observed that human beings are born with two diseases: life, from which we die; and hope, which says the first disease is not terminal. Hope is built into the structure of our personalities, into the depths of our unconscious; it plagues us to the very moment of our death. The critical question is whether hope is self-deception, the ultimate cruelty of a cruel and tricky universe, or whether it is just possibly the imprint of reality.

The parables of Jesus responded to that question. In effect Jesus said: Hope your wildest hopes, dream your maddest dreams, imagine your most fantastic fantasies. Where your hopes and your dreams and your imagination leave off, the love of my heavenly Father only begins. For "eye hath not seen, nor ear heard, neither have entered into the heart of man, the things which God hath prepared for them that love him" (1 Cor. 2:9 KJV).

> May the God of hope fill you with all joy and peace as
> you trust in him, so that you may overflow with hope
> by the power of the Holy Spirit.

ROMANS 15:13

————— 🕆 —————

J esus who lives for those in whom love is dead, and who died that his killers might live, reveals a Father who has no wrath. The Father cannot be offended, nor can he be pleased by what people do. This is the very opposite of indifference. The Lord does not cherish us as we deserve—if that were the case, we would be desolate—but as he must, unable to do otherwise. He is love. Hard as it is for us to believe—because we neither give nor receive love among ourselves in this way— we yet believe, because of the life-death-resurrection of the Carpenter-Messiah, that his Father is more loving, more forgiving, more cherishing than Abraham, Isaac, or Jacob could have dreamed.

What this says simply is that the God and Father of our Lord Jesus Christ is gracious. His love is gratuitous in a way that defies our imagination.

It is for this reason that we can proclaim with theological certainty in the power of the Word: *God loves you as you are and not as you should be!* Do you believe this? That God loves you beyond worthiness and unworthiness, beyond fidelity and infidelity, that he loves you in the morning sun and the evening rain, that he loves you without caution, regret, boundary, limit, or breaking point?

> *And he passed in front of Moses, proclaiming, "The*
> *LORD, the LORD, the compassionate and gracious God,*
> *slow to anger, abounding in love and faithful-*
> *ness. . . ."*

EXODUS 34:6

JESUS' SERVANTS

————[⚕]————

The glory of Jesus lies in this: in weakness, vulnerability, and apparent failure he has called forth disciples to come after him, willing and able to carry the cross and relive his Passion through a life of compassion. They are marginal people, not part of the scene, irrelevant to the "action." In their ministry of quiet presence they do not need to win or compete. They may look like losers even to themselves. The world ignores them. But they are building the Kingdom of God on earth by reaching out in vulnerability and weakness to share the suffering of their brothers and sisters. Where the Compassionate One is, there will his servants be.

> *Even in darkness light dawns for the upright,*
> *for the gracious and compassionate and righteous man.*

PSALM 112:4

———————— [※] ————————

After an interview with someone, Abraham Lincoln remarked to his secretary, "I don't like that man's face."

His secretary reacted in amazement, "But that's what his face is; he's not responsible for his face."

And Lincoln replied tartly, "After forty every man is responsible for his face."

My face is the mirror of my moods. After four decades of dying and rising, I should have acquired sufficient emotional maturity to master my moods and maintain a tranquil facial expression. I think that's what Honest Abe was implying.

I would not be writing this little chapter if a woman had not asked me this morning, "Why are you in such a rotten mood?"

> *All the days of the oppressed are wretched,*
> *but the cheerful heart has a continual feast.*

PROVERBS 15:15

HEART SPEAKS TO HEART

The Rabbi implores, "Don't you understand that discipleship is not about being right or being perfect or being efficient? It's all about the way you live with one another." The success or failure of a given day is measured by the quality of our interest and compassion toward those around us. We define ourselves by our response to human need. The question is not how we feel about our neighbor but what we have done for him or her. We reveal our heart in the way we listen to a child, speak to the person who delivers mail, bear an injury, and share our resources with the indigent.

> But I, with a song of thanksgiving,
> will sacrifice to you.
> What I have vowed I will make good.

JONAH 2:9

————[※]————

Though the Scriptures speak insistently of the divine initiative in the work of salvation, that by grace we are saved, that the Tremendous Lover has taken to the chase, American spirituality still seems to start with self, not with God. Personal responsibility replaces personal response. We seem engrossed in our own efforts to grow in holiness. We talk about acquiring virtue, as if it were some kind of skill that can be acquired through personal effort, like good handwriting or a well-grooved golf swing. In seasons of penance, we focus on getting rid of our hang-ups and sweating through various spiritual exercises, as if they were a religious muscle-building program.

The emphasis is always on what I do rather than on what God is doing in my life. In this macho approach God is reduced to a benign old spectator on the sidelines. The American mystique orients us to attribute any growth in the spiritual life to our own sturdy efforts and vigorous resolutions. We become convinced that we can do a pretty good job of following Jesus if we just, once and for all, make up our minds and really buckle down to it. Well, if that's all there is to Christian discipleship, then in the words of singer Peggy Lee, "Let's break out the booze." All we're doing is transferring the legend of the self-made man from the economic sphere to the spiritual one.

> How can you believe if you accept praise from one
> another, yet make no effort to obtain the praise that
> comes from the only God?

JOHN 5:44

POWER IN HIS WEAKNESS

————————❧————————

The mature Christians I have met along the way are those who have failed and have learned to live gracefully with their failure. Faithfulness requires the courage to risk everything on Jesus, the willingness to keep growing, and the readiness to risk failure throughout our lives. . . .

> In that day the Lord will reach out his hand a second time to reclaim the remnant that is left of his people from Assyria, from Lower Egypt, from Upper Egypt, from Cush, from Elam, from Babylonia, from Hamath and from the islands of the sea.
>
> He will raise a banner for the nations and gather the exiles of Israel; he will assemble the scattered people of Judah from the four quarters of the earth.
>
> ISAIAH 11:11–12

———————————————[⚹]———————————————

Faithfulness to Jesus implies that with all our sins, scars, and insecurities, we stand with him; that we are formed and informed by his Word; that we acknowledge that abortion and nuclear weapons are two sides of the same hot coin minted in hell; that we stand upright beside the Prince of Peace and refuse to bow before the shrine of national security; that we are a life-giving and not a death-dealing people of God; that we live under the sign of the cross and not the sign of the bomb.

> I will sing of the LORD's great love forever;
> with my mouth I will make your faithfulness known
>   through all generations.

PSALM 89:1

ON THE SAME SIDE

———— ⊞ ————

I t was John who said, "Master, we saw a man using your name to expel demons, and we tried to stop him because he is not of our company." Jesus told him in reply, "Do not stop him, for any man who is not against you is on your side." A beautiful ecumenical gesture here. Anyone, regardless of denominational label or theological stance, whether self-righteous, theatrical, pompous, doctrinaire, tract ridden, a fundamentalist, or a Bible banger, anyone who invokes the name of Jesus reverently, is to be accepted as brother or sister in the Lord. Cultural baggage notwithstanding, the person is saying, "I'm on your side."

> Brothers, do not slander one another. Anyone who
> speaks against his brother or judges him speaks against
> the law and judges it. When you judge the law, you
> are not keeping it, but sitting in judgment on it.

JAMES 4:11

———————[※]———————

"Sacrifice and offering you did not desire, but a *body* you prepared for me; holocausts and sin offerings you took no delight in. Then I said, 'As it is written of me in the scroll, Behold, I have come to do your will, O God'" (Heb. 10:5–7 NAB). Psychologists tell us that a man understands himself in terms of his spontaneous body image; what he feels about his *body* and its worth is what he feels about himself. What is my feeling about my body? The question might seem vain, superficial, and pretentious until we ask: How did Jesus Christ understand his body? A body that was broken for us: a sacrificial self, effective only through its destruction. . . .

Look at your body. Is it too fat or too skinny or just trim? Is it flabby or muscular? Are you pleased or displeased? What are your criteria for feeling good about your body? Physical attributes? That's the world. Jesus said, "Sacrifice and offering you did not desire, but a *body* you have prepared for me." A beautiful body in the eyes of the Lord is one spent in self-giving, poured out as a libation in loving service, an instrument of self-donation. You have been gifted with a body fitted for that, Brennan. In this light, your body is truly something beautiful for God, regardless of size, shape, and other dimensions. Like Jesus' body, it is meant to fulfill what is written in the book, "I have come to do your will, O God."

> *But he was pierced for our transgressions,*
> *he was crushed for our iniquities;*
> *the punishment that brought us peace was upon him,*
> *and by his wounds we are healed.*

ISAIAH 53:5

THE PRIMARY TARGET

W hat is indeed crucial to the evangelical enterprise is the awareness that we ourselves are the primary target. It is not "they" who are poor, sinful, and lost. It is ourselves. Unless we acknowledge that we are the sinners, the sick ones, and the lost sheep for whom Jesus came, we do not belong to the "blessed" who know that they are poor and inherit the Kingdom. Enough of our pseudomessianic posturing! Let us be done with our futile attempts to appear righteous before God! The Amen, the faithful, the true Witness says: "I know all about you: you are neither cold nor hot. I wish you were one or the other, but since you are neither, but only lukewarm, I will spit you out of my mouth. You say to yourself, 'I am rich, I have made a fortune, and have everything I want,' never realizing that you are wretchedly and pitiably poor, and blind and naked too" (Rev. 3:15–17 JB).

All of us have become like one who is unclean,
and all our righteous acts are like filthy rags;
we all shrivel up like a leaf,
and like the wind our sins sweep us away.

ISAIAH 64:6

———————[✳]———————

Won't the awareness that God loves us no matter what lead to spiritual laziness and moral laxity? Theoretically, this seems a reasonable fear, but in reality the opposite is true. I know that my wife, Roslyn, loves me as I am and not as I should be. Is this an invitation to infidelity, indifference, an "anything goes" attitude? On the contrary. Love calls forth love. Doing my own thing in complete freedom means, in fact, responding to her love. The more rooted we are in the love of God, the more generously we live our faith and practice it.

It is this love that enables us to love ourselves without excuses and without questioning. We love ourselves as we are because faith has convinced us that God does so. We no longer worry about our spiritual growth (which is just another form of idolatry anyway). In living out being-loved, we move beyond the oppressive demands we impose on ourselves, beyond the idealistic claims of the ego, which tells me who I should be, must be, ought to be. My friend Sister Mary Michael O'Shaughnessy has a banner in her room that says, "Today I will not *should* on myself." I don't have to be somebody else—Mother Teresa, Saint Francis, or Carlo Carretto. As my spiritual director, Larry Hein, says: "Be who you is, because if you is who you ain't, you ain't who you is."

> *"See, he is puffed up;*
> *his desires are not upright —*
> *but the righteous will live by his faith."*

HABAKKUK 2:4

MY BELOVEDNESS

———————[✠]———————

"Who am I?" asked the Trappist monk Thomas Merton, and he responded, "I am one loved by Christ." Herein lies the foundation of the true self. The indispensable condition for developing and maintaining the awareness of our belovedness is time alone with God. In solitude we tune out the nay-saying whispers of our worthlessness and sink down into the mystery of our true self. Our longing to know who we really are—which is the source of most of our discontent—will never be satisfied until we confront and accept silent solitary moments with the Lord. There we discover that the truth of our belovedness is really true. Our primary identity rests in God's relentless tenderness for us revealed in Jesus Christ.

> *I lift up my eyes*
> *to you,*
> *to you*
> *whose throne is*
> *in heaven.*
>
> PSALM 123:1

————— 🔆 —————

The impostor within me is attentive to the size, shape, and color of the bandages that veil my nothingness. The false self persuades me to be preoccupied with my weight. If I binge on a pint of Häagen-Dazs peanut butter vanilla and the scale signals distress the following morning, I am crestfallen. A beautiful day of sunshine beckons, but for the self-absorbed impostor, the bloom is off the rose. I think Jesus smiles at those minor vanities (checking myself out in the storefront window while pretending to look at the merchandise), but they kidnap my attention away from the indwelling God and temporarily rob me of the joy of God's Holy Spirit. Yet the false self rationalizes my preoccupation with my waistline and overall appearance and whispers, "A fat, sloppy image will diminish your credibility in ministry." Cunning.

> *"I tell you that this man, rather than the other, went home justified before God. For everyone who exalts himself will be humbled, and he who humbles himself will be exalted."*

LUKE 18:14

The Incarnation of Compassion

———————————— ✠ ————————————

The Christ who weeps over Times Square is the Man of Sorrows moved in the pit of his stomach for the lostness of the sheep who do not know him. The heart of the crucified Lord of Glory does not turn away in revulsion or disgust at the wretchedness and perversity of the human condition. There is no crime so horrible or sin so despicable that it was left at the foot of the cross. "He took our sickness away and carried our diseases for us." How is this possible?

Because Jesus is God.

He is the incarnation of the compassion of the Father. Meister Eckhart, a fifteenth-century mystic wrote, "You may call God love; you may call God goodness; but the best name for God is Compassion." What do the exalted names—Son of God, Second Person of the Blessed Trinity, Kyrios, Pantocrator, and other christological titles bestowed on Jesus by a later age—signify, but that God was present in the Compassionate One in a unique, extravagant, and definitive way?

> *Christ redeemed us from the curse of the law by becoming a curse for us, for it is written: "Cursed is everyone who is hung on a tree."*
>
> GALATIANS 3:13

————[✤]————

One wintry day shortly before I was ordained, I was sliding down an icy hill in Loretto, Pennsylvania, on the way to class. The road was a sheet of sleet and snow, and the wind whipped through my clothes. Icicles had formed on my eyebrows, and my face was twisted in an Archipelago-style grimace. I did not look or feel as though I was saved.

My companion was seventy-year-old Swiss-born Father Anton Feyer who taught Hebrew, Greek, church history, and whatever else was needed at the seminary. Icicles had formed on his bushy eyebrows too, but his face was bright with laughter as if in the midst of a game he thoroughly enjoyed. His eyes twinkled, his jowls and tummy bobbed up and down, and a mischievous smile played at the corners of his mouth. He looked like Santa Claus leaving the North Pole on Christmas Eve. Annoyed, I asked, "What makes you so happy, Father Feyer?" He looked at me and in his thick German accent answered, "Brudder Brennan, I am a member of a redeemed community!" The conscious awareness of his real identity and his membership in the community of God's people generated a warmth and affability that the frost and ice could not penetrate.

> When Israel came out of Egypt,
> the house of Jacob from a people of foreign tongue,
> Judah became God's sanctuary,
> Israel his dominion.

PSALM 114:1–2

TAKING INVENTORY

———————— ✠ ————————

To discern where you *really* are with the Lord, recall what has saddened you recently. Was it the realization that you don't love Jesus enough? That you do not seek his face in prayer often enough? That you can't honestly say that the greatest thing that ever happened in your life is that Jesus came to you and you heard his voice? That you do not regard finding Jesus as your supreme happiness? That you have denied his last commandment by not loving his people enough?

Or have you been saddened and depressed over a lack of human respect, criticism from an authority figure, financial problems, lack of friends, your bulging waistline?

On the other hand, what has *gladdened* you recently? Reflection on your election to the Christian community? The joy of praying, "Abba, I belong to you"? The afternoon you stole away with the gospel as your only companion? The thrilling awareness that God loves you unconditionally just as you are and not as you should be? A small victory over selfishness? Or were the sources of your gladness and joy a new car, a Brooks Brothers suit, a movie and a pizza, a trip to Paris or Peoria? Are you worshiping idols?

> *Sing to him a new song;*
> *play skillfully, and shout for joy.*

PSALM 33:3

———————[✠]———————

One of the most shocking contradictions in Christian living is the intense dislike many disciples of Jesus have for themselves. They are more displeased, impatient, irritated, unforgiving, and spiteful with their own shortcomings than they would ever dream of being with someone else's. They are fed up with themselves, sick of their own mediocrity, disgusted by their own inconsistency, bored by their own monotony. They would never judge any other of God's children with the savage self-condemnation with which they crush themselves. Through experiencing the relentless tenderness of Jesus, we learn first of all to be with ourselves. To the extent that we allow the compassion of the Lord to invade our hearts, we are freed from the dyspepsia toward ourselves that follows us everywhere, that self-hatred that we are now even ashamed of. It is simply not possible to know the Christ of the Gospels unless we alter our attitude toward ourselves and take sides with him against our own self-evaluation. Would you like to know this moment how Jesus feels about you? Bernard Bush says this is the way you will know: if you love yourself intensely and freely, then your feelings about yourself correspond perfectly to the sentiments of Jesus.

And the divine double take, of course, is that loving ourselves frees us to love others.

> *"Take my yoke upon you and learn from me, for I am gentle and humble in heart, and you will find rest for your souls."*

MATTHEW 11:29

READING THE PROPHETS

———— 🜨 ————

What of our sense of awe and wonder before the lived reality of revelation? Prophetic witness culminating in Jesus of Nazareth declares that the transcendent God who dwells in regions of inaccessible light is like a foolish old man who looks down the road every night for a son who isn't there (Luke 15). God loves, which means, God is loving. But if we are no longer awed by a sunrise, a fiery sun falling into gathering darkness, or a night brilliant with sunshine, will we marvel and be surprised at the astonishing disclosures of God through the prophets? To experience existentially the warmth and tenderness of God's love, the prophets must be tasted and savored in silence. If a shade of their prophetic spirit is to darken our lives with its brilliance, the Word of God must be pondered alone and at length. For as Charles de Foucauld said: "It is in our solitude that God gives himself to us completely." The alternative is a shallow, joyless faith where the reality of a loving Father fades farther and farther into the distance and eventually dies of spiritual consumption. "Not to be accessible to the greatness of the Holy," wrote Baudelaire, "is always the mark of a certain mediocrity of soul."

> *Early the next morning Abraham got up and returned*
> *to the place where he had stood before the* LORD.

GENESIS 19:27

A MYTH ABOUT CONVERSION

————————⁂————————

There is a myth flourishing in the church today that has caused incalculable harm—once converted, fully converted. In other words, once I accept Jesus Christ as my Lord and Savior, an irreversible, sinless future beckons. Discipleship will be an untarnished success story; life will be an unbroken upward spiral toward holiness. Tell that to poor Peter who, after three times professing his love for Jesus on the beach, and after receiving the fullness of the Spirit at Pentecost, was still jealous of Paul's apostolic success.

Often I have been asked, "Brennan, how is it possible that you became an alcoholic after you got saved?" It is possible because I got battered and bruised by loneliness and failure, because I got discouraged, uncertain, and guilt ridden and took my eyes off Jesus. Because the Christ encounter did not transfigure me into an angel. Because justification by grace through faith means I have been set in right relationship with God, not made the equivalent of a patient etherized on a table.

> *For by the grace given me I say to every one of you: Do not think of yourself more highly than you ought, but rather think of yourself with sober judgment, in accordance with the measure of faith God has given you.*

ROMANS 12:3

＊WHEN JESUS' POWER IS FORMED IN ME＊

A m I unjustly criticized, rejected, betrayed by a friend? I can touch the life of Jesus who faced the same things and can will myself to respond as he did. The power of his Spirit passes into my spirit, and the purpose of Pentecost is fulfilled: Christ is formed within me not just in peak moments of transcendental experience but in the nitty-gritty of daily life. I am confined to bed, sick, nauseous, racked with pain, utterly incapable of prayer. I have only to whisper, "It's yours, my Friend," and it is no longer I who lie there, it is Jesus Christ. And so it goes. Jesus slept. I can unite my sleep with his. I'm having a rollicking good time at a Cajun barbecue in New Orleans. I shout with them, *"Laissez les bon temps rouler!"* (Let the good times roll), and connect with Jesus who multiplied the wine at Cana to keep the party going.

> *We are therefore Christ's ambassadors, as though God*
> *were making his appeal through us. We implore you*
> *on Christ's behalf: Be reconciled to God. God made*
> *him who had no sin to be sin for us, so that in him we*
> *might become the righteousness of God.*

2 CORINTHIANS 5:20–21

HUNGER FOR JESUS

———— 🀫 ————

Suppose it were so ordained that your whole future, your eternal destiny, depended on your personal relationship with the bishop of your area. Wouldn't you arrange to spend considerably more time with him than you do now? Wouldn't you try with his help to overcome all the character defects and personality traits that you knew were displeasing to him? And suppose business obligations called you away to that city of saints and scholars, Brooklyn, New York, wouldn't you drop him frequent notes from there and be eager to return to him, "as the deer pants for streams of water" (Ps. 42:1)?

And if he confided to you that he kept a diary of personal memoirs, which were the deepest whisperings of his inner self, wouldn't you be anxious not only to read them but to steep yourself in them so that you might know and love him more?

These are burning questions that every disciple must answer in total candor. Do you hunger for Jesus Christ? Do you yearn to spend time alone with him in prayer? Is he the most important person in your life? Does he fill your soul like a song of joy? Is he on your lips as a shout of praise? Do you eagerly turn to his memoirs, his personal testament, his Gospels, to learn more of him? Are you making the effort to die to anything and everything that would inhibit, diminish, or threaten your friendship?

> I seek you with all my heart;
> do not let me stray from your commands.
>
> PSALM 119:10

SHARING WITH THE POOR

————— 〔✠〕—————

Not every Christian is given the call or the charism to heroic poverty; neither is any Christian excused from the gospel imperative of sharing his material resources with the poor (James 2:15–17). John Woolman, a Quaker who died just before the American Revolution, wrote: "I found by experience that to *keep pace* with the actions of Truth, and *never more but as that opens the way*, is necessary for the true servants of Christ" (*The Journal of John Woolman*). In the concrete circumstances of my life situation, what is the Lord Jesus Christ asking of me in the way of material poverty? Desiring neither more nor less than Truth requires, what gesture (big or little) shall I make today as a sign of my unconditional trust in the Father? The lofty principle of biblical poverty is realized on the pedestrian terrain of our daily experience.

Looking at his disciples, he said:

> "*Blessed are you who are poor,*
> *for yours is the kingdom of God.*"

LUKE 6:20

———— ✠ ————

The Christian is a eucharistic worshiper of the saving love and mercy of the God who has accepted him. He is steeped in gratitude and dependence. His very being is a Eucharist, a permanent and perpetual thanksgiving to God. What does Eucharist mean but thanksgiving? The Lord says that whenever his people are gathered together in an attitude of joyful thanksgiving, he, through his ordained minister, will be present under the species of bread and wine, as the thanks-offering of this assembly. If Eucharist means thanksgiving, Christianity means people who are joyfully grateful people.

> *For long ago, in the days of David and Asaph, there had been directors for the singers and for the songs of praise and thanksgiving to God.*

NEHEMIAH 12:46

JESUS HUMANITY

———————[✠]———————

Jesus had no fear of showing his true emotions. The Gospel portrait of Jesus is that of a man exquisitely attuned to his emotions and uninhibited in expressing them. In Luke's Gospel we see him so offended by a discourtesy in the house of Simon the Pharisee that it provokes him to say, "Simon, I came into your house and you didn't even say, 'Hi.'" In Mark he is so touched, so deeply moved, by the tenderness of the woman who anoints his head with perfume that he turns and says, "Write this down! Wherever the Good News is proclaimed, what she has done will be told also in memory of her.". . .

Scandalous as it may be, this is the Jesus of the Gospels: a man like us in all things but ungratefulness. A man consoled by the tears of a sinful woman, a man who experienced anger, irritation, and fatigue. A man who drank his people's wine and sang their wedding songs. In so many ways and by so many signs did Jesus show us that he is fully human, that he has a sensitive human heart and longs to be treated as one who is human.

> *When Jesus saw her weeping, and the Jews who had*
> *come along with her also weeping, he was deeply*
> *moved in spirit and troubled.*

JOHN 11:33

THE LAW OF THE SPIRIT

It is more than mere coincidence that the prophet and teacher who wrote the letter to the Hebrews should describe Jesus in chapter 2, verse 10 as "the pioneer of our salvation" (RSV). Again in chapter 12, verse 2 of the same letter, Jesus is "the pioneer and perfecter of our faith" (RSV). By looking at Jesus we learn what it is to be on the trail to abundant life.

Jesus liberated his disciples from the tyranny of law. He did this not by abolishing or changing the Law but by dethroning it from its place of primacy, relativizing it, making it subordinate to love and compassion—to the law of the Spirit.

In Romans, chapter 7, verses 1–6, Paul affirms that in Christ we are no longer under the Law's domination. Just as a wife through the death of her husband is no longer bound to the law of matrimony, so the Christian living in the Spirit released by the risen Jesus is no longer bound to the outward letter. In Galatians, chapter 3, Paul vehemently makes war on the position that said if a man observes the Law, he is saved. No, says Paul. The Christian, united to the risen Christ, is dead to the Law, delivered from the Law, freed once and for all. The Christian vocation is a vocation to liberty. Freedom is the cornerstone of Christianity.

"Do not think that I have come to abolish the Law or the Prophets; I have not come to abolish them but to fulfill them."

MATTHEW 5:17

THE NEW LAW

———————[✚]———————

The community formed by Jesus was empowered by God's Word, untrammeled by all the later conventional Christian fetters. It is the school of freedom, where the language of love is spoken and only the daring need apply. It is the home of free men and women, who are a jarring, jolting, and disturbing influence on our Christian commitment. The Spirit escapes human categories. Saint Augustine said that the Ten Commandments are but a coat hanger on which to hang the radical requirements of the New Law.

What is the best outward expression of the law of the Spirit? We take a clue from Jesus' farewell address in the Upper Room on Holy Thursday where he gave love primacy, saying, "This is the 'new' commandment: that you love one another as I have loved you."

> *Therefore show these men the proof of your love and*
> *the reason for our pride in you, so that the churches*
> *can see it.*

2 CORINTHIANS 8:24

———————[✠]———————

I f there is any priority in the personal or professional life of a
Christian more important than the Lordship of Jesus
Christ, he disqualifies himself as a witness to the gospel and
from membership in the gentle revolution. Since the day that
Jesus burst the bonds of death and the messianic era erupted
into history, there is a new agenda, a unique set of priorities,
and a revolutionary hierarchy of values for the believer. The
Carpenter did not simply refine Platonic or Aristotelian ethics,
he did not merely reorder Old Testament spirituality, he did not
simply renovate the old creation. He brought a revolution. We
must renounce all that we possess, not just most of it (Luke
14:33); we must give up our old way of life, not merely correct
some slight aberrations in it (Eph. 4:22); we are to be an alto-
gether new creation, not simply a refurbished version of it (Gal.
6:15); we are to be transformed from one glory to another, even
into the very image of the Lord—transparent (2 Cor. 3:18); our
minds are to be renewed by a spiritual revolution (Eph. 4:23).

> *I do not hide your righteousness in my heart;*
> *I speak of your faithfulness and salvation.*
> *I do not conceal your love and your truth*
> *from the great assembly.*

PSALM 40:10

LOOKING AS THOUGH WE ARE SAVED

————————[✠]————————

One weekend last summer I was vacationing at the Jersey shore with my brother (who, incidentally, is always a delightful surprise). Late Saturday afternoon, I took a walk around an artificial lake in Belmar. One the far side was a banquet hall called "The Barclay," which hosted parties, conventions, wedding receptions, and so forth. More than a hundred people were filing in the front door. They had just left the nuptial liturgy at St. Rose Church and were anticipating the reception. It had already begun. Inside they could hear the music and laughter, drinking and dancing. The looks on their faces! They were jubilant, keyed up, bursting with impatience, sure of their reserved seats; they couldn't wait to get in. They looked as though they were going to a wedding feast.

In Matthew 22 Jesus describes the Kingdom of God as a wedding feast. Do you really trust that you are going to a wedding feast that has already begun?

> *Then I saw a new heaven and a new earth, for the*
> *first heaven and the first earth had passed away, and*
> *there was no longer any sea. I saw the Holy City, the*
> *new Jerusalem, coming down out of heaven from God,*
> *prepared as a bride beautifully dressed for her husband.*

REVELATION 21:1-2

————🈁————

J esus' freedom from public opinion and the nagging concern
of what others might think enabled him to live with honesty and spontaneity. There could be no facade, no mask, no
pretense, no sham, no playing of roles. For the Nazarene
Carpenter, to have integrity meant to be genuine, to communicate authentically, to resonate with his feelings.

The injunction of Paul to "put on Christ" explicitly
means not to conform to the spirit of this passing age. With
utter single-mindedness and purity of heart, Jesus sought only
to please his Father. He was unconcerned about projecting a
"nice guy" image and surely not paranoid about hurting anyone's feelings or stepping on any toes. He knew who he was,
and he permitted nothing and no one to stand in his way of
being himself.

> *So the wall was completed on the twenty-fifth of Elul,*
> *in fifty-two days. When all our enemies heard about*
> *this, all the surrounding nations were afraid and lost*
> *their self-confidence, because they realized that this*
> *work had been done with the help of our God.*

NEHEMIAH 6:15–16

NONVIOLENCE AND LOVE

⸻⸻ 🌞 ⸻⸻

The Christian response to evil—to aggression—is resistance, of course, but nonviolent resistance, the resistance of love, prayer, and accepted suffering. When Christians do anything else, they have parted company with Jesus. Nonviolence is the expression of a faith that the greatest power in human history is the forward movement of love. Nonviolence is as realistic as Jesus himself, and it is one with the cross of Christ's victory over evil. The question of whether or not nonviolent resistance "works" should be referred not so much to the gain of an immediate victory as to the transformation of history from within by the converging forces of love. Gandhi wrote that "Jesus lived and died in vain if he did not teach us to regulate the whole of life by the eternal law of love."

> *"But I tell you, Do not resist an evil person. If someone strikes you on the right cheek, turn to him the other also."*

MATTHEW 5:39

————————[※]————————

The salvation offered by Jesus was purely gratuitous, intended especially for those who had no title to it; for those so conscious of their unworthiness that they had to rely on the mercy of God. The self-righteous imagined that they had earned salvation through observance of the Law. Refusing to give up this madness, they rejected the merciful love of the redeeming God.

In the misery of the sinner Jesus saw the possibility of salvation. He saw the sinner's openness for dialogue, his humility, his need of him. . . . The Kingdom is a pure gift to those who have no right to it. This is the very heart of the gospel and the fundamental theme of the Beatitudes—the nonvalue of the beneficiaries of the Kingdom. To say that man is a cipher is not to denigrate his dignity but to highlight the absolute gratuity of God's promise.

Thus the privileged condition of the children and the sinners sheds considerable light on the primitive meaning of the first Beatitude. Blessed are the poor. Blessed are you who are conscious of your lack of merit and readily open yourselves to the divine mercy.

> A Canaanite woman from that vicinity came to him,
> crying out, "Lord, Son of David, have mercy on me!
> My daughter is suffering terribly from demon-
> possession."

MATTHEW 15:22

COME AND SEE

————————[🕆]————————

Following surgery for prostate cancer, I walked (catheterized) every morning for an hour through our Old Algiers neighborhood in New Orleans with a new pair of glasses. One vital aspect of the postmortem life, it seems, is that everything gets piercingly important. You get stabbed by things, by flowers and babies, by the mighty Mississippi and the inner beauty of your wife, by the loveliness of a plethora of things.

And, of course, it all slowly fades. . . .

The Gospels indicate, however, that at every moment of his life Jesus was aware that everything came from the love of God. He never took his life for granted but each moment received it as a free gift from his Abba.

The nameless gratitude that we feel after a narrow escape from injury or death, Jesus felt each morning as he rose from sleep. He lived without boredom, tranquilizers, or anesthesia, numb to neither the pain nor the joy of the human experience. He was a man with his arms open, his chest uncovered, and his heart exposed; and so the wild world, gift of his prodigal Father, leaped into his eyes, ravished his ears, and pierced his heart.

Jesus said to the two disciples, "Come and see." Come to me and see with my eyes, listen with my ears, and feel with my heart.

> *So God created man in his own image,*
> *in the image of God he created him;*
> *male and female he created them.*

GENESIS 1:27

———— 💮 ————

In days long ago when there were no spiritual directors or brilliant commentaries on Scripture, fidelity to God's will was the whole of spirituality. The two pivotal words in the teaching of Jesus are both A words—*Amen* and *Abba*. *Amen* meaning "yes" and *Abba* meaning "Father." Saying yes to our heavenly Father's will is the essence of the entire moral teaching of Jesus. God will bring good out of evil—even a greater good than if there had been no evil—and the trial will have been an immense good for us.

> *Then Jesus said to the centurion, "Go! It will be done just as you believed it would." And his servant was healed at that very hour.*

MATTHEW 8:13

RESPONSES TO JESUS

————————— 🞖 —————————

Upon being told by her sister, Martha, that Jesus had arrived in Bethany and wanted to see her, Mary got up *quickly* and went to him (John 11:29).

Mary of Magdala was heartbroken and tearful when she found the tomb empty. At the moment of recognition when Jesus called her name, she *clung* to him—"Do not cling to me, because I have not yet ascended to the Father" (John 20:17 JB).

As soon as Peter and John received word of the empty tomb, they *ran* together to the garden, but the other disciple, *running faster than* Peter, reached the tomb first (John 20:3–4).

Peter, the denier of Jesus, a failure as a friend in the hour of crisis, a coward in his soul before the servant girl in the courtyard, *jumped* into the water almost naked once John told him Jesus was on shore. "At these words 'It is the Lord,' Simon Peter, who had practically nothing on, wrapped his cloak around him and jumped into the water" (John 21:7 JB). John notes that the boat was about a hundred yards offshore.

These biblical characters, however clean or tawdry their personal histories may have been, were not paralyzed by the past in their present response to Jesus. Tossing aside self-consciousness, they ran, clung, jumped, and raced to him. Peter denied him and deserted him, but he was not afraid of him.

> *He tends his flock like a shepherd:*
> *He gathers the lambs in his arms*
> *and carries them close to his heart;*
> *he gently leads those that have young.*

ISAIAH 41:11

———————————[✣]———————————

The awareness of our innate poverty, that we were created from the clay of the earth and the kiss of God's mouth, that we came from dust and shall return to dust, pulls away the mask of prestige, of knowledge, of social class, or of strength—whatever it is we use to command attention and respect. (I shudder as I think how often I have worn the clerical collar to serve these very purposes and commanded deference not because of who I was, but because of the clothes I wore.) Poverty of spirit breaks through our human pretenses, freeing us from the shabby sense of spiritual superiority and the need to stand well with persons of importance.

Poverty brings us to the awareness of the sovereignty of God and our absolute insufficiency. We simply cannot do anything alone. Any growth or progress in the spiritual life cannot be traced to our paltry efforts. All is the work of grace. We cannot even acknowledge that Jesus is Lord except through the gift of the Holy Spirit. Life is lagniappe. We are faced with the possibility of genuine humility. I am convinced that without a gut-level experience of our profound spiritual emptiness, it is not possible to encounter the living God.

> [Paul] asked them, "Did you receive the Holy Spirit when you believed?"
>
> They answered, "No, we have not even heard that there is a Holy Spirit."

ACTS 19:2

THE LAW OF MERCY

The Lord abrogated the Law by permitting his disciples to pluck grain on the Sabbath. The Pharisees were furious. "See here! Your disciples are doing what is not permitted on the Sabbath." Jesus replied: "If you understood the meaning of the text, 'It is mercy I desire and not sacrifice,' you would not have condemned these innocent men."

Several years ago when the Friday abstinence was still in force, a beleaguered fan approached me in Yankee Stadium. It was a Friday. "I had a long day, Father. Not even time for lunch. Worked overtime tonight. I was wondering if I could get a hot dog?" Mentally, I thumbed through my moral theology manual for mitigating circumstances: nuclear holocaust, famine, lunar attack, wedding anniversary. . . . What would Jesus have said? "Bring two!"

> Then he said to them, "The Sabbath was made for man, not man for the Sabbath."

MARK 2:27

———— 🈁 ————

Our natural repugnance and ingrained resistance to the inconvenient, unpleasant, and often messy business of compassionate caring is well illustrated by a story told at a recent AA meeting: A construction worker stopped after work for a few beers at the local watering hole and got home just in time for dinner. His little daughter, who had peanut butter and jelly all over her face as well as a deposit in her pants, rushed into his arms. To say that he was "taken aback" would not accurately describe his emotional state. Wheeling around to his wife, he muttered, "How the hell do you love something that smells like this?" Calmly she replied, "In the same way I love a husband who comes home stinking drunk and amorous. You work at it."

> *Love is patient, love is kind. It does not envy, it does not boast, it is not proud. It is not rude, it is not self-seeking, it is not easily angered, it keeps no record of wrongs.*

1 CORINTHIANS 13:4–5

HE CHOSE US

————[☩]————

Through water and the spirit the disciple of Jesus has been bonded to his elder Brother, entered into God's family, become a son of the new covenant, and been given immediate access to the Father's lap. "Blessed be the God and Father of our Lord Jesus Christ. . . . Before the world was made, he chose us in Christ, to be holy and spotless, and to live through love in his presence, determining that we should become his adopted sons, through Jesus Christ" (Eph. 1:3–4).

The problem is: either we don't know it; we know it but don't accept it; we accept it but are not in touch with it; we are in touch with it but do not surrender to it.

> He predestined us to be adopted as his sons through
> Jesus Christ, in accordance with his pleasure and will.
>
> EPHESIANS 1:5

———— ⊹ ————

The Christian growing in consciousness longs with Jesus for the unity of the global community, the dawning of the day when the lion will lie down with the lamb, East will learn the language of the West, black and white will really communicate, cities of apathy, garbage, and despair will experience the sunshine of a better life, and all men will rejoice in the Spirit that makes them one. The sense of cosmic oneness, his own freedom in the Spirit, and the awareness that liberation and liberty are the nucleus of the message of Jesus, direct his attention and focus his energies on the emancipation of the world. The Christian cannot remain insensitive to the oppression of his brothers and oblivious to the world's struggle for redemption, freedom, and peace. He knows that the good done to the poor is done to Jesus himself.

> "The King will reply, 'I tell you the truth, whatever
> you did for one of the least of these brothers of mine,
> you did for me.'"

MATTHEW 25:40

No Holds Barred

————[✺]————

What the world longs for from the Christian religion is the witness of men and women daring enough to be different, humble enough to make mistakes, wild enough to be burned in the fire of love, real enough to make others see how unreal they are. Jesus, Son of the living God, anoint us with fire this day. Let your Word not shine in our hearts, but let it burn. Let there be no division, compromise, or holding back. Separate the mystics from the romantics, and goad us to that daredevil leap into the abyss of your love.

> I turned around to see the voice that was speaking to
> me. And when I turned I saw seven golden lamp-
> stands, and among the lampstands was someone "like a
> son of man," dressed in a robe reaching down to his
> feet and with a golden sash around his chest. His head
> and hair were white like wool, as white as snow, and
> his eyes were like blazing fire. His feet were like
> bronze glowing in a furnace, and his voice was like the
> sound of rushing waters.

REVELATION 1:12–15

————[⚜]————

Remember the Gospel story of the woman with the hemorrhage? Touching only the hem of Christ's garment, she was healed. When Jesus asked, "Who touched me?" Peter was astonished. "Who touched you? You're being jostled and hustled by the crowd on all sides!" But Jesus insisted, "I felt power go forth from me." Among all those in physical contact with Jesus at that moment, this woman's touch was accompanied by faith—faith sufficient to unleash the divine power in the Master.

Far closer is our contact, we who have been made one with Jesus Christ through baptism. There we acquired the potential to participate in the "sacrament of the present moment"—to transform even our most mundane experiences into those of Christ. But we, too, must activate that contact through faith. Strong faith that Jesus can come streaming into our lives and empower us to function, and respond not from our ego-self, but from our Spirit-self. But we must *will* the transformation. Only when we will to live *in Christ* do our actions become his. I am not speaking here of human willpower but of radical reliance on the Holy Spirit, who empowers us to transcend egoism, moodiness, and laziness. . . . I am speaking with the same emphasis as the Trappist monk and psychoanalyst who, when asked by a young Jewish convert, "How do I become a saint?" replied, *"Will it."*

> *The goal of this command is love, which comes from a*
> *pure heart and a good conscience and a sincere faith.*

1 TIMOTHY 1:5

THE WAY OF INTEGRITY

────────🔆────────

While the way of integrity offers no grounds for boasting because it is the work of the Spirit within us (and this is no token acknowledgment; without the Holy Spirit we cannot even see that Jesus is risen), it does call the disciple to rigorous honesty about his attitudes, values, lifestyle, and personal relationships. In my experience of life on the streets, honesty is a rare and precious quality seldom found in society or in the church. Like the alcoholic who denies he has a drinking problem, many of us have been deluding ourselves for so long that dishonesty and self-deception have become an accepted way of life. The *esse quam videri* (to be rather than seem to be) of Saint Gregory Nazianzen has been so convoluted that "seeming to be" becomes the common denominator of ordinary behavior, pretense and sham comprise enough to get by, pious thoughts replace putting on an apron and washing dirty feet, and in the words of Carl Jung, "neurosis is always an adequate substitute for suffering."

> "*They devour widows' houses and for a show make lengthy prayers. Such men will be punished most severely.*"

MARK 12:40

———————— ⌘ ————————

The psalms were born in solitude, in a steady, unflinching gaze at the greatness, tenderness, and fidelity of Yahweh. The basic intuition of the psalms of praise, as one Old Testament scholar points out, is a sense of wonder, awe, and admiration, characteristic of every authentic spiritual life. It is translated into an enthusiasm for Yahweh, his power, goodness, and love. These psalms are pure adoration, the *Amen* of the community in response to God's revelation. And God revealed that he is not only interested, not only patronizing; he is passionately concerned about Israel. Psalm 42 begins, "As the hind longs for the running waters, so my soul longs for you, O God. Athirst is my soul for God, the living God. When shall I go and behold the face of God?" (JB). It is a faith-filled response to the anguished cry of Yahweh recorded by Jeremiah: "Ephraim, a favorite son, my own child, as often as I speak of you, I have to remember you the more. My compassion is aroused. I yearn for you. . . ." In the Song of Songs Yahweh so dispenses with the canons of prudence and discretion as to stir even the insensitive heart.

> *Praise the LORD.*
> *Praise the LORD, O my soul.*
> *I will praise the LORD all my life;*
> *I will sing praise to my God as long as I live.*

PSALM 146:1–2

PREFERRING TO BE
OF LITTLE ACCOUNT

———————[✠]———————

I n canonizing the poor in spirit, Jesus reverses all past ideas of human greatness and offers a totally new idea of human vocation. Jesus says in effect: Like a little child, consider yourself to be of little account. Blessed are you if you love to be unknown and regarded as nothing: all things being equal, to prefer contempt to honor, to prefer ridicule to praise, to prefer humiliation to glory.

To practice poverty of spirit calls us not to take offense or be supersensitive to criticism. The majority of hurts in our lives, the endless massaging of the latest bruise to our wounded ego, feelings of anger, grudges, resentment, and bitterness come from our refusal to embrace our abject poverty, from our obsession with our rights, from our need for esteem in the eyes of others. If I follow the counsel of Jesus and take the last place, I won't be shocked when others put me there, too.

> *Remember how the* LORD *your God led you all the way*
> *in the desert these forty years, to humble you and to*
> *test you in order to know what was in your heart,*
> *whether or not you would keep his commands.*

DEUTERONOMY 8:2

———————❖———————

An attitude of self-acceptance is not self-centered; it is relational. It is not self-regarding, but Christ oriented. The spurious self-contentment that evolves from rigorous mortification and anxious endeavor to achieve purity of heart is bogus spirituality, the counterfeit coin of Christian integrity. As Jesus' unparalleled authenticity and inner serenity were rooted in his Father's good pleasure, so Christian self-acceptance is planted in the conscious affirmation of Jesus in our struggle to be faithful.

> Though he slay me, yet will I hope in him;
> I will surely defend my ways to his face.
> Indeed, this will turn out for my deliverance,
> for no godless man would dare come before him!

JOB 13:15–16

REJOICE! REJOICE!

———⊞———

Through good humor a Christian triumphs over that subtle form of egotism that would make him pose as a martyr or at least a victim, that makes him want to be noticed, consoled, or placed on a pedestal. And it makes community life richer and more delightful.

Paul called good humor a charism and exhorted the Christian community at Philippi to manifest it: Rejoice in the Lord always! Rejoice! Everyone should see how unselfish you are. The Lord is near. Dismiss all anxiety from your minds. Present your needs to God in every form of prayer and in petitions full of gratitude. Then God's own peace which is beyond all understanding, will stand guard over your hearts and minds, in Christ Jesus (see Phil. 4:4–7).

Rejoice in the Lord always. I will say it again: Rejoice!

PHILIPPIANS 4:4

———— [✠] ————

How long have you been a Christian now? How long have you been living in the Spirit now? Do you know what it is to love Jesus Christ? Do you know what it is to have your love unsatisfied, endured in loneliness, and ready to burst your restless, ravenous heart? Do you know what it is to have the pain taken away, the hole filled up, to reach out and embrace this sacred Man and say sincerely, "I cannot let you go. In good times and bad, victory and defeat, my life has no meaning without you"? If this experience has not shown your life darker by its brilliance, then regardless of age, disposition, and state in life, you do not understand what it means to be a Christian.

This and this alone is authentic Christianity. Not a code of dos and don'ts, not a tedious moralizing, not a list of forbidding commandments, and certainly not the necessary minimum requirement for avoiding the pains of hell. Life in the Spirit is the thrill and the excitement of falling in love with Jesus Christ. If the Spirit is not fire, it does not exist. The prayer that rises from my heart is this—if you haven't already, may you come to know in surpassing measure the incredible, passionate joy that I have come to know in the love of Jesus Christ Crucified, the power of God, and the wisdom of God.

I keep asking that the God of our Lord Jesus Christ,
the glorious Father, may give you the Spirit of wisdom
and revelation, so that you may know him better.

EPHESIANS 1:17

A CONSUMING FIRE

———————[☩]———————

Have you ever been sexually aroused to an intense degree? Really stimulated in a sensuous way? Passionately turned on? Both the Scripture and the liturgy of the Christian community say that human sexual arousal is but a pale imitation of God's passion for his people. That is why human love, though it's the best image we have, is still an inadequate image of God's love. Not because it overdoes it, but because human desire with all its emotion cannot compare with the passionate yearning of Jesus Christ. That is why saints can only stutter and stammer about the reality, why Blaise Pascal on his famous night of fire, November 21, 1654, could not speak a word, why Bede Griffiths wrote: "The love of Jesus Christ is not a mild benevolence: it is a consuming fire."

It is only the revelation that God is love that clarifies the happy irrationality of God's conduct and his relentless pursuit. For love tends to be irrational. It pursues in spite of infidelity. The Gospel account of the cleansing of the Temple tells us that sometimes love blossoms into jealousy and anger. Jesus' anger reveals his keen interest, his frantic involvement in his brothers and sisters coming into right relationship with Abba God.

> *For the LORD your God is a consuming fire, a jealous God.*

DEUTERONOMY 4:24

———————✠———————

For Paul, a new creation meant a total renovation of the inner self, a change of mind and heart. It meant far more than the passive union achieved in water baptism. To be "in Christ," he told the Philippians, means to have in you the mind of Christ Jesus, to think as Christ thought, to have the ideals Christ had, to throb with the desires that filled Christ's heart, to replace all your natural actions to persons, events, and circumstances with the response of Jesus Christ. In a word, a christocentric life means to live in the heart of Jesus, to share his tastes and aversions, to have the same interests, affections, and attitudes, to be motivated in everything by his loving compassion. It means making the habitual thought patterns of Jesus Christ so completely your own that truly "I no longer live, but Christ lives in me."

> *Therefore, if anyone is in Christ, he is a new creation;*
> *the old has gone, the new has come!*

2 CORINTHIANS 5:17

PUTTING ON CHRIST

———— ✠ ————

I n the full acceptance of who he was, Jesus is the archetype of personality integration. When we "put on Christ" and fully accept who we are, a healthy independence from peer pressure, people pleasing, and human respect develops. Christ's preferences and values become our own. The Kingdom of God is built on earth when we do the will of our Father in heaven. We become "other Christs" through a life of Christian integrity. The same openness to feelings, simplicity of speech, intimacy with the Father, spirit of humble service, compassionate healing, suffering discipleship, and obedient love are wrought in us by the Paraclete and are precisely what Paul means by "new creation."

> I have been crucified with Christ and I no longer live,
> but Christ lives in me. The life I live in the body, I
> live by faith in the Son of God, who loved me and gave
> himself for me.

GALATIANS 2:20

———————[✳]———————

Peter writes in his first letter: "Clothe yourselves with humility toward one another, because 'God opposes the proud but gives grace to the humble.' Humble yourselves, therefore, under God's mighty hand, that he may lift you up in due time" (1 Peter 5:5b–6).

These words are both frightening and consoling. God resists, refuses, rejects the proud. But he delivers himself up, he gives himself totally to the humble and the little. Not only does he not resist them, but he cannot refuse them anything. The story of the Canaanite woman in Matthew 15:21–28 is a shining example. "Yes, Lord," she said to Jesus, when he pointed out that his mission was to Israel alone, "but even the dogs eat the crumbs that fall from their masters' table." She humbled herself, and Jesus exalted her. "Woman, you have great faith! Your request is granted."

Jesus couldn't resist the humility of this foreign woman, of the good thief, of Mary Magdalene.

> *A man's pride brings him low,*
> *but a man of lowly spirit gains honor.*
>
> PROVERBS 29:23

THE SNARE OF FEARING FAILURE

ou know, in spite of the fact that Christianity speaks of
the cross, redemption, and sin, we're unwilling to admit
failure in our lives. Why? Partially, I guess, because it's
human nature's defense mechanism against its own inadequacies. But even more so, it's because of the successful image our
culture demands of us. There are some real problems with projecting the perfect image. First of all, it's simply not true—we
are not always happy, optimistic, in command. Second, projecting the flawless image keeps us from reaching people who
feel we just wouldn't understand them. And third, even if we
could live a life with no conflict, suffering, or mistakes, it would
be a shallow existence. The Christian with depth is the person
who has failed and who has learned to live with his failure.

Surely you desire truth in the inner parts;
you teach me wisdom in the inmost place.

PSALM 51:6

————[✡]————

A person, in a real sense, is what he or she sees. And seeing depends on our eyes. Jesus uses the metaphor of eyes more often than that of minds or wills. The old proverb, "The eyes are the windows of the soul," contains a profound truth. Our eyes reveal whether our souls are spacious or cramped, hospitable or critical, compassionate or judgmental. The way we see other people is usually the way we see ourselves. If we have made peace with our flawed humanity and have embraced our ragamuffin identity, we are able to tolerate in others what was previously unacceptable in ourselves.

> *"I am sending you to open their eyes and turn them*
> *from darkness to light, and from the power of Satan to*
> *God, so that they may receive forgiveness of sins and a*
> *place among those who are sanctified by faith in me."*

ACTS 26:17–18

ABANDONED TO HIS WILL

oncretely, abandonment to the will of God consists of finding his purpose for you in all the people, events, and circumstances you encounter. If God tears up your beautiful game plan and leads you into a valley instead of onto a mountaintop, it is because he wants you to discover *his* plan, which is more beautiful than anything you or I could have dreamed up. The response of trust is "Thank you, Jesus," even if it is said through clenched teeth.

> *"For I know the plans I have for you," declares the*
> LORD, *"plans to prosper you and not to harm you,*
> *plans to give you hope and a future."*

JEREMIAH 29:11

———————[✳]———————

For many of us, trust does not come easily. Trust does not come from discovering in philosophy or cosmology some proof that God exists. Sometimes it happens when my eyes meet yours or when we share something in common. It is most likely to happen if I love you. Ultimately, we trust God because we love him. Not the other way around: not trust first, then love. Job trusted because he loved.

You will trust God only as much as you love him. And you will love him not because you have studied him; you will love him because you have touched him—in response to his touch. Even then your troubles are not over. You may still wrangle with God. You may cry out with Jesus, "My God, my God, why have you forsaken me?" Only if you love will you make that final leap into darkness: "Father, into your hands I commend my spirit."

And again, Isaiah says,

> *"The Root of Jesse will spring up,*
> *one who will arise to rule over the nations;*
> *the Gentiles will hope in him."*

ROMANS 15:12

LOVE WITHOUT CONDITIONS

————————[✳]————————

The fundamental secret of Jesus in relation to his disciples was his sovereign respect for their dignity. They were persons, not toys, functions, or occasions for personal compensation. In the Lucan account of the Passion, the evangelist notes that after Peter's third denial of Jesus "the Lord turned around and *looked at* Peter. . . ." In that look the reality of recognition was disclosed. Peter knew that no man had ever loved him or no woman could ever love him as Jesus did. The Man whom he had confessed as the Christ, the Son of the living God, looked into his eyes, saw the transparent terror there, watched him act out the dreadful drama of his security addiction, and loved him. The love of Jesus for Peter lay in his complete and unconditional acceptance of him. We who so automatically place conditions on our love ("if you really loved me you would . . . ") fail to see that this is an exchange—not unconditional love. We tack on one of our addictions to finish the sentence. Reality must live up to our expectations.

> And a highway will be there;
> it will be called the Way of Holiness.
> The unclean will not journey on it;
> it will be for those who walk in that Way;
> wicked fools will not go about on it.

ISAIAH 35:8

———————— 🔯 ————————

Genuine Christianity pulls us away from that stupefy-ing, specious religion that points to some future opportunity to practice virtue on some misty ideal. Christ wants Christians to live in the present, to love now, to touch this person in these concrete circumstances. His Word pulls us away from every form of escape from involvement with others. In the Upper Room on the eve of his death, as a final emphasis to his life and ministry, Jesus left us with a clear understanding of Christian life in community. Again and again he repeats, "Love one another . . . love one another as I have loved you. If you love me you will do what I tell you . . . and this is what I tell you (what I demand of you) . . . that you love one another."

Briefly and succinctly Jesus reemphasized the rock foun-dation of the Christian life. And in so doing, he wants us to respect one another and take care of one another; he wants us to fuss and worry about, to be concerned about and involved with, to forgive and make excuses for, to be good to and love one another until the day we die and ever after. "In short, there are three things that last: faith, hope and love; and the greatest of these is love" (1 Cor. 13:13 JB).

> *Judgment without mercy will be shown to anyone who has not been merciful. Mercy triumphs over judgment!*

JAMES 2:13

TAKING HIS HAND

———————[❀]———————

Let me make a suggestion. Each day take a little time to pause and pray, "Jesus, I thank you for everything."

In this simple prayer there is humility, a deep trust in his love, surrender, and thanksgiving. It glorifies Jesus and pleases the Father. It is a cry of abandonment. Actually, it is nothing more than what Paul asked of the Ephesians in chapter 5, verse 20: "Always and everywhere giving thanks to God who is our Father in the name of our Lord Jesus Christ" (JB).

As you pray daily in this way, I believe you will hear the Father say something like this:

"My child, fan the flame of your confidence in me. Keep it burning. I want you to be happy, to come back again and again to this feeling of trust until you are never without it. Trust is an aspect of love. If you love me and believe in my love for you, you will surrender your whole self into my hands like a little child who doesn't even ask, 'Where are you taking me?' but sets off joyously, hand in hand with his mother. How many blessings this happy confidence wins for you, my little one."

> *He trusts in God. Let God rescue him now if he wants*
> *him, for he said, "I am the Son of God."*

MATTHEW 27:43

————————[✠]————————

It is important to recapture the element of delight in creation. Imagine the ecstasy, the veritable orgy of joy, wonder, and delight, when God makes a person in his own image! When God made you! The Father gave you as a gift to himself. You are a response to the vast delight of God. Out of an infinite number of possibilities, God invested you with existence. Regardless of the mess you may have made out of the original clay, wouldn't you agree with Aquinas that "it is better to be than not to be"?

Have I really appreciated the wonderful gift that I am? Could the Father's gift to himself be anything but beautiful?

> *I praise you because I am fearfully and wonderfully*
>   *made;*
> *your works are wonderful,*
> *I know that full well.*

PSALM 139:14

A FATHER'S COMPASSION

———————[✳]———————

"**A**s a father has compassion on his children, so the Lord has compassion on those who fear him." Carl and Norma Prask of North Hollywood, Florida, sent me a sculpture. The artist had chiseled a father cradling his little son on his instep and rocking him back and forth. The child is looking at his father with utter confidence and love. But suppose the little one deliberately slipped off his father's instep and walked away. How would the father feel? How would you feel? Would you miss your little one? Would you call out his name? Would you be eager for his return? In the interim, would you love him in his absence? Well, the Abba of Jesus is at least as nice a person as you.

> *She opened it and saw the baby. He was crying, and she felt sorry for him. "This is one of the Hebrew babies," she said.*

EXODUS 2:6

———————⟨✠⟩———————

"There is no greater love than this, that a man lay down his life for his friends. . . . I call you my friends. . . . Abide in my love. . . . These things I have spoken to you that my joy may be in you, and your joy may be filled. Peace is my gift to you. . . . Don't let your hearts be troubled. Trust in God and trust in me. . . . I'm going now to prepare a place for you, and after I have gone and prepared you a place, I'll return to take you with me, so that where I am you may be too." (Here I'm thinking of a deaf man named Charlie who at the moment of his death said, "For the first time, I hear someone coming.") Jesus says, "You didn't choose me; no, I chose you." *These are phenomenal statements!* What deity of any great world religion has ever spoken with such breathtaking tenderness, incredible familiarity, indomitable confidence, and spellbinding power?

> *" You did not choose me, but I chose you to go and bear fruit."*

JOHN 15:16

FULFILLMENT

————— ⊞ —————

W e recognize that Jesus responds to needs and desires that we've long had, perhaps without being fully aware of them. He speaks to our innermost being, supplies our needs, satisfies our desires. In him the obscure is illuminated, the uncertain yields to the certain, insecurity is replaced by a deep sense of security. In him we find that we have come to understand many things that baffled us. The encounter with Jesus awakens us to possibilities we have never seen, and we know that this person is what we have been seeking.

> *Delight yourself in the* LORD
> *and he will give you the desires of your heart.*

PSALM 37:4

———————❧———————

Gilbert Chesterton met the question squarely. "Christianity has not been tried and found wanting," he wrote. "It has been found difficult and left untried." Mahatma Gandhi once said, "I like your Christ, but I don't like your Christians." He gave as his reason, "They are so unlike your Christ." Unless and until we have men and women who live by the inner dynamism of the Spirit, human torches aglow with the fire of love for Christ, Christianity will be a musty antique of a medieval past.

Only the Holy Spirit conveys the dynamic character of the moral life and nurtures the willingness to accept initiative. External law has bred a don't-get-involved attitude. Stressing the mere and minimal fulfillment of precept, it makes Christians cautious about making waves. Just float through life like a majestic iceberg taking no chances. A prominent American churchman remarked recently: "Other people, often not even Christians, are speaking out the sound principles of Christ in the struggle for racial justice more faithfully than we. They are looked upon as fanatics—yet they are doing a very Christian thing—things we should be doing if we see Christ in our fellow man."

What a strange breed of Christianity the law has ushered in! What little resemblance it bears to the gospel of Jesus Christ!

> *So that with one heart and mouth you may glorify the God and Father of our Lord Jesus Christ.*

ROMANS 15:6

THE LAW OUT OF BALANCE

———— ⛢ ————

Unbalanced emphasis on external law has made the church a haven for the shallow and the insecure. It has fostered legalism and phariseeism by its heavy stress on external formalities. In this golden, postconciliar age, we still have sophisticated Catholics asking, "With this new wrinkle of liturgy of Word and Sacrament, how late can I come to mass now before committing serious sin?" And youth asking, "How long can I neck at the drive-in with my boyfriend before violating chastity?" And grown men asking, "How much can I crib from my employer before it becomes a grave matter?" A small-town mayor in Alabama is outraged that a girl entered church in Bermuda shorts; he is silent on the issue of racial equality. On Ash Wednesday the woman in the Cleveland restaurant scrupulously examines her soup to detect the slightest particle of meat. She is rude, arrogant, coarse, and high-handed with the waitress. What are we doing to the gospel?

> *If I tell the righteous man that he will surely live, but then he trusts in his righteousness and does evil, none of the righteous things he has done will be remembered; he will die for the evil he has done.*

EZEKIEL 33:13

———————[※]———————

The personal transformation of the Christian is a mystery that cannot be pierced, but the effects of the transformation are set forth clearly in the New Testament—so clearly in fact that we try to obscure them. The bottom line is that the transparent Christian resembles Jesus, becomes a professional lover who is motivated by compassion in all that he or she thinks, says, and does. The various ways Paul describes this personal metamorphosis—putting on Christ, living in Christ, Christ living in the Christian, or life in the Spirit—all point to a revolutionary change in our personal lives, our values, our habits, our attitudes. If we are true to this Christian love, it may kill us, impoverish us, or disgrace us. In any event we are sure to lose at least some of the goods of this world, which Jesus took the trouble to point out are of no importance anyway.

> *Therefore we do not lose heart. Though outwardly we are wasting away, yet inwardly we are being renewed day by day.*

2 CORINTHIANS 4:16

THE LIFE OF INTEGRITY

————[✲]————

The life of integrity born of fidelity to the dream has a precise meaning in the mind of Christ. It leaves no room for romanticized idealism, condescending pity, or sentimental piety. When a disciple's every response, word, and decision is motivated by compassion, he has put on Christ and walks in the way of integrity. Biblically, compassion means action. Copious Christian tears for the dehydrated babies in Juarez is heartfelt emotion; when combined with giving them a cup of water it is compassion. The difference between emoting and acting is trenchantly described in the first letter of John: "If a man who was rich enough in this world's goods saw that one of his brothers was in need, but closed his heart to him, how could the love of God be living in him? My children, our love is not to be just words or mere talk, but something real and active" (1 John 3:17–18).

> *The integrity of the upright guides them,*
> *but the unfaithful are destroyed by their duplicity.*

PROVERBS 11:3

———————[❀]———————

A ware of the snares and pitfalls of Pelagianism, semi-Pelagianism, the bootstrap myth, the Horatio Alger legend of the self-made man, and do-it-yourself spirituality, I found Simon's answer addressing a real imbalance in my own interior life. Conscious that God takes the initiative and that by his grace we are saved, I am addressing the sincerity, seriousness, and ferocity of my determination to correspond with his saving grace. Apart from him I can do nothing. But without my cooperation he can do nothing. Christ will not sanctify me against my will. I believe that he will finally give me exactly what I choose and that the tendencies and desires my choices imply will be mine, irretrievably so. Obedience to the Word, the habit of constant prayer, the daily practice of Christian virtue, require active collaboration on my part.

> Then he told her, "For such a reply, you may go; the demon has left your daughter."

MARK 7:29

WHAT JESUS FELT

————————[❋]————————

The Greek verb *splangchnizomai* is usually translated "to be moved with compassion." But its etymological meaning is more profound and powerful. The verb is derived from the noun *splangchna*, which means "intestines, bowels, entrails," that is to say, the inward parts from which the strongest emotions arise. In American argot we would call it a gut reaction. That is why English translations resort to active expressions like "he was *moved* with pity" or "his heart *went out* to them." But even these verbs do not capture the deep physical flavor of the Greek word for compassion. The compassion that Jesus felt was quite different from superficial and ephemeral emotions of pity or sympathy. His heart was torn, his gut wrenched, the most vulnerable part of his being laid bare.

> "Is not Ephraim my dear son,
> the child in whom I delight?
> Though I often speak against him,
> I still remember him.
> Therefore my heart yearns for him;
> I have great compassion for him,"
> declares the LORD.

JEREMIAH 31:20

ONE OF US

————————————————

To those who envisage life in Christ as sweetly insipid or airily otherworldly, the cleansing of the Temple, described in chapter 2 of John's Gospel, is a most disconcerting scene. It presents us with the inescapable portrait of an angry Savior. The magnanimous Jesus who said, "Forgive your neighbor seventy times seven," the meek Lamb of God who said, "Learn from me for I am gentle and humble of heart," has fashioned a homemade whip and is tearing through the Temple overturning stalls and showcases, thrashing the merchants, and roaring, "Get out of here! This isn't Winn Dixie! You will not turn sacred space into a supermarket!"

It would be an understatement to say that Jesus was upset. Blazing wrath, unmitigated rage are more accurate. Like fear, love, and hatred, anger is an emotion both basic and necessary to human nature. When God drew aside the curtain of eternity and stepped into human history in the man Jesus, he fully assumed the human condition down to the last joyful or painful experience. The Word was made flesh. He was really one of us. Jesus is no stained-glass figure, no pastel face on a religious card.

Jesus wept.
Then the Jews said, "See how he loved him!"

JOHN 11:35–36

THE REIGN OF GOD

————[✠]————

Through meal sharing, storytelling, miraculous healing, preaching, teaching, and a life of compassion that knew no frontiers, boundaries, or sectarian divisions, Jesus inaugurated in his person the reign of God. In Jesus' own conduct the new age dawned, the messianic era erupted into history. His disciples' loving concern, nonjudgmental attitude, and compassionate care for their brothers and sisters is the visible form in which the reign of God is manifested today. What makes the Kingdom come is heartfelt compassion. It is the way that God's lordship takes.

> This is what the LORD Almighty says: "Administer true justice; show mercy and compassion to one another."
>
> ZECHARIAH 7:9

———⟨✠⟩———

The unity so ardently desired and expressed by Jesus Christ in his high-priestly prayer presupposes freedom in all its forms. The Church as the visible body of the Lord is committed to global freedom, to active participation in the construction of a just social order, and to stimulating and radicalizing the dedication of Christians. The holy alliance between charismatic spirituality and liberation theology serves to vitalize the Church's action in the world and to make its commitment to the Lordship of Jesus deeper and more radical.

The Christian in the unitive center of consciousness views his life and growth in the Spirit quite simply. He knows, to paraphrase Pascal, that all the liberation and revolution theologies, all the charismatic, Asiatic, and apophatic spiritualities, all the burial mounds of rhetoric, enfeebled good intentions, mumbling, and fumbling of cerebral Christians busy cultivating their own idolatries, are not worth as much as one loving act that emancipates one slave from one moment of exile in Egypt.

> *Guard the good deposit that was entrusted to you—*
> *guard it with the help of the Holy Spirit who lives in us.*

2 TIMOTHY 1:14

YAHWEH'S PASSION

In Isaiah, chapter 54, and later in Hosea, chapter 2, God pictures himself as husband and lover of his people. These images provide a profound insight into Jewish religious experience, an insight that has led one modern Scripture scholar to say that the fantastic humanness of the Incarnation is really not so surprising in a religious tradition of which Hosea was a part.

What God did through this prophet was to appropriate sexual imagery to himself. Yahweh is as intimately involved with Israel as a husband with his wife—and no model wife, either. Israel was a harlot, unfaithful to her husband, whoring around with false gods. But Yahweh's passion for his bride was such that he simply could not give her up. He desired her with a longing that her infidelity couldn't cool. He permitted her to exercise a power over him that aroused his ardor even when she had become a prostitute. As one Christian put it, "Yahweh was hooked on his bride." He could not have enough of her, and his passion could not be dampened by her many betrayals.

For your Maker is your husband—
the LORD *Almighty is his name—*
the Holy One of Israel is your Redeemer;
he is called the God of all the earth.

ISAIAH 54:5

WHO AM I?

————— 图 —————

J ohn the Baptist knew who he was and what he was called to be. "I am not the Messiah; I am sent before him. It is the groom who has the bride. The groom's best man waits there, listening for him, and is overjoyed to hear his voice. That is my joy, and it is complete. He must increase, while I must decrease."

Who am I? What are my reasons for wanting to go on living? What are my goals, dreams, desires, aspirations? What is stirring, moving, surfacing in my soul? In a broad stroke of the brush, I would say, paraphrasing Thoreau, that as the hour of my particular sunset approaches, I would be appalled to discover that I had died without having lived.

For to me, to live is Christ and to die is gain.

PHILIPPIANS 1:21

————— ✠ —————

A fellow Franciscan once challenged me: "Do you ever reflect upon the fact that Jesus feels proud of you? Proud that you accepted the faith that he offered you? Proud that you chose him for a friend and Lord? Is he proud of you that you haven't given up? Proud that you believe in him enough to try again and again? Proud that you trust that he can help you? Do you ever think that Jesus appreciates you for wanting him, for wanting to say no to so many things that would separate you from him? Do you think that Jesus can ever be grateful to you for pausing to smile, comfort, give to one of his children who have such great need to see a smile, to feel a touch? Do you ever think of Jesus being grateful to you for learning more about him so that you can speak to others more deeply and truly about him? Do you ever think that Jesus can be angry or disappointed in you for not believing that he has forgiven you totally? He said, 'I do not call you servants, but friends. . . .' Therefore, there is the possibility of every feeling and emotion that can exist between friends to exist here and now between Jesus and you."

> Yet the LORD longs to be gracious to you;
> he rises to show you compassion.
> For the LORD is a God of justice.
> Blessed are all who wait for him!

ISAIAH 30:18

———————[⚹]———————

There is a wondrous open-mindedness about children and an insatiable desire to learn from life. An open attitude is like an open door—a welcoming disposition toward the fellow travelers who knock on our door during the middle of a day, the middle of the week, or the middle of a lifetime. Some are dirt balls, grungy, disheveled, and bedraggled. The sophisticated adult within me shudders and is reluctant to offer them hospitality. They may be carrying precious gifts under their shabby rags, but I still prefer clean-shaven Christians who are neatly attired and properly pedigreed and who affirm my vision, echo my thoughts, stroke me, and make me feel good. Yet my inner child protests: "I want new friends, not old mirrors."

When our inner child is not nurtured and nourished, our minds gradually close to new ideas, unprofitable commitments, and the surprises of the Spirit. Evangelical faith is bartered for cozy, comfortable piety. A failure of nerve and an unwillingness to risk distorts God into a bookkeeper, and the gospel of grace is swapped for the security of religious bondage.

"Unless you become as little children . . ." Heaven will be filled with five-year-olds.

> After the crowd had been put outside, he went in and
> took the girl by the hand, and she got up.

MATTHEW 9:25

CHRISTIAN MARRIAGE

Our human experience tells us that Christian marriage is usually not lived to a lyrical beat; it often comes to awkward expression in our fumbling attempts to forgive and make peace, to walk a mile in the other's moccasins, and to share the frightened, lonely, insecure, and sometimes neurotic journey of our spouse through the way of compassion. We can find echoes of ourselves in the petty, strange, and broken syllables of their story. With remarkable insight Vincent DePaul wrote: "Be compassionate and you will become a saint."

Let us draw near to God with a sincere heart in full assurance of faith.

HEBREWS 10:22

———————[卐]———————

I realize that I don't love as much as I could or should. I miss cues. Sometimes I hear what a woman says but not what she means and wind up giving sage counsel to a nonproblem. Distracted by a disturbing phone call, I left the monastery to give a talk to the inmates of the Trenton State Penitentiary and began with the outrageous greeting: "Well, it's nice to see so many of you here!" And so it goes. Frequently not in form, on top, or in control. That is part of my poverty as a human being. His impoverished spirit prevents the poor man from being a tyrant to himself.

In fact, if you asked a man who is poor in spirit to describe his prayer life, he might well answer, "Most of the time my prayer consists in experiencing the absence of God in the hope of communion." He is not richly endowed with extraordinary graces and mystical experience. Yet the experience of absence does not mean the absence of experience. Like the soldier in combat sneaking a look at his wife's picture tucked in his helmet, the experience of her absence does not mean at that moment the absence of an experience of her. And somehow the poor man perceives that the goal of the spiritual life is not religious experience but union with God through love.

> One thing I ask of the LORD,
> this is what I seek:
> that I may dwell in the house of the LORD
> all the days of my life,
> to gaze upon the beauty of the LORD
> and to seek him in his temple.

PSALM 27:4

JEREMIAH'S CALL

J eremiah reminds us that a vocation is whatever God wants. It is accepting ourselves just as he made us, with our talents, disposition, and character or the lack of them. God may give us one talent for teaching and five talents for compassion. His demands may be so ordinary, so common, that they stir little response in our emotions. Yet in God's will alone can we find peace. Even though God's will is hidden from us, following it can only mean success. The prophet Jeremiah is a shining example of a successful failure.

> But if I say, "I will not mention him
> or speak any more in his name,"
> his word is in my heart like a fire,
> a fire shut up in my bones.
> I am weary of holding it in;
> indeed, I cannot.

JEREMIAH 20:9

———————[⚕]———————

I ntensity of desire is of paramount importance. The Christian's dedication to his growth into higher consciousness is the single most important determinant of his spiritual development. Without an intense inner commitment, he is a dilettante playing spiritual games. When the pearl of great price is the most treasured value in his life, and the grace of surrender is sought through Jesus the Liberator in persevering prayer, in sacramental healing, and in the healing power of the Christian community, the miracle of transparency, love, and oneness will unfold in his life. . . . It is God's will that we grow in holiness (1 Thess. 4:3), know the truth that makes us free (John 8:32), and rejoice with a joy that no one can take from us (John 16:22).

You hear, O LORD, the desire of the afflicted;
you encourage them, and you listen to their cry.

PSALM 10:17

THE RULE OF LAW

————————✠————————

Why, then, if Paul declares the Christian freed from the rule of law, does the Christian religion still contain a code of laws? In his letter to Timothy Paul answers that "the law is not meant for those who live innocent lives." The law is for the unjust. The Spirit does not dwell within the unjust man, so he needs other laws to guide him. The commandments of God and the precepts of the Church make the sinner conscious of his sinfulness. The awareness of his miserable, unhappy existence leads him to grope for God. Thus, the purpose of external law is to lead the sinner to the internal law of love.

> *Through him everyone who believes is justified from everything you could not be justified from by the law of Moses.*

ACTS 13:39

————————[✿]————————

The experience of God's Spirit as tenderness was mirrored to me at a couple's forty-fifth wedding anniversary. The husband and wife quietly exited midway through the reception. On the way to the rest room I passed a sheltered alcove. They were sitting on a love seat and the man was staring intently at his spouse. He knew everything about her there was to know: her virtues and her character defects, her occasional moodiness and her sense of humor, her pettiness and her magnanimity.

The expression on his face conveyed unconditional acceptance, steadfast forgiveness, inexhaustible patience, and a tender love that kept no score of past failings. Not a word was exchanged. She sighed, then cried. They embraced.

The spirituality of accepted tenderness brings an intermittent awareness of the loving gaze of the Abba of Jesus with the aforementioned qualities infinitely magnified. It is a spirituality without manuals and navel-gazing, goals and game plans, stress and distress. It simply rejoices in the gift. And it is all the work of the Holy Spirit defined as given tenderness.

> Yahweh is tender and compassionate, slow to anger,
> most loving. As tenderly as a father treats his children,
> so Yahweh treats those who fear him.

PSALM 103:8, 13 JB

OUR IMAGE OF JESUS

————————⌘————————

My brothers and sisters, Jesus is our God. He and the Father are one. He is the image of the invisible God. Our Jesus image makes all the difference. If we let the Lion of Judah run loose as Lord of our lives, he will not want us to be poor, broken, or sad. Yet he may allow it, knowing that in these conditions we are more likely to let him make us rich, whole, and happy. If you let the real Jesus into your life, the God whose supreme desire is your happiness and fulfillment, you'll want to throw out anything that is going to stop you from reaching his Kingdom. The brutal hyperboles about plucking out the eye and cutting off the hand or foot become understandable in this context—and in no other. Jesus' teaching is full of wild exaggerations, for Jesus is a wild man. And he says to us, "It has pleased my Father to give you the Kingdom."

For he has not despised or disdained
the suffering of the afflicted one;
he has not hidden his face from him
but has listened to his cry for help.

PSALM 22:24

RISE, O SLEEPER!

———————————

One definition of salvation is "an ongoing process of becoming increasingly conscious." Many of us remain in a state of psychic numbness throughout our lives. We are sleepwalkers like the zonked pedestrians on the mechanical sidewalk in the Atlanta airport. Kierkegaard saw that the basic human problem is that all men are bored.

Jesus is always calling on us to wake up. "Why are you sleeping?" (Luke 22:46). It is daily meditation that leads us to full wakefulness. We learn to wake up to the reality of our existence and the reality of God. Spiritual maturity is simply living in harmony with ourselves and with God. When we meditate, our eyes are taken off ourselves. We are not concerned with our own perfection or our own wisdom or even our own happiness. Our eyes are fixed on Jesus, and we receive from him everything, literally everything, we need to run the race and to make light of the difficulties we have, whatever they are.

Meditation makes us lighthearted because we know that there is only one thing essential to life and that is to be in harmony with God and ourselves (see Luke 10:42; 12:31). This is what leads to the discovery that we cannot lose once we realize that everything that happens to us has been designed to teach us holiness.

> So then, let us not be like others, who are asleep, but
> let us be alert and self-controlled.

> I THESSALONIANS 5:6

THE HEALING PROCESS

———————— 🔯 ————————

To live in the wisdom of accepted tenderness is to let go of cares and concerns, to stop organizing means to ends and simply *be* in each moment of awareness as an end in itself. It is to hear with the heart the word of Paul to Titus: "The tenderness and love of God our Savior has dawned in our lives: he saved us not because of any righteous deeds we had done but because of his mercy" (3:4–5 JB). We can embrace our whole life story in the knowledge that we have been graced and made beautiful by the providence of our past history. All the wrong turns in the past, the detours, mistakes, moral lapses, everything that is irrevocably ugly or painful, melts and dissolves in the warm glow of accepted tenderness. As theologian Kevin O'Shea writes, "One rejoices in being unfrightened to be open to the healing presence, no matter what one might be or what one might have done."

When I am most afraid,
I put my trust in you;
in God whose word I praise,
in God I put my trust, fearing nothing.

PSALM 56:3–4 JB

———————— 🕂 ————————

It is important to note that submission is not surrender. The former is the acceptance of reality consciously, not unconsciously. There is a superficial yielding, but tension continues. I say that I accept who I am, but I do not accept it so fully that I am willing to act on it—to actually act out who I am. Surrender is a moment when the unconscious forces of resistance cease effectively to function. The Christian now no longer evades the call of the Spirit but accepts it. "The emotional state of surrender," writes Dr. Harry S. Tiebout, "is a state in which there is a persisting capacity to accept reality. It is a state that is really positive and creative."

When the Christian surrenders to the Spirit on the unconscious level, there is no residual battle, and relaxation ensues with freedom from strain and conflict. Submission, on the other hand, is halfhearted acceptance. It is described by such words as *resignation, compliance, acknowledgment, concession*, and so forth. There remains a feeling of reservation, a tug in the direction of nonacceptance. Surrender produces wholehearted acceptance.

> *Who, by the power that enables him to bring every-*
> *thing under his control, will transform our lowly bod-*
> *ies so that they will be like his glorious body.*

PHILIPPIANS 3:21

THE DREAM OF LIFE

—————[✠]—————

Even when preoccupied, distracted, or salivating, we each have a dream, a vision of life that corresponds to our convictions, embodies our uniqueness, and expresses what is life-giving within us. Whether altruistic or ignoble, the dream gives definition to our lives and influences the decisions we make, the steps we take, and the words we speak. If security represents our highest aspirations, we may be owned and indentured by Aetna Life and Casualty; if pleasure is our priority, we will distribute our time and money in hedonistic pursuits; if scholarship rules, we will be properly pedigreed and securely settled in an academic environment. Even if the dream is unrealistic or temporarily on hold due to uncontrollable circumstances, it prods our consciousness, nurtures our fantasies, and inchoately sustains our will-to-meaning in the world.

The dream of Jesus Christ is the Kingdom of God, and the committed Christian buys into his dream.

Commit your way to the LORD;
trust in him and he will do this.

PSALM 37:5

————————⚜————————

Every religion has three elements: the intellectual element, the ritual or sacramental element, and the personal or mystical element. The intellectual element comprises what a religion believes, its doctrines or dogmas. The ritual element consists in the sacrifices and ceremonies of worship, and the mystical element is the personal relationship with the God we adore. In Christianity Jesus stands at the center of each of these aspects. He is the intellectual element, for he is the doctrine we believe.

He *is* the revelation. He is also the ritual element. When the Christian community gathers for the communal meal, Jesus *is* the Eucharist. The other sacraments are his gestures prolonged in time and space. As Saint Augustine said: "It is Christ alone who baptizes, confirms, forgives, and heals." And Jesus is the center of the mystical life. In him we live and move and have our being. Outside of Jesus there is no personal communion with God, no mystical life. We are sons and daughters of Abba only in Christ Jesus; we inherit the Kingdom only in Christ Jesus. Christian mysticism is essentially a personal relationship in which one member is a human being and the other is the eternal God revealed in Jesus.

> *Religion that God our Father accepts as pure and*
> *faultless is this: to look after orphans and widows in*
> *their distress and to keep oneself from being polluted*
> *by the world.*

JAMES 1:27

No Apologies

———— 🕀 ————

Living out of the center means sharing Jesus' intimate experience of God as Father. One meaning of the word *father* in the Scriptures is lord and ruler, full control and authority. Jesus acknowledged the absolute sovereignty of his Father. He never attempted to justify God for all the muddle, pain, and tragedy in the world. In Luke 13, when people tell Jesus about some Galileans murdered by Pilate, he does not defend God or justify his reasons for allowing people to suffer. Indeed, he reminds them about the eighteen on whom the tower of Siloam fell. Jesus makes no effort to exonerate God from the scandal of suffering, to bail him out, to rationalize or minimize the presence of tragedy in his world. He surrenders without reservation to the infinite wisdom and awesome majesty of God.

> *He will stand and shepherd his flock*
> *in the strength of the LORD,*
> *In the majesty of the name of the LORD his God.*
> *And they will live securely, for then his greatness*
> *will reach to the ends of the earth.*

MICAH 5:4

THE NEW LIFE

———————[※]———————

J ust as a mother does not think in terms of law and obligation when, in the middle of the night, she runs to the bedside of her crying child, but rather responds naturally to the internal law of her maternal being, so for the Christian, law is perfectly compatible with liberty. Christian existence means that we have been transformed. Through the Spirit we live in Christ Jesus. Life is doing what comes supernaturally. Our new being must overflow into action as the natural expression of our real self. "Walk in the Spirit," Paul says, "and you will not fulfill the lusts of the flesh." What matters is Christian being. The new law is the internal principle of operation.

> *Carry each other's burdens, and in this way you will fulfill the law of Christ.*

GALATIANS 6:2

LAW AND GRACE

————————[✳]————————

P aul rejects the Law because it has become an occasion of sin. It tells man not to covet, but it leaves him helpless in avoiding covetousness. Though Paul is speaking here of the Mosaic Law, his argument pertains to all law. Rules and regulations provide sinful man with just another opportunity to sin. The disciplinary law says, "Do not eat meat on Good Friday," but it gives me no power to push the hamburger away.

What then? Is the Christian, a man without law, free to sin? Paul's answer is an unequivocal *no*. "Do not use your freedom to indulge the sinful nature" (Gal. 5:13).

Is there any norm at all by which a Christian can guide his actions and shape his behavior? What determines right from wrong? Paul answers that the law of the Spirit giving life has replaced the old law of sin and death. And he identifies the law of grace with the law of the Spirit. "You are not under law, but under grace" (Rom. 6:14).

> *The one who sows to please his sinful nature, from that*
> *nature will reap destruction; the one who sows to*
> *please the Spirit, from the Spirit will reap eternal life.*

GALATIANS 6:8

————⊞————

I n the discipline of consciousness-focusing the Christian psychologically distances himself from himself and the surrounding world. In a detached way he reviews his performance in the various centers of consciousness, almost like watching an actor on the stage of life. He doesn't pat himself on the back or criticize in any way. He impartially witnesses himself. In peace and calm before the Lord he discerns where he has been and where he is. Such focusing can free him from the enslavement of addictions that keep his emotions churning in self-destructive ways. It can free his consciousness from involvement in lower levels so that the Spirit of God may more and more dominate his self-awareness. It can enable him to change from someone who is asleep to someone who is awake, from a Christian acting like an automatic robot to one celebrating his freedom in Christ Jesus. The discipline of consciousness-focusing concludes with the petition to surrender to the way of the Spirit throughout the day and the prayer of praise.

> *For I am full of words,*
> *and the spirit within me compels me.*

> JOB 32:18

A Pilgrim People

————————[✠]————————

The Church of Jesus Christ is a place of promise and possibility, of adventure and discovery, a community of love on the move, strangers and exiles in a foreign land en route to the heavenly Jerusalem. We are a pilgrim people who have checked into the hotel of Earth overnight with bags packed and ready to go. Regrouping and retrenching, squatting and discussing are not the poses or postures of a wandering Aramean or the lifestyle of the Lord Jesus. "The foxes have their holes, the birds of the air their nests, but the Son of Man has nowhere to lay his head."

This is what the LORD says:

> "Maintain justice
> and do what is right,
> for my salvation is close at hand
> and my righteousness will soon be revealed."

ISAIAH 56:1

JUST RECEIVE

———————[✻]———————

Perhaps the most fundamental religious question I can ask myself today is: Do I really believe the Good News of Jesus Christ? Do I hear his word spoken to my heart: "Shalom, be at peace. I understand your fears, your failures, your brokenness. I don't expect you to be perfect. I have been there. All is well. You have my love. You don't have to pay for it, and you can't deserve it. You only have to open and receive it. You only have to say yes to my love—a love beyond anything you can intellectualize or imagine."

> O Lord, open my lips,
> and my mouth will declare your praise.

PSALM 51:15

"COME TO ME"

───────────[✝]───────────

The dominant theme of the Book of Glory, the second part of John's Gospel, is union with the Lord. Through the beautiful imagery of the vine and the branches, Jesus calls all men to himself. "Abide in me, dwell in me, resort to me, come to me." Significantly, Jesus does not say, "Come to a day of renewal, a retreat, a prayer meeting, a liturgy," but "come to me." Is this the self-flattering superiority of a religious fanatic? Yes, if he is not the Savior of the world. He is either a bigot or the Risen Lord who must be proclaimed as the world's only hope.

Who else would dare to say, "I am the way, I am truth and life. . . . I am the light of the world. . . . I am the bread of heaven. He who eats of this bread will never know what it is to die. . . . He who believes in me will have everlasting life; and the one who does not believe in me will be condemned"?

> When he had gone indoors, the blind men came to him, and he asked them, "Do you believe that I am able to do this?"
>
> "Yes, Lord," they replied.

MATTHEW 9:28

DIVIDED WITHIN MYSELF

————————☙————————

The proof par excellence of the Christian who has experienced God's unbearable forgiveness and infinite patience is that he is able to be forgiving and patient with others. Whatever other gifts he may possess, this sign given by Jesus stamps his life as being "in the Spirit."

Francis Macnutt has said: "If the Lord Jesus Christ has washed you in his own blood and forgiven you all your sins, how dare you refuse to forgive yourself?" Self-hatred is a sin. Anything that causes division in the Body of Christ is sinful. When I am divided within myself, when I am so preoccupied with my own sins, egocentricity, and moral failures that I cannot hear the anguished cry of others, then I have subtly reestablished self as the center of my focus and concern. Biblically, that is idolatry.

Be merciful, just as your Father is merciful.

LUKE 6:36

CONVERSION DAILY

————————[※]————————

There is nobody in the Christian community who is not called to continual conversion. There is no one who does not still have before him the labor of building up the image of Jesus Christ in his life by the steady practice, day by day, of Christian virtues. And, as Edward O'Connor remarks, "You don't sing your way around that stuff." Paul writes in First Corinthians, "I bruise my body and make it know its master, for fear that after preaching to others I should find myself rejected." To the Colossians, "Christ is the Master whose slaves you must be." To the Galatians, "Make no mistake about this: God is not to be fooled; a man reaps what he sows."

> *The body is a unit, though it is made up of many*
> *parts; and though all its parts are many, they form one*
> *body. So it is with Christ.*

1 CORINTHIANS 12:12

MY REAL SELF

————[✠]————

In my final year at the seminary, I developed a bad case of hay fever. Every morning at 5:30, just as the cleric master began to lead sixty seminarians in prayer, I would have an attack of coughing and sneezing. One day he called me into his office and accused me of insubordination, claiming that I was deliberately disrupting morning prayer with my antics. He warned me that my future actions would be monitored and that my ordination to the priesthood, just four months away, was in jeopardy. It was a devastating moment. I left his office angry and frightened, filled with self-pity and confusion. I stumbled to the chapel, sank to my knees, began to silently whisper the name Jesus over and over. Then something wondrous happened. In a moment of truth and breathtaking freedom, I realized that ordination to the priesthood was not so almighty important. It pleased Jesus more to have me as my real self— hay fever allergies and all—than to have a cowed and intimidated priest. I left the chapel and never once looked over my shoulder. I was ordained the following May, still sneezing.

In the history of Christian discipleship, this little incident scarcely ranks alongside the heroism of the martyrs and saints. Still, it gave me a taste for living out of the center and experiencing the freedom of the sons of God.

> *I will make an everlasting covenant with them: I will*
> *never stop doing good to them, and I will inspire them*
> *to fear me, so that they will never turn away from me.*

JEREMIAH 32:40

ACTING ON THE WORD

————— ✠ —————

Most failures to act on the Word can be traced to ignorance, inattention, or insufficient esteem for the
Person of the Word. A boozy goodwill toward the
world replaces the radical conversion and explicit death to self
that the gospel demands. We do not want a God who would
change us. Authentic Christianity rings in the First Letter to
the Corinthians, "Jews call for miracles, Greeks look for wisdom; but we proclaim Christ—yes, Christ nailed to the cross;
and though this is a stumbling block to the Jews and folly to the
Greeks, yet to those who have heard his call, Jews and Greeks
alike, he is the power of God and the wisdom of God." If the
People of God are not hearing the call to repentance and the
power to fulfill it, is it because we ministers of the Word are
preaching another Christ from the pulpit?

> "I have not come to call the righteous, but sinners to
> repentance."

LUKE 5:32

———————𝌤———————

J esus' self-awareness and unflagging zeal in the ministry must be seen in direct and unceasing relation to his interior life of growing intimacy with the Father. We must not lose sight of this logical link: the primacy of mission and the consuming zeal for proclaiming the reign of God derive not from theological reflection, the desire to edify others, or trendy spirituality; its wellspring is the Father's holiness and Jesus' self-awareness of his relation to the Father. This is not a question of words or pious sentiments, but a burning and divine reality.

How did he stay centered in self-awareness? It is highly significant that at the outset of his public ministry, the Gospels are punctuated with numerous references to his withdrawal from the mainstream of activity to pray. The Gospels indicate that Jesus needed this special kind of intimate touch with his Father. His own interior growth and sense of mission and direction depended very much on these times of prayer.

> And a voice from heaven said, "This is my Son, whom
> I love; with him I am well pleased."

MATTHEW 3:17

LIVING OUT OF THE CENTER

L iving out of the center frees us from the tyranny of peer pressure. Living to please the Father, as Jesus did, becomes the basic impulse of a Christian's life—more important than pleasing people. And this requires a remarkable degree of freedom. Jesus was not intimidated by public opinion, by what "others will think." In order to be free for the outcasts, the sinners, the marginals in his social world, Jesus had to keep his distance from the expectations and the moralizing judgments of the authorities and the respectable. When he walked with the notorious sinner Zacchaeus through the streets of Jericho, he was not fazed by the scandalized murmurs of the crowd. He wasn't looking around anxiously, fearing what people might say. He was neither afraid of their rejection nor concerned about stepping on toes. He was going to the home of Zacchaeus because this sinner was a child of his Father, that was all. And that's the name of that tune.

> *Be strong and courageous. Do not be afraid or terrified*
> *because of them, for the LORD your God goes with you;*
> *he will never leave you nor forsake you.*

DEUTERONOMY 31:6

———— 🕆 ————

"**B**lessed are those who know that they are poor" (NEB). We must know who we are. How difficult it is to be honest—to accept that I am unacceptable, to renounce self-justification, to give up my preposterous pretending that my paltry prayers, spiritual insights, knowledge of Scripture, and blustering successes in ministry have made me pleasing to God. No antecedent beauty enamors me in his eyes. I am lovable because he loves me. Period. The first step in liberation from self-hatred is to move from the darkness of self-delusion into the daylight of God's truth.

Everyone who loves has been born of God and knows God.

1 JOHN 4:7

INFLUENCED BY WHOSE OPINION?

———————[✝]———————

The Word of God to the Church of Ephesus is pointed: "I have this against you: you have lost your early love. Think from what a height you have fallen; repent, and do as you once did." Paul expresses similar displeasure and apprehension over the faith of the Corinthians: "I am afraid that your thoughts are being corrupted and that you are losing your single-minded devotion to Christ."

Here was a man who truly acted on the Word of God. He cared only for the judgment of Jesus Christ on his behavior, and nothing for the judgment of men. He was more concerned about the good pleasure or displeasure of the living God than his neighbors' approval. Paul is a courageous witness to the reality of the invisible God, and a powerful example to many of us who are so influenced by the opinion of others; who are so interested in keeping a certain image in the community's eye; who desire only to be liked, accepted, and approved by any group with which we associate; who are not especially careful about our image in God's sight, or otherwise we would not so often neglect the things that he alone sees, like private prayer and secret acts of kindness.

> *Those who are far away will come and help to build the temple of the LORD, and you will know that the LORD Almighty has sent me to you. This will happen if you diligently obey the LORD your God.*

ZECHARIAH 6:15

———————⊞———————

It is symptomatic that in the Western world where the Church is 2000 years old, the mass of people still pass Christianity by. Why? Because the visible presence of Jesus Christ through the Holy Spirit in Christians as a whole, apart from a few individuals, is no longer present.

> *What then shall we say, brothers? When you come together, everyone has a hymn, or a word of instruction, a revelation, a tongue or an interpretation. All of these must be done for the strengthening of the church.*

1 CORINTHIANS 14:26

MOVED BY THE SPIRIT?

———— 🜨 ————

So often we become self-moved and -motivated rather than moved and motivated by the Spirit. Is the security center operating in this decision in order to win approval, avoid criticism, or escape rejection? Are my cuteness and coyness in this personal relationship signs of entrapment in the sensation center? Am I role-playing King Baby through a subtle power ploy in the office or in the prayer community? Dietrich Bonhoeffer wrote, "Satan's desire is to turn me in on myself to the extent that I become enslaved and become a destructive force in community. The thrust from Jesus Christ is the opposite—to enhance my freedom so that I can become a creative force of love. It is the spirit of self-centeredness and selfishness versus the spirit of openness and self-sacrifice for the good of others." Again, the goal is a continually discerning heart.

> *All the believers were one in heart and mind. No one claimed that any of his possessions was his own, but they shared everything they had.*

> ACTS 4:32

———— ✠ ————

L iving for God finds its foremost expression in prayer. The heart of discipleship lies in commitment and worship, not reflection and theory. The Spirit of Jesus provides a way for us to live on the surface and out of the depths at the same time. On the surface we can think, dialogue, plan, and be fully present to the demands of the daily routine. Simultaneously, and deeply within, we can be in prayer, adoration, thanksgiving, and attentiveness to the Spirit. The secret places of the heart become a sanctuary of praise in the noisy playpen of the marketplace. What masters of the interior life recommend is the discipline of "centering down" throughout the day: a quiet, persistent turning to God while driving, cooking, conversing, writing, and so on. After weeks and months of practice, relapses, discouragement, and returns to the center, this discipline becomes a habit. Brother Lawrence called it "the practice of the presence of God."

> *O you who hear prayer,*
> *to you all men will come.*

PSALM 65:2

A SOUL OF PRAYER

———————[※]———————

The late theologian Romano Guardini was once asked by a student why he cherished such deep devotion to Francis of Assisi. "Because he allowed Jesus Christ to become transparent in his personality," he replied. Francis energized a religious revolution throughout thirteenth-century Europe. Why? Because he was a mirror of Christ, one of the most perfect replicas of Jesus that the world has ever seen. And anyone even remotely acquainted with the life of the Poverello need not be told that he was par excellence a man of prayer. To this day the Umbrian hills are dotted with the secluded hermitages and cavelike retreats where Francis passed weeks and often months in prayer. These silent places bear deafening witness that the First Other had first claim on his time, interest, love, and attention. The visitor to Assisi must pass beyond the walls of the city to the primitive *Carceri* if he is to discover the soul of Saint Francis and the secret of his unparalleled apostolic influence.

> *O LORD, God of Israel, there is no God like you in heaven above or on earth below—you who keep your covenant of love with your servants who continue wholeheartedly in your way.*

> 1 KINGS 8:23

————[✚]————

I suspect I am not alone here. The narcissistic obsession with weight watching in North America is a formidable ploy of the impostor. Despite the valid and important health factor, the amount of time and energy devoted to acquiring and maintaining a slender figure is staggering. No snack is unforeseen, no nibble spontaneous, no calorie uncharted, no strawberry left uncounted. Professional guidance is procured, books and periodicals scrutinized, health spas subsidized, and the merits of the protein diet debated on national television. What is spiritual ecstasy compared to the exquisite pleasure of looking like a model? To paraphrase Cardinal Wolsey, "Would that I had served my God the way I have watched my waistline!"

> *May God himself, the God of peace, sanctify you*
> *through and through. May your whole spirit, soul and*
> *body be kept blameless at the coming of our Lord Jesus*
> *Christ.*

1 THESSALONIANS 5:23

RIGHT RELATIONSHIP

————[✻]————

The promised peace that the world cannot give is located in being in right relationship with God. Self-acceptance becomes possible only through the radical trust in Jesus' acceptance of me as I am. Befriending the impostor and the Pharisee within marks the beginning of reconciliation with myself. . . .

In the Rabbi's embrace our evil impulses are converted and transformed into good. Just as the unbridled lust of the sinful woman in Luke's Gospel was transformed into a passion for intimacy with Jesus, so our possessiveness about money metastasizes into greed for the treasure in the field. Our inner murderer becomes capable of murdering homophobia, bigotry, and prejudice. Our vindictiveness and hatred are transformed into intolerance and rage at the caricatures of God as a petty accountant. Our chronic niceness is converted into heartfelt compassion for those who have lost their way.

And the meaning of the Rabbi's words, "Behold, I make *all* things new," becomes luminously clear.

Trust in the LORD with all your heart
and lean not on your own understanding.

PROVERBS 3:5

————🈁————

S ubstituting theoretical concepts for acts of love keeps life at a safe distance. This is the dark side of putting *being* over *doing*. Is this not the accusation that Jesus leveled against the religious elite of his day?

The Christian commitment is not an abstraction. It is a concrete, visible, courageous, and formidable way of being in the world, forged by daily choices consistent with inner truth. A commitment that is not visible in humble service, suffering discipleship, and creative love is an illusion. Jesus Christ is impatient with illusions, and the world has no interest in abstractions. "Everyone who listens to these words of mine and does not act on them will be like a stupid man who built his house on sand" (Matt. 7:26 JB). If we bypass these words of the Great Rabbi, the spiritual life will be nothing more than fantasy.

The one who talks, especially if he talks to God, can affect a great deal, but the one who acts really means business and has more claims on our attention.

> *He will show you mercy because you obey the LORD*
> *your God, keeping all his commands that I am giving*
> *you today and doing what is right in his eyes.*

DEUTERONOMY 13:17–18

MAKING THE CHOICE

———— [✠] ————

The crisis of American spirituality, put bluntly, is Spirit versus flesh. . . . We do not choose decisively between God and Mammon, and our procrastination constitutes a decision itself. We carefully distribute ourselves between flesh and Spirit with a watchful eye on both. The unwillingness to sustain ourselves in the continual self-awareness that we are sons of the Father in Christ Jesus through the power of the Holy Spirit, causes a spiritual schizophrenia of the most frightening kind. It is not that I am afraid to tell you who I am; I simply cannot tell you because I don't know who I am. I have not given the deep inner assent to my Christian identity. I am afraid of losing my life for fear of finding my real self—a reality that will not begin to exist until I assent to it. God calls me by my name, and I do not answer. I do not know my name.

> Him who overcomes I will make a pillar in the temple
> of my God. Never again will he leave it. I will write
> on him the name of my God and the name of the city
> of my God, the new Jerusalem, which is coming down
> out of heaven from my God; and I will also write on
> him my new name.

REVELATION 3:12

———————※———————

The crowd does not take kindly to nonconformity. It is the scorn of our peers probably more than anything else that hinders our living out of the center. The fear of ridicule paralyzes us more effectively than flat-out opposition. How much good is left undone because of this fear! The irony is that the opinions we fear most are not those of people we really respect, yet these very persons influence our lives more than we want to admit. This desire to stand well with "them" can lead to an appalling mediocrity and a frightening unfreedom.

Living out of the center shapes and forms a liberated Christian. Albert Camus once said, "The only way to deal with an unfree world is to become so absolutely free that your very act of existence becomes an act of rebellion." There is nothing more maddening to the mob than a free person.

> Though I am free and belong to no man, I make myself
> a slave to everyone, to win as many as possible.

  1 CORINTHIANS 9:19

WEARING MASKS

———————◼︎———————

In the struggle with self-hatred, we obviously do not like what we see. It is uncomfortable, if not intolerable, to confront our true selves, and so, like runaway slaves, we either flee our own reality or manufacture a false self, which is mostly admirable, mildly prepossessing, and superficially happy. Defense mechanisms become useful allies here. These unconscious ploys warp our perception of reality and protect us from fear, loss, and emotional pain. Through the smoke screen of rationalization, projection, displacement, insulation, intellectualization, and generalization, we remain on the merry-go-round of denial and dishonesty. Those of us who have played this game wear a thousand masks to disguise the face of fear.

> *There is no fear in love. But perfect love drives out*
> *fear, because fear has to do with punishment. The one*
> *who fears is not made perfect in love.*

1 JOHN 4:18

———————[⚓]———————

P aul writes to the Thessalonians: "We have passed God's scrutiny, and he has seen fit to entrust us with the work of preaching; when we speak, it is with this in view; we would earn God's good opinion, not man's, since it is God who can read our inmost thoughts."

Here is the essence of perfect sincerity in conduct—to care for nothing but God's judgment on our actions; not to vary our attitude to suit the company we are in, not to hold one opinion when alone and adopt another in conversation, but to speak and act as in the sight of God who can read our inmost thoughts. Sincerity means trying to make the outward man more and more like the inner man, by simply being true to oneself, so that no human respect can make us false.

> And this is my prayer: that your love may abound
> more and more in knowledge and depth of insight, so
> that you may be able to discern what is best and may
> be pure and blameless until the day of Christ.

PHILIPPIANS 1:9–10

SINS OF OMISSION

———————[茶]———————

One night at Coney Island a group of us were standing outdoors at Nathan's munching hot dogs. A few yards away in the center of the boardwalk, a man was pouring a can of beer on the head and down the blouse of a pregnant girl of maybe fifteen. He was describing aloud in lurid detail how he had sexually abused her and what he had in mind later. She appeared slightly intoxicated; at any rate, she was crying.

"What a zoo!" one of our group said. "Let's split."

We started toward the car when, like a bell sounding deep in my soul, I heard, *Who are you?*

I stopped as if my shoes were stuck to the pavement. "I am a son of my Father," I said.

That girl is my daughter.

I went back, drew the girl aside, and spoke with her for several minutes. Some bystanders began to taunt: "Pimp! Whoremonger!" That night I wept, not for them but for myself, for the countless times I have played the silent sentinel, afraid to acknowledge the presence of the Son of Man in the least of my brothers and sisters. How often I've seen human dignity being degraded and been content to moralize about the situation and walk away. James writes in his letter: "When a man knows the right thing to do and does not do it, he sins."

> *"So, because you are lukewarm—neither hot nor cold—I am about to spit you out of my mouth."*

REVELATION 3:16

———————[✳]———————

Suppose for a moment that in a flash of insight you discovered that all your motives for ministry were essentially egocentric, or suppose that last night you got drunk and committed adultery, or suppose that you failed to respond to a cry for help and the person committed suicide. What would you do?

Would guilt, self-condemnation, and self-hatred consume you, or would you jump into the water and swim a hundred yards at breakneck speed toward Jesus? Haunted by feelings of unworthiness, would you allow the darkness to overcome you, or would you let Jesus be who he is—a Savior of boundless compassion and infinite patience, a Lover who keeps no score of our wrongs?

John seems to be saying that the disciples of Jesus ran to him because they were crazy about him; or, in the more restrained prose of Raymond Brown, "Jesus was remembered as one who exhibited love in what he did and was loved deeply by those who followed him."

The beloved disciple sends a message both to the sinner covered with shame and to the local church tentative and slow to forgive for fear of appearing lax or liberal. The number of people who have fled the church because it is too patient or compassionate is negligible; the number who have fled because they find it too unforgiving is tragic.

> Love is patient, love is kind. It does not envy, it does not
> boast, it is not proud. It is not rude, it is not self-seeking,
> it is not easily angered, it keeps no record of wrongs.

1 CORINTHIANS 13:4–5

DISCERNING THE FATHER'S WILL

———[✠]———

The Father cares. He knows each of us by name. He is deeply involved in the little drama of our personal existence. "Even the hairs of your head have all been counted" (Luke 12:7 JB). Within this climate of trust the Christian confidently searches to discern the Father's will. It is the atmosphere in which all his decisions become clear and from which all his actions spring. The outcome is less vague, ambiguous, and uncertain than one might suppose. The sounds of inner peace, harmony, and consonance resonate in the heart attuned to the Father's will, while agitation, conflict, dissonance, and contretemps resonate in the untuned heart singing its own song.

> *"I know your deeds, your hard work and your perseverance. I know that you cannot tolerate wicked men, that you have tested those who claim to be apostles but are not, and have found them false."*

REVELATION 2:2

L iving out of the center enables us to blend for a moment into a greater background than our own fears, to merely be still, and to know that God is God. It means that I don't figure out, I don't analyze. I simply lose myself in the experience of just being alive, of being in a community of believers, simply knowing that it's good to be there, even if I don't know where "there" is or why it's good. An inner stillness assures me that it is enough right now to be centered, to be in Christ Jesus, and that gratefulness is both the heart of living and the heart of prayer.

> *He makes me lie down in green pastures,*
> *he leads me beside quiet waters.*

PSALM 23:2

SUCCESS IN FAILURE

———————[※]———————

I n my days of wine and roses, sour wine and withered roses, when I was stashing vodka bottles in the bathroom, the glove compartment, and the geranium pot, I saw my life as a complete waste—not only for the things I was doing, but for the things I wasn't doing, the meager, paltry, stingy response I was making to Christ in the least of my brothers. It was a long winter of discontent, guilt, fear, shame, and unbearable hypocrisy. The future held out only the bleak prospect of a wet brain and an alcoholic shuffle, commitment to the funny farm, or premature death. The disease meant failure with no redeeming aspect whatsoever.

But living out of the center has taught me that every failure *succeeds in some way.* It provides the opportunity not only to humble the self, but also to be with the failure of others. If your life or mine were an untarnished success story, an unbroken upward spiral toward holiness, we might never come to understand the human heart.

> *Better to be lowly in spirit and among the oppressed*
> *than to share plunder with the proud.*

PROVERBS 16:19

———————🈂———————

Paul wrote to the Philippians: "I tell you now with tears in my eyes, that there are many whose way of life makes them enemies to the cross of Christ. They are heading for destruction, appetite is their god, and they glory in their shame. Their minds are set on earthly things." Paul's cheeks are still streaked because of the ignorance of God's Word, tepidity, rank insincerity, spiritual adultery, indifference to prayer, comfortable piety, and apostolic sloth that dapple the Christian life in America today.

When Jesus Christ reveals himself through his Word, which is acting and creative, he calls for a spontaneous response. His message is not a reassurance to keep right on doing what we have been doing but, writes Edward O'Connor, "a summons to the labor of eliminating from our lives, faithfully and perseveringly, everything in us that is opposed to the work and will of his Holy Spirit for us. Faith means that we be ready to act on the Word."

We did not give in to them for a moment, so that the
truth of the gospel might remain with you.

GALATIANS 2:5

LEARNING TO LOVE

————————※————————

Religious formation often focused on abstractions, impersonal ethics, and fixed formulae because no one believed that "one learns to love God by loving men." The apostle Paul was not taken seriously: "Help carry one another's burdens; in that way you will fulfill the law of Christ." Community life was not perceived as a radical imitation of the Blessed Trinity who is dialogue, spontaneous love, and community. The light of John the Evangelist illumines the darkness: "No one has ever seen God; but if we love each other, God lives in us and his love is made complete in us" (1 John 4:12). An arresting thesis! To love one another means that the love of God has reached full growth in us.

> *"But love your enemies, do good to them, and lend to them without expecting to get anything back. Then your reward will be great, and you will be sons of the Most High, because he is kind to the ungrateful and wicked. Be merciful, just as your Father is merciful."*

LUKE 6:35–36

———————— 🌣 ————————

J esus skewered his opponents with words to this effect: "The harlots who have no imagined righteousness to protect will be dancing into the Kingdom, while you have your alleged virtue burned out of you! Hear me well: I have come to announce the dawn of a new age, an era of incredible generosity. Allow yourselves to be captivated by joy and wonder at the surpassing greatness of my Father's love for the lost; set it over against your own joyless, loveless, thankless, and self-righteous lives. Let go of your impoverished understanding of God and your circumscribed notion of morality. Strike out in a new direction. Cease from your loveless way, and be compassionate. Celebrate the homecoming of the lost, and rejoice in my Father's munificence."

> *That I may declare your praises*
> *in the gates of the Daughter of Zion*
> *and there rejoice in your salvation.*

PSALM 9:14

GOOD HUMOR

————[✠]————

Effectiveness in the ministry is enhanced by good humor. Remember the prayer of Teresa of Avila—"From silly devotions and sour-faced saints, spare us, O Lord." Good humor is not a superficial smile, a grin-and-bear-it attitude, or the "ginger-peachy" mentality. It is rooted securely in the faith conviction that I am loved by God as I am, not as I should be. This disposition invites others to love and admire the gospel style of life. A good-humored Christian who accepts others as they are, not as they should be, is an evangelist. A zealous but ill-humored evangelist can cause others to say: "If that's what religion does to you, sit on it!"

> *A cheerful heart is good medicine,*
> *but a crushed spirit dries up the bones.*

PROVERBS 17:22

————— 🎋 —————

I f the Pharisee is the religious face of the impostor, the inner child is the religious face of the true self. The child represents my authentic self and the Pharisee the inauthentic. Here we find a winsome wedding of depth psychology and spirituality. Psychoanalysis aims to expose clients' neuroses, to move them away from their falseness, lack of authenticity, and pseudosophistication, toward a childlike openness to reality, toward what Jesus enjoins us to be: "unless you become like little children."

The inner child is aware of his feelings and uninhibited in their expression; the Pharisee edits feelings and makes a stereotyped response to life situations. On Jacqueline Kennedy's first visit to the Vatican, Pope John XXIII asked his secretary of state, Giuseppi Cardinal Montini, what was the proper way to greet the visiting dignitary, wife of the U.S. president. Montini replied, "It would be proper to say 'Madame' or 'Mrs. Kennedy.'" The secretary left, and a few minutes later the First Lady stood in the doorway. The Pope's eyes lit up. He trundled over, threw his arms around her, and cried, "Jacqueline!"

> For he who was a slave when he was called by the
> Lord is the Lord's freedman; similarly, he who was a
> free man when he was called is Christ's slave.

1 CORINTHIANS 7:22

THE ONE WHO SAVES

———————— 🕆 ————————

Living out of the center is not a rarefied, spaced-out state. It has helped me achieve connections and insight into the Word of God that were hitherto hidden. For example, Jesus told us to consider ourselves the least of all. He also told us that what we do for the least brother we do for him. Since whatever is done for the least is done for the Lord, our compassion must start with ourselves. Before I am asked to show compassion toward my brothers and sisters in their suffering, I am asked to accept the compassion of Jesus in my own life, to be transformed by it, and to become caring and compassionate toward myself in my own failure and hurt, in my own suffering and need. His love is not conditioned by what we are or do. He will be gracious and compassionate toward us no matter what our track record, for that is what *Jesus* means—"the One who saves." Those who live out of the center know in their bones that they are poor and sinful, but theirs is a spirit of self-acceptance without self-concern. This is the heart of the gospel—that we can be gracious and compassionate toward ourselves.

> *Finally, all of you, live in harmony with one another;*
> *be sympathetic, love as brothers, be compassionate and*
> *humble.*

1 PETER 3:8

———————[⚜]———————

Т he disciple is not above the Master. Upon the disciples'
jubilant return from the active ministry, Jesus' directive
for preserving their humanness and for centering in
their self-awareness was, "'Come with me by yourselves to a
quiet place and get some rest.' So they went away by themselves in a boat to a solitary place" (Mark 6:31–32).

It is important to keep these times of withdrawal in the
context and rhythm of Jesus' very active and busy life. Such
moments of prayer are always oriented to his active life and
presence in the world. The major decisions of his life (for
example, the selection of the twelve men who would enter the
intimate circle of his friendship and share in his mission) were
always preceded by a night alone on the mountaintop. . . .

One cannot but think of the number of wrong mar-
riages, wrong employments, wrong personal relationships, and
all the concomitant suffering that would be avoided if
Christians submitted their decision-making processes to the
Lordship of Jesus Christ and shared in his intimate trust of the
Father's Will.

> Now you are the body of Christ, and each one of you
> is a part of it.

I CORINTHIANS 12:27

FELLOWSHIP AT THE TABLE

I once met a pastor in the hills of Colorado who invites a family to his rectory every Sunday afternoon for a home-cooked meal. Frequently the guests are unchurched or exchurched. During my visit the fare was simple but the company and conversation stimulating. This family shared the deep hurt inflicted on them by a previous pastor and consequently had discontinued churchgoing. But that afternoon they received consideration instead of expected condemnation, a merciful acquittal rather than an anticipated verdict of guilty. They returned to the worshiping community the following week. They had been healed by an ordinary Sunday meal. Table-sharing with the pastor brought them into fellowship with God.

> *They devoted themselves to the apostles' teaching and to the fellowship, to the breaking of bread and to prayer.*

ACTS 2:42

TRUSTING OUR FATHER

B ut what is faith? Is it merely a matter of the mind? Is it intellectual assent to a dusty pawnshop of dogmatic beliefs? Is it notional acceptance of a closed system of well-defined teachings, like original sin, Immaculate Conception, communion of saints, and so forth? Is it a set of abstract opinions we express in such formulas as "I believe in God"? Muslims, Buddhists, and Shintoists believe in God. Is there anything unique about the Christian credo?

In the magnificent sixth chapter of Matthew's Gospel, faith is described as the unconditional acceptance of the God revealed by Jesus Christ as loving Father. Unless we surrender in faith to his saving truth and live buoyed up by its assurance, we have not made the Christian profession of faith. The term *Father* occurs eleven times in this one chapter, and it is in this Father that the disciples of Jesus are to place unwavering trust. The disciples are called men of "little faith" if they do not trust their Father who knows their needs and provides for the birds of the air and the lilies of the field.

> *Then he touched their eyes and said, "According to your faith will it be done to you."*
>
> MATTHEW 9:29

THE EMERGING CHILD

———— 卍 ————

"Unless you become as little children . . ." The spiritual life might be defined as the development of personality in the realm of faith and grace. My Christian personality is not just a vegetative existence; I am a unique and radiant center of personal thought and feeling. Rather than living a routine existence in mere conformity with the crowd, the emerging child reminds me I have a face of my own, gives me the courage to be myself, protects me against being like everybody else, and calls forth that living, vibrant, magnificent image of Jesus Christ that is within me waiting only to unfold and be expressed.

> "Therefore, whoever humbles himself like this child is
> the greatest in the kingdom of heaven. And whoever
> welcomes a little child like this in my name welcomes me."

MATTHEW 18:4-5

COME DINE WITH ME

————[✠]————

T he scandal that Jesus caused in first-century Palestinian Judaism can scarcely be appreciated by the Christian world today. The class system was enforced de rigueur. It was legally forbidden to mingle with sinners who were outside the Law; the prohibition on table-fellowship with beggars, tax collectors, and prostitutes was a religious, social, and cultural taboo. Unfortunately, the meaning of meal sharing is largely lost on society today. In the East, to share a meal with someone is a guarantee of peace, trust, brotherhood, and forgiveness; the shared table is a shared life. To say "I would like to have dinner with you" means to an orthodox Jew, "I would like to enter into friendship with you." Even today an American Jew will share a doughnut and a cup of coffee with you, but to extend a dinner invitation is to say: "Come to my *mikdash me-at*, my miniature sanctuary, my dining room table, and we will celebrate the most beautiful experience that life affords—friendship." That is what Zacchaeus heard when Jesus called him down from the sycamore tree, and that is why Jesus' practice of table-fellowship caused hostile comment from the outset of his ministry.

> *Jesus came, took the bread and gave it to them, and did the same with the fish.*

JOHN 21:13

THE SNARE OF SPIRITUALISM

————— ✠ —————

All of Satan's temptations to Jesus are to *spiritualism*. First, he tries to appeal to the divinity in Jesus. (As a matter of fact, Satan always tries to stress our spiritual strength, our divine character. He has done this from the very beginning. "You will be like God" is the slogan of the Evil One. It is *the* temptation he sets before us in countless variations, urging us to reject the truth of the humanity we have been given.)

How true in my own life! Every time that I try to soar above the inherent limitations of my human nature and pretend I'm an *angel*, I wind up playing the *beast*. Alcoholism is a good example—a futile attempt to escape the poverty, loneliness, and frustration that are so much a part of the human condition. The same may be said of the drug culture. The name of the game doesn't change. Intellectual pride fits into this category. I attempt to bridge the vast gulf that separates creature from Creator by disavowing my limited, finite intelligence, and I take myself so seriously that I feel superior to others. I presume that I am more important in the eyes of God than the brother who cooks in the kitchen. Insidiously, Satan stresses my charismatic gifts and ensnares me in spiritualism.

> *For everything in the world—the cravings of sinful man, the lust of his eyes and the boasting of what he has and does—comes not from the Father but from the world.*

1 JOHN 2:16

My brother or sister, if you live out of the center, you win. On a given day you might be more depressed than anything else, but when your life is hidden with Christ in God, you win. The roof might collapse, the empire may crumble, you may be transferred to Pago Pago, but with Christ in you, your hope of glory, you win. You might be thinking low thoughts in high places—sitting in church wondering about the preacher's hairstyle, or what you would say if Ronald Reagan gave you a phone call, or what other name you might have chosen for yourself, or could you witness to Christ if you were being tortured with electric shock, or with a little body work could you look like Rambo.

But if you live out of the center on and off during the day, you win. In our kitchen we have a saying enclosed in an old beaten-up wooden frame: "God will not look you over for medals, diplomas, or honors, but for scars.". . . All you may have are your wounds and your last shred of hope. But with the risen victorious Jesus at the center of your life, you win. That was all the early Christian community had against Jerusalem, Rome, and Athens—and the Christians won. That's not rhetoric; that's history. They had only Jesus, and we keep thinking that we need something else.

*I consider that our present sufferings are not worth
comparing with the glory that will be revealed in us.*

ROMANS 8:18

THE ANSWER

———————[✷]———————

I n order to be free to be faithful to this sacred man and his dream, to others and ourselves, we must be liberated from the damnable imprisonment of self-hatred and freed from the shackles of projectionism, perfectionism, moralism/legalism, and unhealthy guilt. Freedom for fidelity demands freedom from enslavement.

It is a tired cliché, a battered bumper sticker, an overused and often superficial slogan, but it is the truth of the gospel: Jesus is the answer. Is there any price too exorbitant, any cost too extravagant to pay for the privilege of being able to make your own personal response to his haunting question: Who do you say that I am?

So we say with confidence,

> *"The Lord is my helper; I will not be afraid.*
> *What can man do to me?"*

HEBREWS 13:6

———————[※]———————

I t is the charism of saints, who are enlightened and inspired
by the Holy Spirit, to trust radically. Paul pours out his
whole heart in Philippians 4:13 in the cry, "I can do everything through him who gives me strength." That is raging confidence.

When Jesus says in John 16, "Have confidence in me, be
brave, cheer up," he is calling us to unconditional abandonment to God's mercy over the sins of our past, and to unwavering confidence that they have not only been forgiven, but
entirely forgotten.

> For it is we who are the circumcision, we who worship
> by the Spirit of God, who glory in Christ Jesus, and
> who put no confidence in the flesh.

PHILIPPIANS 3:3

THE DESERT TEMPTATIONS

———————— ✥ ————————

The temptations in the desert challenged the authenticity of the Jordan experience. All three add up to the same thing—"If you are the Son. . . ." Is Jesus really Son-Servant-Beloved? Was the Jordan experience illusion? Did anyone else hear the voice that he heard? Satan launches a frontal assault on the religious identity of Jesus. The Gospel periscope does not dwell on the inner struggle and fierce conflict in the human heart of Jesus, but the issue was tumultuous. George Aschenbrenner notes, "He is asked here in risk and trust to ratify, and thus to embrace, at the level of mission and action, His own relation to the Father." In the starkness and simplicity of the vast uncluttered wilderness, Jesus interpreted his existence and his mission in the world at a new and decisive level and emerged from the desert with the Breath of the Father on his face.

> Jesus answered, "It is written: 'Man does not live on bread alone, but on every word that comes from the mouth of God.' "

MATTHEW 4:4

————[⚓]————

Homophobia and racism are among the most serious and vexing moral issues of this generation, and both church and society seem to limit us to polarized options.

The anything-goes morality of the religious and political Left is matched by the sanctimonious moralism of the religious and political Right. Uncritical acceptance of any party line is an idolatrous abdication of one's core identity as Abba's child. Neither liberal fairy dust nor conservative hardball addresses human dignity, which is often dressed in rags.

Abba's children find a third option. They are guided by God's Word and by it alone. All religious and political systems, Right and Left alike, are the work of human beings. Abba's children will not sell their birthright for any mess of portage, conservative or liberal. They hold fast to their freedom in Christ to live the gospel—uncontaminated by cultural dreck, political flotsam, and the filigreed hypocrisies of bullying religion. Those who are bent on handing gays over to the torturers can lay no claim to moral authority over Abba's children. Jesus saw such shadowed figures as the corrupters of the essential nature of religion in his time. Such exclusive and divisive religion is a trackless place, Eden overgrown, a church in which people experience lonely spiritual alienation from their best human instincts.

> As for those who seemed to be important —whatever they were makes no difference to me; God does not judge by external appearance—those men added nothing to my message.

GALATIANS 2:6

THE FATHER'S WORKS

I n the man Jesus there is an utter single-mindedness toward his Father and the reign of God. . . . "The words that I speak are not spoken of myself; it is the Father who lives in me accomplishing his works.". . . "Father, if it is your will, take this cup from me; yet not my will but yours be done.". . . In the temple Jesus tersely replies to his mother, "Why did you search for me? Did you not know I had to be in my Father's house?". . .

We must not allow these words to be interpreted as allegory. The will of the Father is reality. It is like a river of life coming down from the Father to Jesus—a bloodstream from which he draws life even more profoundly and more powerfully than he draws life from his mother. And whoever is ready to do the will of the Father becomes a part of this bloodstream, and he is united to the life of Christ Jesus more truly, deeply, and strongly than the way in which Jesus was united to his mother.

Here we find an utter lack of human sentimentality in Jesus. The two focal points of his ministry are the Father and himself. Again, this is as it should be. The New Testament is the *kairos*—the hour of salvation—and its essential lines are through Jesus Christ to the Father from whom salvation comes.

> "My food," said Jesus, "is to do the will of him who
> sent me and to finish his work."

JOHN 4:34

————— ✥ —————

The inner child is capable of a spontaneous breakthrough of emotions, but the Pharisee within represses them. This is not a question of being an emotional person or a subdued one. The issue is, Do I express or repress my authentic feelings? John Powell once said with sadness that if he had to write an epitaph for his parents' tombstone, he would have to write: "Here lie two people who never knew one another." His father could never share his feelings, so his mother never got to know him. To open yourself to another person, to stop lying about your loneliness, to stop lying about your fears and hurts, to be open about your affection, and to tell others how much they mean to you—this is the triumph of the child over the Pharisee and the dynamic presence of the Holy Spirit at work.

> *Neither circumcision nor uncircumcision means any-*
> *thing; what counts is a new creation.*
>
> GALATIANS 6:15

JESUS' COMPASSION

————————[❧]————————

The extraordinary perception and exquisite sensitivity of Jesus enabled him to read the human heart with piercing clarity. . . . Jesus knew what hurt people. He knew then and he knows now. He loves with a depth that escapes human comprehension.

Several years ago, when a minister-friend of mine bottomed out, resigned his church, and abandoned his family, he fled to a logging camp in New England. One wintry afternoon as he sat shivering in his aluminum trailer, the portable electric heater suddenly quit and died. Cursing this latest evidence of a hostile universe, the minister shouted, "God, I hate you!" then sank to his knees weeping. There in the bright darkness of faith, he heard Christ say: "I know; it's okay." Then this shattered man heard Jesus weeping within him. The minister stood up and started home.

The Lord is fine-tuned to the hates and loves, disappointments and delights, brokenness and togetherness, the fears, joys, and sorrows of each of us. That he knows what hurts the human heart shows up all through his earthly ministry: with the brokenhearted Magdalene crying at his feet, the adulterous woman fearing for her life, the Samaritan woman with her history of failed relationships, the women weeping along the road to Calvary. . . .

> *He did not need man's testimony about man, for he*
> *knew what was in a man.*

JOHN 2:25

————— 🕂 —————

The early American Indians had a unique practice in training young braves. On the night of a boy's thirteenth birthday, after his fortitude and maturity had been tested by various trials in hunting, fishing, and scouting, he was placed in the center of a dense forest to spend the entire night alone. It was equivalent to his bar mitzvah or confirmation in the Judeo-Christian tradition, the sign of his adulthood. In a wood so thick that even the moonlight could not penetrate, he was left to the terrors of the darkness. Every twig that snapped seemed like a wild animal ready to pounce. Through the night he looked anxiously toward the east, awaiting the dawn. After what seemed more like a month than a single night, the first ray of sunlight exposed the interior of the forest. Slowly the young boy began to distinguish the bushes, the flowers, the path. Then to his utter astonishment, he saw his father standing just a few feet away behind a tree, armed with a bow and arrow.

Don't you suppose the boy thought, "If only I had known my father were there, I wouldn't have been afraid of anything"? Hundreds of years earlier, Jesus had said to the sinking Peter and to the terrified disciples shipping water on Lake Genesareth, "Where is your faith? Don't you know that my heavenly Father stands beside you night and day, armed not with a bow and arrow but with the love and power of his Spirit to ward off any danger?"

> *So do not fear, for I am with you;*
> *do not be dismayed, for I am your God.*
> *I will strengthen you and help you;*
> *I will uphold you with my righteous right hand*

ISAIAH 41:10

PARTAKERS OF HIS NATURE

The relentless tenderness of Jesus challenges us to give up our false faces, our petty conceits, our irritating vanities, our preposterous pretending and become card-carrying members of the messy human community. Jesus calls us to be tender with one another because he is tender. He invites us into the fellowship of saved sinners wherein our identity and glory lie not in titles, trinkets, honorary degrees, and imaginary differences, but in our "new self" in Christ irrevocably bonded to our brothers and sisters in the family of God.

As the first letter of Peter puts it, we are "partakers of the divine nature," caught up in the very life of God himself, enabled to transcend our automatic emotions of fear, distaste, and all the judgmental junk we carry, empowered to be unrelentingly tender as the Lion-Lamb is relentless and tender.

And his compassion knows no frontiers or boundaries and extends to all. Even to myself.

Remember, O LORD, your great mercy and love,
for they are from of old.

PSALM 25:6

————[❖]————

The obsession with erotica in book, film, play, and entertainment signals entrapment in the sensation center. The carnal man is blatantly in the flesh and lives and walks according to the flesh. Yet many committed Christians who decry the rampant pornography of our sensate culture still dabble discreetly in the fleshpots and paralyze the power of the Spirit in their lives!

An ambivalent "prudence of the flesh" seeks a sort of gilded mediocrity where the self is carefully distributed between flesh and spirit with a watchful eye on both. Paul calls these "men of imperfect spiritual vision." They have received the Spirit, but they remain spiritual men in embryo because they do not subject themselves fully to the domination of the Spirit; they yield to sexual passion and other drives, thus confining themselves to an infantile spirituality.

They never become adults. Paul compares them to babies unable to take solid food (1 Cor. 3:2).

"The perfect Christian," writes Jean Mouroux, "is he who does not normally yield to the demands of the flesh, and who is normally docile to the impulses of the Spirit."

> But among you there must not be even a hint of sexual
> immorality, or of any kind of impurity, or of greed,
> because these are improper for God's holy people.

EPHESIANS 5:3

THE CORE OF MY EXISTENCE

———— ⌈⚹⌉ ————

My identity as Abba's child is not an abstraction or a tap dance into religiosity. It is the core truth of my existence. Living in the wisdom of accepted tenderness profoundly affects my perception of reality, the way I respond to people and their life situations. How I treat my brothers and sisters from day to day, whether they be Caucasian, African, Asian, or Hispanic; how I react to the sin-scarred wino on the street; how I respond to interruptions from people I dislike; how I deal with ordinary people in their ordinary unbelief on an ordinary day will speak the truth of who I am more poignantly than the pro-life sticker on the bumper of my car.

We are not for life simply because we are warding off death. We are sons and daughters of the Most High and are maturing in tenderness to the extent that we are for others—all others—to the extent that no human flesh is strange to us, to the extent that we can touch the hand of another in love, to the extent that for us there are no "others."

> *Be very careful, then, how you live—not as unwise*
> *but as wise, making the most of every opportunity,*
> *because the days are evil.*

EPHESIANS 5:15–16

———————[✠]———————

The communitarian notion of Christianity has suffered severely under legalistic morality. Why have we had such difficulty in launching the liturgical renewal? Because we have lost sight of the awareness that the eucharistic celebration is the assembly of God's holy and worshiping family gathered around their Elder Brother who leads them to the Father in loving submission. Religion has become kind of a telephone booth affair, a private communication between God and me that has no reference to my brother. I go to mass while the world goes to hell. When external law drugs me into such insensitivity that I can no longer hear the anguished cry of my brother; when American Christians can grow fat and selfish in their superabundance—while a few streets away their white, black, and Chicano brothers are submerged in grinding poverty and depersonalizing squalor—and still salve their consciences with the Sunday masses they have attended; when Americans can spend thirty billion dollars on their own vacations and parcel out measly millions in antipoverty bills, then Karl Marx was right—religion is the opium of the people.

> *If you really keep the royal law found in Scripture,*
> *"Love your neighbor as yourself," you are doing right.*
> *But if you show favoritism, you sin and are convicted*
> *by the law as lawbreakers.*

JAMES 2:8–9

JESUS' ACCEPTANCE
OF THE HUMAN CONDITION

———— 🉁 ————

The poverty of Jesus' spirit is captured beautifully in his spontaneous reply to the rich young man. "Why do you call me good? No one is good but God alone." This is the inner attitude of Jesus that ravished the heart of his Father: "I solemnly assure you, the Son cannot do anything by himself—he can only do what he sees the Father doing." Jesus acknowledges that everything is a loving gift from the Father's hand. And he cries out—this is the basic attitude for admission to the Kingdom. "How pleasing you are in my Father's eyes when you have this be-attitude, this attitude of being poor like me, when you accept the limits of your humanity."

Of course, the Evil One gets upset when we cling to our humanness. He was very distressed with Jesus in the desert for this very reason. He wanted Jesus to renounce his poverty, his humanness. Satan already knew that when Jesus accepted the poverty of the human condition, the saga of salvation-history was moving toward its climax. And Jesus held nothing back, clung to nothing, permitted nothing to shield him—even his true origin. He "did not count equality with God a thing to be grasped, but emptied himself" (Phil. 2:6–7). And Satan is furious.

> For you know the grace of our Lord Jesus Christ, that
> though he was rich, yet for your sakes he became poor,
> so that you through his poverty might become rich.
>
> 2 CORINTHIANS 8:9

———— 卐 ————

The incontrovertible sign of the Christian who has experienced forgiveness is that he can love his enemies. This is an extraordinary charism and the infallible sign of the activity of the Holy Spirit. "Love your enemies, do good to them. . . . Then . . . you will be sons of the Most High, because he is kind to the ungrateful and wicked" (Luke 6:35). . . . Jesus Christ crucified is not merely a heroic example to the church; he is the power of God, a living force transforming our lives through his Word, "Father, forgive them, for they do not know what they are doing" (Luke 23:34).

> You see, at just the right time, when we were still
> powerless, Christ died for the ungodly. Very rarely
> will anyone die for a righteous man, though for a good
> man someone might possibly dare to die. But God
> demonstrates his own love for us in this: While we
> were still sinners, Christ died for us.

ROMANS 5:6–8

JESUS' WORK IN US

———— 🔯 ————

T he compassionate love of Jesus at work within us empowers us to suffer with, endure with, struggle with, partake of, be moved in the depths of our being for the hunger, nakedness, loneliness, pain, squalid choices, and failed dreams of our brothers and sisters in the human family. We don't have to join the work of Mother Teresa in Calcutta or Bruce Ritter in Times Square or the Medical Missionaries in El Salvador. The Passion of Christ is being played out in our own communities, perhaps in our own homes, in anyone who is in agony of flesh or spirit. Jesus is there not in some vague eerie way but as a real presence—for what we do for the least of our brothers and sisters, we do for him. On that Calvary next door where Christ still hangs, I will minister to my Savior and my Lord.

> *But Zacchaeus stood up and said to the Lord, "Look, Lord! Here and now I give half of my possessions to the poor, and if I have cheated anybody out of anything, I will pay back four times the amount."*

LUKE 19:8

———— 図 ————

J esus brings freedom from the money game, the power game, the pleasure game, and the pervasive sense of self-hatred that racks our torn conscience. With insight that defies imagination, he proposes a new agenda that proffers peace and a joy that the world would never dare promise: "Turn to my Father, set your heart on his kingdom, and these other things will be given you as well" (see Luke 12:31).

This is a glimpse of the Jesus that I have met over the years on the slopes of my self, the Christ of my interiority. There is a beauty and enchantment about the Nazarene that draw me irresistibly to follow him. He is the Pied Piper of my lonely heart. It is not pious prattle to say: the only valid reason I can think of for living is Jesus Christ. Paul puts it so well: "There is only Christ and he is everything."

> *You are all sons of God through faith in Christ Jesus,*
> *for all of you who were baptized into Christ have*
> *clothed yourselves with Christ.*

GALATIANS 3:26–27

FREE FROM FEAR

————————[※]————————

Becuase of the God-revelation of Jesus, fear and worry are emphatically precluded from the Christian life by him. "Do not let your hearts be troubled.". . . "Do not live in fear, little flock. It has pleased your Father to give you the kingdom.". . . "I warn you then: do not worry about your livelihood." In the twilight of his years the evangelist John pens these lyrical lines: "God is love, and he who abides in love abides in God, and God in him. . . . Love has no room for fear; rather perfect love casts out all fear. And since fear has to do with punishment, love is not yet perfect in one who is afraid" (see 1 John 4:16, 18). Anxiety about tomorrow is explicitly forbidden by Jesus. For the same reason doubts, uncertainty, and misgivings in petitionary prayer are indecent luxuries no Christian can afford: "Ask and you will receive. Seek and you will find. Knock and it will be opened to you. For the one who asks receives. The one who seeks, finds. The one who knocks, enters" (see Matt. 7:7–8). Whether Jesus refers to the sparrow not falling from the sky without permission, to the birds that are fed and the flowers that are clothed, or to praying for today's bread and entrusting tomorrow to another's hands, the underlying mystery is always expressed in the words "Your Father in heaven."

> "Do not be like them, for your Father knows what you need before you ask him."

MATTHEW 6:8

———————[✣]———————

The unglamorous and little-publicized works of mercy: the ministry of small things, feeding and sheltering, visiting the sick and incarcerated, educating, correcting, speaking a healing word, bearing wrongs, listening creatively, counseling, washing dirty feet, praying with people, are all ways of living the life of compassion. This is no minor matter. When Jesus tells us in Matthew 5:48, "Be perfect . . . as your heavenly Father is perfect," the same commandment is translated in Luke 6:36 (JB) as: "Be compassionate as your Father is compassionate."

> *"The poor you will always have with you, and you can help them any time you want. But you will not always have me."*

MARK 14:7

INVISIBLE CONVICTION

——————⟨✳⟩——————

The paternal love of the Father and the fraternal love of Jesus, "our beloved Lord and Brother," as de Foucauld liked to say, were not bluff, myth, or pious rhetoric to him. His trust in the Father was not merely theoretical or verbal. It was so operative that it banished fear, worry, and discouragement from his life and, at the same time, instilled boldness, daring, and boundless trust that God would provide for his daily needs. "Is it possible that he who did not spare his own Son but handed him over for the sake of us will not grant us all things besides?" became the shaping spirit of his prayer. The martyr of the Sahara lived in the desert of the present moment, seeing God alone, occupied only with doing what he wanted. In complete fidelity to the here and now, all the rest was left, forgotten, abandoned to Providence. On a dark December night on the lonely sands of Tamanrasset, he went to his death with courage and calm. Faith that his risen Lord had conquered death and the invincible conviction that "in dying we no longer perish for the Resurrection will render our corruptible bodies incorruptible" (Saint Athanasius) transformed the experience of death from end to beginning, a transition into the only experience worthy of the name life.

"But he who stands firm to the end will be saved."

MATTHEW 24:13

——————[图]——————

J esus brought a revolution in the understanding of God. It is impossible to exaggerate the extravagance of the Father's compassion and love. From Flannery O'Connor's short story "The Turkey," the god of Little Ruller—Something Awful— and all other false images are blown away. Projection is exposed for the idolatry that it is. To pray to any god other than a Father who finds sheer delight in reconciliation is illusion, cowardice, and superstition. For the disciple, God is no other than as he is seen in the person of Jesus.

You shall have no other gods before me.

Exodus 20:3

IN TOUCH WITH OUR FEELINGS

———————[✠]———————

Before going out to dinner my wife, Roslyn, will often say, "I just need a few moments to put on my face." A Pharisee must wear his or her religious face at all times. The Pharisee's voracious appetite for attention and admiration compels him to present an edifying image and to avoid mistakes and failure studiously. Uncensored emotions can spell big trouble.

Yet, emotions are our most direct reaction to our perception of ourselves and the world around us. Whether positive or negative, feelings put us in touch with our true selves. They are neither good nor bad: they are simply the truth of what is going on within us. What we do with our feelings will determine whether we live lives of honesty or of deceit. When submitted to the discretion of a faith-formed intellect, our emotions serve as trustworthy beacons for appropriate action or inaction.

> David, wearing a linen ephod, danced before the LORD
> with all his might.

> 2 SAMUEL 6:14

———————— ✠ ————————

I find myself threatened, challenged, and exhilarated by Christ's freedom from human respect, his extraordinary independence, indomitable courage, and unparalleled authenticity. In preaching the gospel I have been graced to speak fearlessly in the knowledge and conviction that the Word of God must not be fettered, compromised, or watered down; but in my personal life, my fears and insecurities lead me voraciously to seek the approval of others, to assume a defensive posture when I am unjustly accused, to feel guilty over refusing any request, to doggedly live up to others' expectations, to be all things to all men in a way that would make the apostle Paul shudder.

> *On the contrary, we speak as men approved by God to*
> *be entrusted with the gospel. We are not trying to*
> *please men but God, who tests our hearts.*

1 THESSALONIANS 2:4

ABBA!

————————[✻]————————

I n his book *God and Man*, Edward Schillebeecx focuses on the findings of child psychologists to make strikingly obvious what is obviously striking. The average American child begins to speak at the age of eighteen months. Invariably, the first word formulated is "Da, da, dad, daddy." At the same age level, a Jewish child in first-century Palestine would say in Aramaic, "Ab, Ab, Abba, Abba." The revolutionary revelation of Jesus lies precisely in this: the infinitely holy God in whose presence Moses had to remove his shoes, the God from whose fingertips universes fall, the God beside whose beauty the Grand Canyon is only a shadow, the God beside whose power the nuclear bomb is nothing, may be addressed with the same intimacy, familiarity, tenderness, and reverence as an eighteen-month-old child resting on his father's lap.

> For you did not receive a spirit that makes you a slave
> again to fear, but you received the Spirit of sonship.
> And by him we cry, "*Abba, Father.*"

ROMANS 8:15

————[⚕]————

D oes the church have any more urgent ministry than providing time and making space for the critical question of the Johannine Christ, "Do you love me?" Is there any creedal, codal, or cultic priority that supersedes the personal relationship between the believer and Jesus Christ? Is there any hope for radical Christian renewal and the implementation of the social gospel if Jesus Christ is not Lord of my life? Do we set this decisive question aside in favor of moralizing, philosophizing, organizing, and erecting new temples to an unknown god?

The third time he said to him, "Simon son of John, do you love me?"

Peter was hurt because Jesus asked him the third time, "Do you love me?" He said, "Lord, you know all things; you know that I love you."

Jesus said, "Feed my sheep."

JOHN 21:17

No More Games

————[✠]————

A fringe benefit for the believer en route to higher Christian consciousness is that ninety-nine percent of the emotional suffering caused by his addictive programming to security, sensation, and power disappears from his daily dance. He is able to drop all deceptive manipulative lower-order games—the money game, the security game, the male-female game, the power game, the knowledge game, the expert game, and so forth—and he presents himself simply to others: "Here I am." Free from any false self-image, he says, "It's all I've got."

> *Therefore, since we have been justified through faith,*
> *we have peace with God through our Lord Jesus*
> *Christ, through whom we have gained access by faith*
> *into this grace in which we now stand. And we rejoice*
> *in the hope of the glory of God.*

ROMANS 5:1–2

————[✝]————

There are three ways of committing suicide—taking my own life, letting myself die, and *letting myself live without hope*. This last form of self-destruction is so subtle that it often goes unrecognized and therefore unchallenged. Ordinarily it takes the form of boredom, monotony, drudgery, feeling overcome by the ordinariness of life.

We begin by admitting in the inner sanctum of our hearts that the Christian calling is too demanding, that life in Christ Jesus is too sublime. We settle into a well-worn groove and lose the stuff of gospel greatness. We become like everyone else, fail ourselves and the community by failing to respond to the living, vibrant, magnificent image of Christ that is within us waiting only to be expressed.

> *O Israel, put your hope in the LORD,*
> *for with the LORD is unfailing love*
> *and with him is full redemption.*
>
> PSALM 130:7

BREAKING THE PRIMITIVE CONCEPT

———————[✠]———————

According to Hosea, God is willing to maintain the relationship even when his spouse has become an adulteress or a prostitute. This conviction is carried into the New Testament. The adulterous woman is brought before Jesus. The god of the authorities, who never quite got over Hosea's contribution, is expected to judge her. She has been unfaithful, and this divine posture embodied in leadership would stone her. The god of the Pharisees is interested in the contract. He wants justice first and foremost. Let us kill the woman for the contract's sake. The person is expendable in this primitive concept of God. Sinai revisited.

But in the man Jesus we see the actual face of God—one in keeping with the whole Old Testament revelation. The Lord is interested in the woman, in her. His love moves one step beyond justice and proves more salvific than spelling out the ground rules all over again. . . .

The revelation of God's love comes to full term in Jesus Christ who declares that God is Father. He invites all men to enter the same Father-Son relationship that he himself shares. Paul echoes this teaching in Romans: "All who are led by the Spirit of God are sons of God. You did not receive a spirit of slavery leading you back into fear, but a spirit of adoption through which we cry out, 'Abba!'"

> "Do not judge, or you too will be judged. For in the same way you judge others, you will be judged, and with the measure you use, it will be measured to you."

MATTHEW 7:1–2

———— 🎋 ————

Y ou cannot apply human logic or justice to Yahweh. Human logic is based on human experience and human nature. Yahweh does not conform to this kind of order. If Israel is unfaithful, God remains faithful. This Being of Revelation remains faithful against all logics and all limits of justice because *He Is* and is unchanging. It is only this note of love that clarifies the happy irrationality of God's conduct and his persistence. Love tends to be a bit irrational. It pursues despite infidelity; it blossoms into envy, jealousy, anger—frantic anger, which betrays keen interest. The notion of love not only gives a fuller notion of divine nature, but by blossoming into other notions of passion, wrath, and eagerness, it widens our notion of God. The more complex and emotional the image of God becomes in the Bible, the bigger he grows and, paradoxically, the more we approach the mystery of his indefinability.

> *God looks down from heaven*
> *on the sons of men*
> *to see if there are any who understand,*
> *any who seek God.*

PSALM 53:2

REALLY HUMAN, REALLY POOR

————————[✠]————————

The Christian who is really human is really poor. How does this poverty of spiritism reflect itself in day-to-day living?

In conversation, the poor man always leaves the other person with the feeling, "My life has been enriched by talking with you." And it has. He is not all exhaust and no intake. He doesn't impose himself on another; he doesn't overwhelm him with his wealth of insights; he doesn't try to convert him by concussion with one sledgehammer blow of the Bible after another. He listens well because he realizes he is poor and has so much to learn from others. His poverty enables him to enter the existential world of the other, even when he cannot identify with that world. Being poor, he knows how to receive and can express appreciation and gratitude for the slightest gift.

Atomic physicist and spiritual writer Peter van Breeman has written: "The poor man accepts himself. He has a self-image in which the awareness of his limitations is very vivid but that does not depress him. This consciousness of his own insufficiency without feelings of self-hatred is typical of the poor in spirit."

> *Hear, O LORD, and answer me,*
> *for I am poor and needy.*
> *Guard my life, for I am devoted to you.*
> *You are my God; save your servant*
> *who trusts in you.*

> PSALM 86:1–2

———————— 🀆 ————————

The journey to transparency begins with an honest confrontation with the truth, which is not something but Someone. It may mean the humble and peaceful acknowledgment to the Lord that I am inordinately preoccupied with security, sensation, and power. It will require genuine compassion for others when we see them acting out their addictions and emotion-backed demands. They are a mirror of ourselves. Their little drama is either where we are or where we've been. It is our inner solidarity in darkness that reduces self-righteousness and irritability and makes compassion possible.

Answer me, O LORD, out of the goodness of your love;
in your great mercy turn to me.

PSALM 69:16

A HEART FIXED ON JESUS

———————[✠]———————

I n biblical symbolism the heart is the eye of the body. The anxious, darting, filmy eyes of many Christians are the psychosomatic manifestations of a heart beclouded by the vanities of this world. The translucent eyes of others radiate the simplicity and joy of a heart fixed on Jesus Christ, the Light of the world. When the author of Hebrews enjoins the reader, "Let us fix our eyes on Jesus, the author and perfecter of our faith" (12:2), he not only gives a simple prescription for Christian transparency, but also insists on a reappraisal of one's whole value system, for "where your treasure is, there your heart will be also" (Luke 12:34).

> *My heart is steadfast, O God;*
> *I will sing and make music with all my soul.*

> PSALM 108:1

————— 🉀 —————

The gospel declares that no matter how dutiful or prayerful we are, we can't save ourselves. . . .

Maybe this is the heart of our hang-up, the root of our dilemma. We fluctuate between castigating ourselves and congratulating ourselves because we are deluded into thinking we save ourselves. We develop a false sense of security from our good works and scrupulous observance of the law. Our halo gets too tight, and a carefully disguised attitude of moral superiority results. Or, we are appalled by our inconsistency, devastated that we haven't lived up to our lofty expectations of ourselves. The roller-coaster ride of elation and depression continues.

Why?

Because we never lay hold of our nothingness before God, and, consequently, we never enter into the deepest reality of our relationship with him. But when we accept ownership of our powerlessness and helplessness, when we acknowledge that we are paupers at the door of God's mercy, then God can make something beautiful out of us.

> *Surely God is my salvation;*
> *I will trust and not be afraid.*
> *The LORD, the LORD, is my strength and my song;*
> *he has become my salvation.*

ISAIAH 12:2

THE SPIRITUALITY OF
SELF-SUFFICIENCY

————[✤]————

The spirituality of self-sufficiency, the attitude of "everything depends on me" bears no resemblance to the gospel of Jesus Christ. Witnessing the multiplication of the loaves, the apostles were utterly and completely dumbfounded—their minds were closed to the power of the Spirit at work in Jesus to make the impossible possible.

The self-reliant rely on their own limited human resources. This is not the spirituality of Paul as he writes to the Ephesians: "I pray that your inward eyes may be illumined that you may realize how vast are the resources of his power open to us who believe in him." The early Christians considered themselves supermen not because of superhuman willpower but because of reliance on the supernatural power of the Spirit.

> *Jesus answered, "I tell you the truth, you are looking*
> *for me, not because you saw miraculous signs but*
> *because you ate the loaves and had your fill."*

JOHN 6:26

THE TRANSFORMATION

———— ❊ ————

The incarnation of the Father's freedom calls us beyond admiration to transformation. A recent convert to Jesus was approached by an unbelieving friend: "So you have been converted to Christ?"

"Yes."

"Then you must know a great deal about him. Tell me, what country was he born in?"

"I don't know."

"What was his age when he died?"

"I don't know."

"How many sermons did he preach?"

"I don't know."

"You certainly know very little for a man who claims to be converted to Christ."

"You are right. I am ashamed at how little I know about him. But this much I know: Three years ago I was a drunkard. I was in debt. My family was falling to pieces; they dreaded the sight of me. But now I have given up drink. We are out of debt. Ours is a happy home. My children eagerly await my return home each evening. All this Christ has done for me. This much I know of Christ!"

To know is to be transformed by what one knows.

He replied, "Whether he is a sinner or not, I don't know. One thing I do know. I was blind but now I see!"

JOHN 9:25

GOD'S GIFTS

———— 🎴 ————

The God of biblical revelation is ours. Not only does he love his people, but through Jesus Christ he has given us his whole being without reserve. He has given us the clarity of his knowledge, the freedom of his love, the bliss of his trinitarian life. *He has given us himself, and his name is Holy Spirit.* The God who fed the Israelites in the desert invites the New Israel to feast as table companions of Jesus in the messianic banquet. The God who yearned for Ephraim's love now yearns for ours. The God who started salvation-history on its course longs to bring it to a brilliant conclusion in a heaven where no sun in the sky will be needed to warm and brighten our existence, for the Lamb in our midst will be our light and our warmth.

> *Those who are led by the Spirit of God are sons of God.*

ROMANS 8:14

———— ❖ ————

The spell of self-hatred cast by moralism/legalism is broken when a Christian is no longer seduced by secular standards of human greatness and makes the glorious breakthrough into the lackey lifestyle of the Master and desires to serve rather than be served. The stark realism of the gospel allows for no romanticized idealism or sloppy sentimentality here. Servanthood is not an emotion or mood or feeling; it is a decision to live the life of Jesus. It has nothing to do with what we feel; it has everything to do with what we do—humble service. When this metanoia is effected in our lives by the power of the Spirit, freedom from the tyranny of self-hatred is the first fruit. "It is for freedom that Christ has set us free. Stand firm, then, and do not let yourselves be burdened again by a yoke of slavery" (Gal. 5:1).

> O LORD, truly I am your servant;
> I am your servant, the son of your maidservant;
> you have freed me from my chains.
>
> PSALM 116:16

THE PHARISEE WITHIN

————————[✻]————————

The Pharisee who pardons himself is condemned. The tax collector who condemns himself is acquitted. To deny the Pharisee within is lethal. It is imperative that we befriend him, dialogue with him, inquire why he must look to sources outside the Kingdom for peace and happiness.

At a prayer meeting I attended, a man in his midsixties was the first to speak: "I just want to thank God that I have nothing to repent of today." His wife groaned. What he meant was he had not embezzled, blasphemed, fornicated, or fractured any of the Ten Commandments. He had distanced himself from idolatry, drunkenness, sexual irresponsibility, and similar things; yet, he had never broken through into what Paul calls the inner freedom of the children of God.

If we continue to focus solely on the sinner/saint duality in our person and conduct, while ignoring the raging opposition between the Pharisee and the child, spiritual growth will come to an abrupt standstill.

> *Dear friends, now we are children of God, and what*
> *we will be has not yet been made known. But we*
> *know that when he appears, we shall be like him, for*
> *we shall see him as he is. Everyone who has this hope*
> *in him purifies himself, just as he is pure.*

1 JOHN 3:2–3

————— 楽 —————

One way I have come to know Jesus is by empathetic identification with marginal characters in the Gospel narrative. My background as a sergeant in the Marine Corps lends to relatively easy rapport with the centurion. Remember the day that Jesus healed his servant? The military man fell down and said, "Sir, I am not worthy to have you enter under my roof. Just give an order and my boy will get better." But the most revealing line in that story, according to Matthew, is that "Jesus was astonished." He spun round and cried out, "I tell you solemnly, nowhere in Israel have I found faith like this." At last, Jesus was saying, finally there is someone who understands me and what I want to be for my people—a Savior of boundless compassion, unbearable forgiveness, infinite patience, and healing love. Will the rest of you let me be who I am and stop imposing your small, silly, and self-styled ideas of who you think I should be!

> "Yes, Lord," she told him, "I believe that you are the
> Christ, the Son of God, who was to come into the
> world."

JOHN 11:27

KNOWING JESUS PERSONALLY

———————[☩]———————

Our experience of God's unconditional love must be shaped by the Scriptures. God's written Word must take hold of us as his spoken Word took hold of Isaiah and Jeremiah, Ezekiel and Hosea; as the spoken Word of Christ mesmerized Matthew and Mary Magdalene and captivated Simon Peter and the Samaritan woman.

The Word we study has to be the Word we pray. My personal experience of the relentless tenderness of God came not from exegetes, theologians, and spiritual writers, but from sitting still in the presence of the living Word and beseeching him to help me understand with my head and heart his written Word. Sheer scholarship alone cannot reveal to us the gospel of grace. We must never allow the authority of books, institutions, or leaders to replace the authority of *knowing* Jesus Christ personally and directly. When the religious views of others interpose between us and the primary experience of Jesus as the Christ, we become unconvicted and unpersuasive travel agents handing out brochures to places we have never visited.

> *Do your best to present yourself to God as one*
> *approved, a workman who does not need to be*
> *ashamed and who correctly handles the word of truth.*

2 TIMOTHY 2:15

————[⚹]————

Healthy guilt adds not a single paragraph to the script for self-hatred. The conviction of personal sinfulness leads to realistic confrontation, ruthless honesty, and self-knowledge; it stimulates compunction, contrition, the desire for reconciliation, and inner peace. As in any lovers' quarrel, the making up not only absolves the past, but also brings a new depth of trust and security to the relationship. There is more power in sharing our weaknesses than our strengths. The forgiveness of God is gratuitous and unconditional liberation from the domination of guilt. He overlooks our past, takes away present or future consequences of past transgressions, and causes us to cry out, "*O felix culpa!*" The sinful and repentant prodigal son experienced an intimacy and joy with his Father in his brokenness that his sinless self-righteous brother would never know.

> "*Blessed are those who mourn,*
> *for they will be comforted.*"

MATTHEW 5:4

UNHEALTHY GUILT

———— ⌘ ————

Preoccupation with self is always a major component of unhealthy guilt and recrimination. It stirs our emotions, churning in self-destructive ways, closes us in upon the mighty citadel of self, leads to depression and despair, and preempts the presence of a compassionate God. The language of unhealthy guilt is harsh. It is demanding, abusing, criticizing, rejecting, accusing, blaming, condemning, reproaching, and scolding. It is one of impatience and chastisement. Christians are shocked and horrified because they have failed. Unhealthy guilt becomes bigger than life. The image of the childhood story "Chicken Little" comes to mind. Guilt becomes the experience in which people feel the sky is falling.

Yes, we feel guilt over sins, but healthy guilt is one that acknowledges the wrong done and feels remorse but then is free to embrace the forgiveness that has been offered. Healthy guilt focuses on the realization that all has been forgiven, the wrong has been redeemed.

> *Therefore no one will be declared righteous in his sight*
> *by observing the law; rather, through the law we*
> *become conscious of sin.*

> ROMANS 3:20

————— ⊞ —————

The habit of moralizing spoils religion. Personal responsibility to an inviolable moral code replaces personal response to God's loving call. Moralism and its stepchild, legalism, reduce the love story of God for his people to the observance of burdensome duties and oppressive laws. The legalist deformation of religion concerns itself with shadow not substance. At the funeral home, a well-intentioned friend eulogizes the deceased: "John was a wonderful Catholic. He never missed Sunday mass, was married only once, and of course he never told a dirty joke." Here the criterion for holiness and the ultimate sign of religious surrender is observance of the law. The Pharisees did as much!

> *There is not a righteous man on earth*
> *who does what is right and never sins.*

ECCLESIASTES 7:20

BEAUTY SPEAKS

———[✳]———

Commenting on Psalm 148, which celebrates the manifestation of God in the works of creation, Saint Augustine asked, "Does God proclaim himself in these wonders?" "No," he answered, "the things themselves proclaim him. All things speak."

Saint Francis sensed that the beauty of sensible things was the voice by which they announced God. "It is you who made me beautiful, not I, but you." When did creation cry aloud to Francis like that? At the moment he discovered what created things concealed. It was his reflection upon them and the attention paid them that opened their voices to cry, "How beautiful is the one who made us!" In chatting amiably with the birds, scolding the wolf of Gubbio for disturbing the neighborhood, keeping a lamb at the Portiuncula to remind the brothers of the Lamb of God, and writing a lyrical canticle to Brother Sun, Francis communed with God in nature and revealed a cosmic consciousness of surpassing sensitivity.

> *Some of the Pharisees in the crowd said to Jesus,*
> *"Teacher, rebuke your disciples!"*
>
> *"I tell you," he replied, "if they keep quiet, the stones*
> *will cry out."*

LUKE 19:39-40

————— 🕀 —————

The perfectionist interprets weakness as mediocrity and inconsistency as a loss of nerve. The desire for perfection transcends the desire for God. The painful consciousness of having sold out for small comforts that now seem indispensable and the small compromises growing more numerous that now seem irreversible is a source of deep distress. A compassionate attitude of self-acceptance is simply unacceptable. The notion that sin and grace can coexist simultaneously in the same person, that imperfection and inspiration are not mutually exclusive, is a maudlin concession valid only for those not striving for spiritual excellence. Yet the apostle Paul writes, "Though the will to do what is good is in me, the performance is not, with the result that instead of doing the good things I want to do, I carry out the sinful things I do not want." Father Bernard Bush notes, "It has never been expressed so succinctly. Saint Paul can even find the hand of God and a response of praise in the contemplation of his own sinfulness."

> "Watch and pray so that you will not fall into temptation. The spirit is willing, but the body is weak."

MARK 14:38

The Geography of Nowhere

————[✿]————

To live in "nowhere"—composed of the two words *now* and *here*—is to live in the temple of the present moment. Paying attention to the gift that arrives right now, right here, is one of the premier skills of the spiritual life.

To live in the present means to trust deeply that what is most important in life is the here and now. We are constantly distracted by things that might have happened in the past or that might happen in the future. It is not easy to dwell in the temple of nowhere, to remain focused on the present. Our mind is hard to master and keeps pulling us away from engagement with the present.

When Jesus tells us to become like little children, he is inviting us to forget what lies behind and to forgo concern about the future. It is only *now* that we are in the presence of God.

> *"But when you give to the needy, do not let your left hand know what your right hand is doing, so that your giving may be in secret. Then your Father, who sees what is done in secret, will reward you."*

MATTHEW 6:3–4

GOD'S CONSTANCY WITH HIS REBELLIOUS PEOPLE

—————[☩]—————

Thus, God raised up the prophets, burned into their consciousness a lively awareness of his presence, and sent them to his people to reveal him in a warmer, more passionate manner. Though Israel was faithless and ungrateful, though she had played the prostitute whoring after idols, the prophets cry the constancy of God in face of man's infidelity. Image upon image reveals a near sense of frustration in God as he deals with his rebellious people. We have the image of the solitary harvester who returns home alone in the evening, weary and fatigued at the effort of the day and apparently discouraged. We have the picture of God treading the winepress alone, his garments red with the stain of grapes. We have Isaiah's daring image comparing God to a woman in labor, undergoing anguish to bring forth a people worthy of the divine vocation. In the prophecy of Hosea a gush of tears seems almost to overwhelm God as he cries out in agony: "How could I give you up, O Israel, or deliver you up, O Ephraim?" "How could I treat you like Adama, or make you like Seboim?" Finally, just when men would say, "I owe you nothing, for you have broken contract," just when human beings would declare, "So much, no more. I cannot forgive you any longer. I will not let you keep taking advantage of me," then the overwhelming *hesed*, the steadfast, enduring love of Yahweh, sweeps forward and the triumphant line rings out, "I am God, not man!"

> *What is man that you are mindful of him,*
> *the son of man that you care for him?*

PSALM 8:4

I t is hard to speak of beauty without speaking of Saint Francis. In his personality was mirrored a generous measure of the transcendent beauty of God. If God is an illimitable ocean of beauty, Francis was a small spring shooting up, such as the world had never seen before. His gestures are the revelation of his soul. One day he arrives in the village square. A large crowd follows him. As everyone knows, the village priest has not been living a life of rectitude. As Francis reaches the square, the priest by chance happens out of the church. The crowd watches and waits. What will Francis do? Denounce the priest for the scandal he has created, sermonize the villagers on human frailty and the need for compassion, simply pretend he doesn't see the priest and continue on his way? No. He steps forward, kneels in the mud, takes the priest's hand, and kisses it. That's all. And that is magnificent. Toward the end of his life, Francis gathers two branches—one represents a violin, the other a bow. And what a marvelous melody he plays. Interiorly, of course. But what is the music of Mozart and Bach beside this? The words and gestures of Francis are manifestations of a soul completely surrendered to God. As we see the beauty streaming from his soul, one realizes anew the truth of the words of Leon Bloy, "The only real sadness in life is not to be a saint."

> Cast your cares on the LORD
> and he will sustain you;
> he will never let the righteous fall.

PSALM 55:22

LOVE'S RESPONSE

———————☒———————

Confronted with the radical demands of the Christian commitment, our natural response is fear, anguish, insecurity. But confronted with the lived truth of God's enveloping love, insecurity is swallowed up in the security of agape, anguish gives place to hope, fear to desire. The Christian has become aware that God's appeal for unlimited generosity from his people has been preceded from his side by a limitless love, a love so intent upon a response that he has empowered us to respond through the gift of his own Holy Spirit.

> *But because of his great love for us, God, who is rich in mercy, made us alive with Christ even when we were dead in transgressions—it is by grace you have been saved.*

EPHESIANS 2:4-5

GROWING A KINGDOM

————[✻]————

With serene confidence and sovereign authority Jesus explains, "The Kingdom is not what you expected—a dazzling and dramatic intervention of unbearable glory. You see, it begins very small, tiny like a mustard seed. And it takes time to grow, so be patient."

Again Jesus says, "It's like a farmer who plants a seed and goes away, and later it sprouts." Ask any farmer in Pennsylvania or Vermont when he plants the wheat, and he will answer, "In late September or early October." Ask him what he does in the interim until harvest, and his surprised reply to your naive question will be, "Nothin'! It grows by itself."

That's the way it is with the reign of God, Jesus explained. The Kingdom will grow by itself. What the father planted will be harvested, and nothing will get in the way. Not heresies, schisms, ecclesiastical blunders, defections, moral failures; not if the budget isn't balanced; not if I can't find a way to end this book; not persecutions or nuclear holocausts—nothing will obstruct the coming of the Kingdom. That is certain. Human effort is as nothing compared to the inexorable plan of God.

> *I have put my words in your mouth*
> *and covered you with the shadow of my hand—*
> *I who set the heavens in place,*
> *who laid the foundations of the earth,*
> *and who say to Zion, "You are my people."*

ISAIAH 51:16

———————[✻]———————

God does not condemn but forgives. The sinner is accepted even before he repents. Forgiveness is granted to him, he need only accept the gift. This is real amnesty—gratis. The gospel of Jesus Christ is the love story of God with us. It begins with unconditional forgiveness: the sole condition is trusting faith. Christianity happens when men and women experience the unwavering trust and reckless confidence that come from knowing the God of Jesus. There is no reason for being wary, scrupulous, cautious, or afraid with this God. As John writes in his first letter: "In love there can be no fear, but fear is driven out by perfect love: because to fear is to expect punishment, and anyone who is afraid is still imperfect in love" (1 John 4:18 JB).

> "He causes his sun to rise on the evil and the good,
> and sends rain on the righteous and the unrighteous."

MATTHEW 5:45

MY CHRISTIAN PERSONALITY

————————[✠]————————

The spiritual life might be defined as the development of personality in the realm of faith and grace. My Christian personality is not just a vegetative existence; I am a unique and radiant center of personal thought and feeling. Rather than living a routine existence in mere conformity with the crowd, the emerging child reminds me I have a face of my own, gives me the courage to be myself, protects me against being like everybody else, and calls forth that living, vibrant, magnificent image of Jesus Christ that is within me, waiting only to unfold and be expressed.

> *Your attitude should be the same as that of Christ Jesus.*

PHILIPPIANS 2:5

FAITH? OR FORMULA?

————————————🔯————————————

If we could rid our minds for a moment of all the definitions of faith that we have grown up with and that have caused more trouble than they were ever worth, we might discover with alarm that the essence of biblical faith lies in trusting God.

The difference between faith as belief in a series of doctrinal formulations—such as incarnation, salvation, redemption—and faith as unconditional trust in God is enormous. An unshakable trust in God is the remedy for much of our sickness, melancholy, and self-hatred. The heart converted from mistrust to trust in the irreversible forgiveness of Jesus Christ is redeemed from the corroding power of fear. So awesome is this ultimate act of confidence in Christ's acceptance that one can only stutter and stammer about its protean importance. Unfaltering trust in the merciful love of the redeeming God deals a mortal blow to skepticism, cynicism, self-condemnation, and despair. It is our decisive *yes!* to Jesus' summons, "Trust in the Father and trust in me" (see John 14:1).

The words of Angelus Silesius, "If God stopped thinking of me, he would cease to exist," are strictly orthodox; God, by definition, is thinking of me.

The merchant of mistrust dismisses these words as hyperbole and remains sullen.

Abba's child trusts them and goes daft for joy.

> *"I tell you the truth, whoever hears my word and*
> *believes him who sent me has eternal life and will not*
> *be condemned; he has crossed over from death to life."*

JOHN 5:24

DISTANCING OURSELVES
FROM THE GOSPEL

———————[✠]———————

Any legalistic distortion of the gospel erects a protective screen of piety between the worshiper and that life-changing encounter. It ensures that the Word of God no longer rustles like refreshing rain on the parched ground of our souls. It no longer sweeps like a wild storm into the comfortable corners of our well-fed virtue. The gospel becomes just a pattering of pious platitudes spoken by a Jewish carpenter in the distant past.

A case in point: when Jesus, the new Moses, climbed the mountain to deliver his inaugural address, he began his sermon with the words, "Blessed are the poor in spirit: the kingdom of heaven is theirs." This spells out the game plan for a radically different lifestyle of constant prayer, total unselfishness, buoyant, creative goodness, and unbridled involvement in the material and spiritual well-being of God's children.

> Let us examine our ways and test them,
> and let us return to the LORD.
>
> LAMENTATIONS 3:40

THE DIFFICULTY OF
STANDING UP FOR WHAT IS RIGHT

———— 🔯 ————

Anyone who has ever stood up for the truth of human dignity, no matter how disfigured, only to find previously supportive friends holding back, even remonstrating with you for your boldness, feels the loneliness of the poverty of uniqueness. This happens every day to those who choose to suffer for the absolute voice of conscience, even in what seem to be small matters. They find themselves standing alone. I have yet to meet the man or woman who enjoys such responsibility.

> *I called on your name, O LORD,*
> *from the depths of the pit.*
> *You heard my plea: "Do not close your ears*
> *to my cry for relief."*
> *You came near when I called you,*
> *and you said, "Do not fear."*
> *O Lord, you took up my case;*
> *you redeemed my life.*

LAMENTATIONS 3:55–58

STANDING ALONE

———— 🔀 ————

The poverty of uniqueness is the call of Jesus to stand utterly alone when the only alternative is to cut a deal at the price of one's integrity. It is a lonely *yes* to the whispers of our true self, a clinging to our core identity when companionship and community support are withheld. It is a courageous determination to make unpopular decisions that are expressive of the truth of who we are—not of who we think we should be or whom someone else wants us to be. It is trusting enough in Jesus to make mistakes and believing enough that his life will still pulse within us. It is the unarticulated, gut-wrenching yielding of our true self to the poverty of our own unique, mysterious personality.

In a word, standing on our own two feet is often a heroic act of love.

> LORD, *who may dwell in your sanctuary?*
> *Who may live on your holy hill?*
> *He whose walk is blameless*
> *and who does what is righteous,*
> *who speaks the truth from his heart.*

PSALM 15:1–2

———————[⚛]———————

R ecently I directed a three-day silent retreat for six women in Virginia Beach. As the retreat opened, I met briefly with each woman and asked her to write on a sheet of paper the one grace that she would most like to receive from the Lord. A married woman from North Carolina, about forty-five years old, with an impressive track record of prayer and service to others told me she wanted more than anything to actually experience just one time the love of God. I assured her that I would join her in that prayer.

The following morning this woman (whom I'll call Winky) arose before dawn and went for a walk on the beach. She noticed a teenage boy and a woman walking in her direction. In less than a minute the boy had passed by to her left, but the woman made an abrupt ninety-degree turn, walked straight toward Winky, embraced her deeply, kissed her on the cheek, whispered "I love you," and continued on her way. Winky had never seen the woman before. Winky wandered along the beach for another hour before returning to the house. She knocked on my door. When I opened it, she was smiling. "Our prayer was answered," she said simply.

> *He will love you and bless you and increase your num-*
> *bers. He will bless the fruit of your womb, the crops of*
> *your land—your grain, new wine and oil—the calves*
> *of your herds and the lambs of your flocks in the land*
> *that he swore to your forefathers to give you.*

DEUTERONOMY 7:13

EMBRACING JESUS' HUMANITY

————————[✠]————————

Fearing that I would miss the divinity of Jesus, I distanced myself from his humanity, like an ancient worshiper shielding his eyes from the holy of holies. My uneasiness betrays a strange hesitancy of belief, an uncertain apprehension of a remote deity, rather than intimate confidence in a personal Savior.

As John leans back on the breast of Jesus and listens to the heartbeat of the Great Rabbi, he comes to know him in a way that surpasses mere cognitive knowledge.

What a world of difference lies between *knowing about* someone and *knowing him!* We may know all about someone—name, place of birth, family of origin, educational background, habits, appearance—but all those vital statistics tell us nothing about the person who lives and loves and walks with God.

In a flash of intuitive understanding, John experiences Jesus as the human face of the God who is love. And in coming to know who the Great Rabbi is, John discovers who *he* is—the disciple Jesus loved.

> *"No, the Father himself loves you because you have*
> *loved me and have believed that I came from God."*

JOHN 16:27

————— 🕀 —————

We are plunged into mystery—what Abraham Heschel called "radical amazement." Hushed and trembling, we are creatures in the presence of ineffable Mystery above all creatures and beyond all telling.

The moment of truth has arrived. We are alone with the Alone. The revelation of God's tender feelings for us is not mere dry knowledge. For too long and too often along my journey, I have sought shelter in hand-clapping liturgies and cerebral Scripture studies. I have received knowledge without appreciation, facts without enthusiasm. Yet, when the scholarly investigations were over, I was struck by the insignificance of it all. It just didn't seem to matter.

But when the night is bad and my nerves are shattered and Infinity speaks, when God Almighty shares through his Son the depth of his feelings for me, when his love flashes into my soul and when I am overtaken by Mystery, it is *kairos*—the decisive inbreak of God in this saving moment of my personal history. No one can speak for me. Alone, I face a momentous decision. Shivering in the rags of my fifty-nine years, either I escape into skepticism and intellectualism or with radical amazement I surrender in faith to the truth of my belovedness.

> *"His master replied, 'Well done, good and faithful servant! You have been faithful with a few things; I will put you in charge of many things. Come and share your master's happiness!'"*

MATTHEW 25:21

THIS SACRED SEASON

———————✠———————

Once a year the Christmas season strikes both the sacred and secular spheres of life with sledgehammer force: suddenly Jesus Christ is everywhere.

For approximately one month his presence is inescapable. You may accept him or reject him, affirm him or deny him, but you cannot ignore him. Of course he is proclaimed in speech, song, and symbol in all the Christian churches. But he rides every red-nosed reindeer, lurks behind every Cabbage Patch doll, resonates in the most desacralized "season's greetings." Remotely or proximately, he is toasted in every cup of Christmas cheer. Each sprig of holly is a hint of his holiness, each cluster of mistletoe a sign he is here.

For those who claim his name, Christmas heralds this luminous truth: The God of Jesus Christ is our absolute future. Such is the deeply hopeful character of this sacred season. By God's free doing in Bethlehem, nothing can separate us from the love of God in Christ Jesus. Light, life, and love are on our side.

> *"The virgin will be with child and will give birth to a son, and they will call him Immanuel"—which means, "God with us."*

MATTHEW 1:23

IS MY BELIEF MY OWN?

————————[⚶]————————

I f there is one thing I have learned in the gathering mist of midlife it is that the journey from Haran to Canaan is a personal one. Each one of us bears the responsibility of responding to the call of Christ individually and committing ourselves to him personally. Do I believe in Jesus or in the preachers, teachers, and cloud of witnesses who have spoken to me about him? Is the Christ of my belief really my own or that of theologians, pastors, parents, and Oswald Chambers? No one—not parents or friends or church—can absolve us of this ultimate personal decision regarding the nature and identity of the son of Mary and Joseph. His question to Peter—Who do you say that I am?—is addressed to every would-be disciple.

> *Therefore, my dear friends, as you have always*
> *obeyed—not only in my presence, but now much more*
> *in my absence—continue to work out your salvation*
> *with fear and trembling.*

PHILIPPIANS 2:12

PREPARING FOR JESUS

———————— 🔯 ————————

The primitive confession of faith "Jesus is Lord" is not an abstract theological proposition but a highly personal statement. It puts my integrity on the line and profoundly affects the way I celebrate Advent, the four weeks of preparation for the birth of Christ. If Jesus is Lord of my life and my Christmas, I am challenged to submit all the priorities of my personal and professional life to this primary fact.

> *Submit yourselves, then, to God. Resist the devil, and he will flee from you.*

JAMES 4:7

———————— 🕀 ————————

Christmas is a vision that enables the Christian to see beyond the tragic in his life. It is a reminder that he needs the laughter of God to prevent him from taking the world too seriously. The Christian law of levity says that whatever falls into the earth will rise again. Christian laughter is the echo of Christmas joy in us.

If you really accept the mystery of Bethlehem, "glad tidings of great joy," your heart will be filled with the laughter of the Father. "You are sad now but I shall see you again, and your hearts will be full of joy, and that joy no one shall take from you" (John 16:22 JB).

> "Rejoice in that day and leap for joy, because great is
> your reward in heaven. For that is how their fathers
> treated the prophets."

LUKE 6:23

A PEOPLE OF HOPE

———————[❀]———————

"Jesus Christmases in us whenever people come home to themselves in our presence, and when they feel a little less hopeful and joyful because we are absent."

These words, scribbled in a journal several years ago in solitude, lay hold of me with prophetic power when the great season of hope begins. Christians are a people of hope to the extent that others can find in us a source of strength and joy. If not, our profession of faith "by the power of the Holy Spirit He was born of the Virgin Mary and became man" is as academic, tentative, and hopeless as the alcoholic who promises, "I'll quit tomorrow."

Be filled to the measure of all the fullness of God.

EPHESIANS 3:19

———————[✠]———————

I n the face of pessimistic appraisals that we have nothing
going for us anymore, Christmas says that we have everything going—Jesus, the journey, and the dream. Richard
Rohr says, "The Christian never loses, because he has nothing
to lose."

My brothers and sisters in Christ Jesus, if you have been
struck by the grace of Christmas, if the Lord in his mercy has
given you the courage to accept acceptance, if you are con-
victed that Christmas is the decisive breakthrough of the passionate love of God in Jesus, if you trust that God is faithful to
his promises, that he will finish what he began, that amazin'
grace is at work right now, that you have only checked into the
hotel of earth overnight and you are en route to the heavenly
Jerusalem, then in the immortal words of John Powell, "Please
notify your face!"

On the other hand, if you have not been struck by the
grace of Christmas, ask for it and it will be given. . . .

> "In that day you will no longer ask me anything. I tell
> you the truth, my Father will give you whatever you
> ask in my name."

JOHN 16:23

WHEN GOD ENTERED HUMAN HISTORY

The world has been irreparably changed by Jesus Christ. When preached purely, his Word exalts, frightens, shocks, and forces us to reassess our whole life if we are sincere. The gospel breaks our train of thought, shatters our comfortable piety, cracks open our capsuled truths. The flashing spirit of Jesus Christ breaks new paths everywhere. His sentences stand like quivering swords of flame because he did not come to bring peace but revolution. The gospel is no Pollyanna tale for the harmless but a cutting-edge, rolling thunder, convulsive earthquake in the world of the human spirit.

In entering human history God has shattered all previous conceptions of who God is and what man is supposed to be. . . . The life he has planned for Christians is a Christian life, much like the life he lived. He was not poor that we might be rich. He was not mocked that we might be honored. He was not laughed at so that we could be lauded. On the contrary, he was revealing the Christian picture of man, one that is meant to include you and me. "We are to fill up what is wanting," Paul says, "in the suffering of Christ."

> *"Praise be to the Lord, the God of Israel,*
> *because he has come and has redeemed his people."*

LUKE 1:68

———— 图 ————

To Jesus' haunting question, "But who do you say that I am?" tumultuous events in my personal life in recent years have forged this reply: "You are the incarnation of the Father's freedom, the unfettered creative response to his love."

In choosing to be born in utter obscurity, the King of the universe ignored conventional expectations. He celebrated in his own birthday the freedom to be unorthodox. In failing to live up to people's presuppositions ("From Nazareth?" asks Nathanael. "Can anything good come from that place?"), Jesus became a stumbling block to many of his contemporaries. The housebroken Jewish imagination cringed at the crib, shuddered at the ersatz salvation of a humble, unpredictable God. A king in rags was an insult to the finely honed intellect of the Pharisee and the rational mind of the scribe. Simpleminded shepherds and the rabble who did not know the Law might be hoodwinked, but those who studied the Scriptures could not be deceived. There is a fascinating principle at work here in very religious people: "Messiah, you get our allegiance only when you fulfill our expectations."

> When the angels had left them and gone into heaven,
> the shepherds said to one another, "Let's go to
> Bethlehem and see this thing that has happened, which
> the Lord has told us about."

LUKE 2:15

THE PEACE OF CHRIST

This is a point of capital importance for those who would fully experience the grace of Christmas. When we are in right relationship with Jesus, we are in the peace of Christ. Except for grave, conscious, deliberate infidelity, which must be recognized and repented of, the presence or absence of *feelings* of peace is the normal ebb and flow of the spiritual life. When things are plain and ordinary, when we live on the plateaus and in the valleys (which is where most of the Christian life takes place) and not on the mountaintops of peak religious experiences, this is no reason to blame ourselves, to think that our relationship with God is collapsing, or to echo Magdalene's cry in the garden, "Where has my beloved gone?" Frustration, irritation, fatigue, and so forth may temporarily unsettle us, but they cannot rob us of living in the peace of Christ Jesus. As the playwright Ionesco once declared in the middle of a depression: "Nothing discourages me, not even discouragement."

> *Finally, brothers, good-by. Aim for perfection, listen to my appeal, be of one mind, live in peace. And the God of love and peace will be with you.*

2 CORINTHIANS 13:11

———————[☩]———————

Christian hope, the spirit that dominates the Advent/ Christmas season, is not reserved merely for some splendid future yet to come. It is much more than an otherworldly matter, a promise of heavenly reward after death. Jesus does not ask us to wait until later, until the end for help and healing. Hope is the good news of transforming grace now. We are freed not only from the fear of death but from the fear of life; we are freed for a new life, a life that is trusting, hopeful, and compassionate.

> For you have been my hope, O Sovereign LORD,
> my confidence since my youth.
>
> PSALM 71:5

THE LAST LAUGH

------[⚜]------

Years ago in the seminary in Loretto, Pennsylvania, I was taught that the name *Isaac* (*Yishaq* in Hebrew) means "laughter." Abraham and his wife Sarah had given up on God's promise of a child because of their advanced years. When Sarah was told that she would soon be pregnant, she laughed in disbelief. But God had the last laugh. A son was born to them in their old age, and the mirthless human laugh of despair turned into the Father's laughter of love. . . .

Isaac, son of the promise made to Abraham, was a prophetic foreshadowing of Jesus in whom the promise is fulfilled. Jesus is God's final laughter. Laughter is the celebration of incongruity, dissonance, lack of harmony. Nothing could be more incongruous in the Hebrew tradition than a virgin having a baby.

Christmas is a faith-experience that enables us to see beyond the tragic in our lives. It is a reminder that we need the laughter of God to prevent us from taking the world too seriously, the world of cerebral head trips played in dead earnest, the game of one-upmanship escalated to mortal combat, the illusions of self-importance. God's laughter is his loving act of salvation begun in Bethlehem.

> Our mouths were filled with laughter,
> our tongues with songs of joy.
> Then it was said among the nations,
> "The LORD has done great things for them."
>
> PSALM 126:2

————❈————

There is no need to multiply examples of what is so patently an essential condition of the Christian walk. We are saved through faith—an unflagging, unwavering attachment to the person of Jesus Christ.

What is the depth and quality of your faith commitment? In the last analysis, faith is not a way of speaking or even of thinking; it is a way of living. Maurice Blondel said, "If you want to know what a person really believes, don't listen to what he says but watch what he does." Only the practice of faith can verify what we believe. Does faith permeate the whole of your life? Does it form your judgments about death, about success? Does it influence the way you read the newspaper? Do you have a divine sense of humor that sees through people and events into the unfolding plan of God? When things are turbulent on the surface of your life, do you retain a quiet calm, firmly fixed in ultimate reality? As Thérèse of Lisieux said, "Let nothing disturb you, let nothing frighten you. All things are passing. God alone remains." Does your faith shape your Advent season this year?

> In him and through faith in him we may approach
> God with freedom and confidence.

 EPHESIANS 3:12

HIS PRESENCE AT CHRISTMAS

———————⊞———————

The crisis of Christmas in the Christian community is truly a crisis of faith. Many of us will continue to ignore the invitation, dodge the truth, evade reality, and postpone the decision about Jesus—which is a decision itself.

Yet Christmas is the birthday of the Son of God. What will separate the men from the boys, the women from the girls, the mystics from the romantics this Christmas will be the depth and quality of our passion for Jesus. The insensitive will eat, drink, and be merry; the superficial will follow social customs in a religious setting; the defeated will be haunted by ghosts from the past.

And the victorious minority who are not intimidated by the cultural patterns of the lockstepping, anonymous, and unbelieving majority will celebrate as though he was near—near in time, near in place, the witness of our motives, our speech, our behavior. As indeed he is.

> But as for me, it is good to be near God.
> I have made the Sovereign LORD my refuge;
> I will tell of all your deeds.

PSALM 73:28

———————— ⌘ ————————

I t is one thing to know Jesus Christ loves us and another thing to *realize* it. In prayer we slow down to a human tempo and make time to listen. In prayer we discover what we already have. You start from where you are and realize that you are already there. We already have everything, but many of us don't know it and therefore don't experience it. Everything has been given to us by the Father in Jesus. All we need now is to experience what we already possess. The most precious moments of prayer consist in letting ourselves be loved by the Lord.

During the Christmas season we don't have to seek after God in prayer. We could not seek him unless we had already found him. Abba, Jesus, and the Spirit have been there all the time, and if we create the opportunity in prayer, God will make himself known to us. "We learn to pray," said the late Thomas Merton, "by praying."

> *May my prayer be set before you like incense;*
> *may the lifting up of my hands be like the evening*
> *   sacrifice.*

PSALM 141:2

THE AUTHENTIC MYSTIC

I n our technological world the word *mystic* has fallen on hard times. Used mostly in a pejorative sense, *mystic* has come to mean someone who is spaced out in a dreamy metaphysical fog. An authentic mystic, however, is not a person who engages in unusual forms of prayers accompanied by visions, ecstasies, and levitations. A mystic, in the words of the German theologian Karl Rahner, is someone who has experienced something. A mystic is aglow with passionate longing for Jesus Christ, who is sought, loved, and worshiped for himself alone. *A mystic is a person whose life is ruled by thirst.* That thirst is slaked in prayer, in the knowing-loving-and-delighting in a person. "This is eternal life: that they may know you, the only true God, and Jesus Christ, whom you have sent" (John 17:3).

The contemplative at Christmas grows quiet before "the light [that] shines in the darkness" (John 1:5). He stills his soul and becomes tranquil like a child in its mother's arms. He interiorizes and appropriates to himself the mercy, forgiveness, reconciliation, and love that are embodied in the Child of Bethlehem. He surrenders to the grace of the Word made flesh. He accepts acceptance.

He stilled the storm to a whisper;
the waves of the sea were hushed.

PSALM 107:29

————————————[卂]————————

The traditional hymn sung in many churches on Sunday morning, "Christ Jesus Victor, Christ Jesus *Ruler*, Christ Jesus Lord and Redeemer," implies that the relationship with Jesus is the most intense and intimate of all my relations. Is this really true? In gut-level honesty, what rules our lives as we prepare for Christmas? What has power over us?

First, I suppose, it's people. Those who speak to me; the men and women whose words I read. Those with whom I associate or would like to associate; those who give to me and those who refuse; those who help and those who hinder; those whom I like and those whom I do not like. Such people occupy my attention, fill my thoughts, in a sense, *rule* in me.

Jesus Christ? Well, he counts, but only after I have finished with the others. Only when they and their claims leave me time for him. Sometimes these others occupy so much of my time that the whole day slips by without a thought of the Lord of my life. Even at worship, I can be so distracted by my friends and enemies that I forget to lift up my mind and heart to him. Oh, I may recite a few mechanical prayers, but my thoughts are somewhere else. "This people gives me lip service," Isaiah heard the God of Israel say, "but their heart is far from me." Like King Claudius in Shakespeare's *Hamlet*: "My words fly up, my thoughts remain below. Words without thoughts never to heaven go."

> *The people to whom I am sending you are obstinate and stubborn. Say to them, "This is what the Sovereign LORD says."*

EZEKIEL 2:4

HOPE IN MY SAVIOR

———— 🕀 ————

The Christmas contemplative knows that hope is a gift, an undeserved gift of peace, but that it is also a call to decision—the decision to trust. . . .

Hope thrives on the difficult and challenges the conclusion that our only contribution to the world will be, in the words of T. S. Eliot, "an asphalt driveway in front of our home and a thousand lost golf balls." Hope convinces us that in clinging to a miserable sense of security and status quo, the possibility of growth and greatness is utterly defeated. Hope says that I no longer need be dismayed over my personal dishonesty and self-centeredness and feeble life of faith. That I no longer need to feel defeated, insensitive, and superficial.

Because the question no longer is: Can I do it? Am I able? Can I overcome my moodiness, my laziness, my sensuality, my grudges, and resentments? The only question is: Is Jesus Christ able? Can my Savior, the Lord of my life, revive my drooping spirit and transform me at Christmas as he transformed the world through his birth in Bethlehem?

> "I have told you these things, so that in me you may
> have peace. In this world you will have trouble. But
> take heart! I have overcome the world."

JOHN 16:33

THE SINGLE MOST IMPORTANT CONSIDERATION

———————[❀]———————

I wonder, if we were to stop people at random in the street on December 24th and ask them what they want most for Christmas, how many would say, "I want to see Jesus"?

I believe that the single most important consideration during the sacred season of Advent is *intensity of desire*. Paraphrasing the late Rabbi Abraham Heschel, "Jesus Christ is of no importance unless he is of supreme importance." An intense inner desire is already the sign of his presence in our hearts. The rest is the work of the Holy Spirit.

> *They came to Philip, who was from Bethsaida in*
> *Galilee, with a request. "Sir," they said. "we would*
> *like to see Jesus."*

JOHN 12:21

THE GIGANTIC SECRET

———[✠]———

"**C**hristmas for the pagans is small publicity," Chesterton said, "for the Christian it is a gigantic secret."

And the gigantic Christmas secret is that Emmanuel, God-with-us, is a baby boy "wrapped in swaddling clothes and lying in a manger." When Jesus Christ is born in me, hope burns brightly and everything else fades into twilight. The roof can collapse, winter heat become unavailable, fair-weather friends shift their allegiance, popularity wane. The Kingdom of Christ Jesus remains alight within me. As Don Quixote tells Aldonza in *The Man from La Mancha:* "Wins and losses don't matter, all that matters is following the quest."

> *Through him you believe in God, who raised him from the dead and glorified him, and so your faith and hope are in God.*

1 PETER 1:21

———— 🕂 ————

Jesus calls us at Christmas to enter into the Kingdom of Liberty, to be set free by his Father's love. There is a refreshing quality about the Nazarene without which Christianity would never have become a fact of history. The surprise of his birth in Bethlehem fires a longing to be free from self and free for others. It sparks a search for intelligent and imaginative ways to celebrate an unconventional Christmas.

The wailing Infant bears witness to a God whose Word is fresh and alive, who is not the defender of the old, the already settled, the well established and familiar. The God we encounter in Jesus is free from preoccupation with his own glory, free to be for us, free to be gracious, free to love and let be.

This Christmas such a God might well expect us to be creatively responsive and thus truly Christlike. Indeed, he might call us to set free captives bound by loneliness and isolation, to share our hope with prisoners of gloom and despair, to invite the unlovely to our table, to celebrate our freedom in forgetfulness about our comfort and convenience, to cry the gospel by ministering to widows and orphans, to be the Church by bringing soup to the poor, to ignore conventional expectations, to call his Son out of Egypt once more.

He is able to deal gently with those who are ignorant
and are going astray, since he himself is subject to
weakness.

HEBREWS 5:2

EVERYTHING WILL BE ALL RIGHT

———— ✥ ————

Christmas is the promise that the God who came in history and comes daily in mystery will one day come in glory. God is saying in Jesus that in the end everything will be all right. Nothing can harm you permanently, no suffering is irrevocable, no loss is lasting, no defeat is more than transitory, no disappointment is conclusive. Jesus did not deny the reality of suffering, discouragement, disappointment, frustration, and death; he simply stated that the Kingdom of God would conquer all of these horrors, that the Father's love is so prodigal that no evil could possibly resist it.

> *He will wipe every tear from their eyes. There will be*
> *no more death or mourning or crying or pain, for the*
> *old order of things has passed away.*

REVELATION 21:4

————— 🜲 —————

The shipwrecked at the stable are the poor in spirit who feel lost in the cosmos, adrift on an open sea, clinging with a life-and-death grip to one solitary plank. Finally they are washed ashore and make their way to the stable, stripped of the old spirit of possessiveness in regard to anything. The shipwrecked find it not only tacky, but utterly absurd to be caught up either in tinsel trees or in religious experiences—"Doesn't going to church on Christmas make you feel good?" They are not concerned with their own emotional security or with any of the trinkets of creation. They have been saved, rescued, delivered from the waters of death, set free for a new shot at life. At the stable in a blinding moment of truth, they make the stunning discovery that Jesus is the plank of salvation they have been clinging to without knowing it!

All the time they were battered by wind and rain, buffeted by raging seas, they were being held even when they didn't know who was holding them. Their exposure to spiritual, emotional, and physical deprivation has weaned them from themselves and made them reexamine all they once thought important. The shipwrecked come to the stable seeking not to possess, but to be possessed, wanting not peace or a religious high, but Jesus Christ.

> To the church of God in Corinth, to those sanctified in Christ Jesus and called to be holy, together with all those everywhere who call on the name of our Lord Jesus Christ —their Lord and ours.

I CORINTHIANS 1:2

THE INFANT JESUS

———————[✠]———————

The Bethlehem mystery will ever be a scandal to aspiring disciples who seek a triumphant Savior and a prosperity gospel. The infant Jesus was born in unimpressive circumstances, no one can say exactly where. His parents were of no social significance whatsoever, and his chosen welcoming committee were all turkeys, losers, and dirt-poor shepherds. But in this weakness and poverty the shipwrecked at the stable would come to know the love of God.

Sadly, Christian piety down the centuries has prettified the Babe of Bethlehem. Christian art has trivialized divine scandal into gingerbread crèches. Christian worship has sentimentalized the smells of the stable into dignified pageant. . . . Pious imagination and nostalgic music rob Christmas of its shock value, while some scholars reduce the crib to a tame theological symbol. But the shipwrecked at the stable tremble in adoration of the Christ child and quake at the inbreak of God almighty. Because all the Santa Clauses and red-nosed reindeer, fifty-foot trees, and thundering church bells put together create less pandemonium than the infant Jesus when, instead of remaining a statue in a crib, he comes alive and delivers us over to the fire that he came to light.

> By myself I have sworn,
> my mouth has uttered in all integrity
> a word that will not be revoked:
> Before me every knee will bow;
> by me every tongue will swear.

ISAIAH 45:23

———————[✤]———————

In 1980, the day before Christmas, Richard Ballenger's mother in Anderson, South Carolina, was busy wrapping packages and asked her young son to shine her shoes. Soon, with the proud smile that only a seven-year-old can muster, he presented the shoes for inspection. His mother was so pleased that she gave him a quarter.

On Christmas morning as she put on the shoes to go to church, she noticed a lump in one shoe. She took it off and found a quarter wrapped in paper. Written on the paper in a child's scrawl were the words, "I done it for love."

When the final curtain falls, each of us will be the sum of our choices throughout life, the sum of the appointments we kept and the appointments we didn't keep. The glory of the shipwrecked will be that they habitually failed to turn up for duty. In their defense they claim they were detained by a baby in swaddling clothes. When interrogated as to why they hung out at the stable, they answer, "We done it for love."

In their integrity the shipwrecked preserve the meaning of Christmas in its pristine purity—the birthday of the Savior and the eruption of the messianic era into history.

This Christmas, may you belong to their number.

We love because he first loved us.

1 JOHN 4:19

KNEELING IN HIS PRESENCE

——————[✠]——————

I s there anyone in our midst who pretends to understand the awesome love in the heart of the Abba of Jesus that inspired, motivated, and brought about Christmas? . . .

God entered into our world not with the crushing impact of unbearable glory, but in the way of weakness, vulnerability, and need. On a wintry night in an obscure cave, the infant Jesus was a humble, naked, helpless God who allowed us to get close to him.

> *"This will be a sign to you: You will find a baby wrapped in cloths and lying in a manger."*

LUKE 2:12

———————[✠]———————

There is a beautiful story recounted every Christmas in the forests of Provence in southern France. It's about the four shepherds who came to Bethlehem to see the Child. One brought eggs, another brought bread and cheese, the third brought wine. And the fourth brought nothing at all. People called him L'Enchanté. The first three shepherds chatted with Mary and Joseph, commenting how well Mary looked, how cozy the cave was and how handsomely Joseph had appointed it, what a beautiful starlit night it was. They congratulated the proud parents, presented them with their gifts, and assured them that if they needed anything else, they had only to ask. Finally someone asked, "Where is L'Enchanté?" They searched high and low, up and down, inside and out. Finally, someone peeked through the blanket hung against the draft, into the crèche. There, kneeling at the crib, was L'Enchanté— the Enchanted One. Like a flag or a flame taking the direction of the wind, he had taken the direction of love. Through the entire night, he stayed in adoration, whispering, "Jesu, Jesu, Jesu—Jesus, Jesus, Jesus."

> *To whom, then, will you compare God?*
> *What image will you compare him to?*

ISAIAH 40:18

THE SPIRIT OF CHRISTMAS

————————[✦]————————

One of the many documented miracles that have occurred in Lourdes, France, took place in 1957. A French father took his ten-year-old son, blind from birth, on a pilgrimage from Brittany to Lourdes. At the shrine, the child begged his father to pray for him. His dad prayed aloud, "Lord, give my boy his sight." Instantly, the boy could see. He looked around. He saw flowers, trees, green grass, the open sky. Then he looked into his father's eyes, the eyes that went with the only voice he had known during ten long years of darkness and loneliness.

When he saw his father, do you know what he said?

"Oh boy! Everybody's here!"

This is the spirit of Christmas. Everybody's here! The deep, passionate love of Jesus Christ, our Lord and brother, is the breakthrough of Bethlehem and the heartbeat of the Christian life.

Jesus replied, " You may go. Your son will live." The man took Jesus at his word and departed.

JOHN 4:50

————— 🜊 —————

A central theme in the personal life of Jesus Christ, which lies at the very heart of the revelation that he is, is his growing intimacy with, trust in, and love of his Abba.

After his birth in Bethlehem, Jesus was raised in Nazareth by Mary and Joseph, according to the strict monotheistic tradition of the Jewish community. Like every devout Jew, Jesus prayed the Shema Israel, "Hear, O Israel, the Lord your God is one God" (see Deut. 6:4), three times a day. Jesus was surrounded with the Absolute, dominated by the One, the Eternal, the "I Am Who I Am."

In his human journey, Jesus experienced God in a way that no prophet of Israel had ever dreamed or dared. Jesus was indwelt by the Spirit of the Father, and gave a name for God that would scandalize both the theology and public opinion of Israel. The name that escaped the mouth of the Nazarene Carpenter: *Abba.*

> *Therefore God exalted him to the highest place*
> *and gave him the name that is above every name.*
>
> PHILIPPIANS 2:9

COMING IN GLORY

————————[※]————————

Contemplating the crib (meaning, looking at Jesus while loving him), the Christian's faith flames into joyous expectation that the Christ who came in history will one day come in glory. Paul writes in Colossians: "When Christ, who is your life, appears, then you also will appear with him in glory" (Col. 3:4). Here, Paul refers to a future event. Christmas arouses longing for the Parousia, the Second Coming. It awakens hope in that heralded upheaval, that upcoming earthquake that makes radical discipleship possible, ushering in as it will the ultimate fulfillment of human history.

> *"I am coming soon. Hold on to what you have, so that no one will take your crown."*

REVELATION 3:11

———————[⚛]———————

The faith that Jesus inspired in his disciples had such a profound impact on them that the disciples found it impossible to believe anyone could be equal or greater to him, not even Moses or Elijah, not even Abraham. That a prophet or judge or messiah should come after Jesus and be greater than Jesus was inconceivable. It was not necessary to wait for someone else. Jesus was everything. Jesus was everything the Jews ever had hoped and prayed for. Jesus had fulfilled or was about to fulfill every promise and every prophecy. If anyone is to judge the world in the end, it must be he. If anyone is to be appointed Messiah, King, Lord, Son of God, how could it be anyone but Jesus?

> *On his robe and on his thigh he has this name written:*
> KING OF KINGS AND LORD OF LORDS.
>
> REVELATION 19:16

THE WORD MADE FLESH

————⊠————

One night a dear friend of Roslyn's named Joe McGill was praying over this passage in John: "In the beginning was the Word, and the Word was with God and the Word was God. . . . The Word was made flesh, he lived among us. . . ." (John 1:1, 14). In the bright darkness of faith, he heard Jesus say: "Yes, the Word was made flesh. I chose to enter your broken world and limp through life with you."

On the last day, when we arrive at the Great Mansion in the Sky, many of us will be bloodied, battered, bruised, and limping. But, by God and by Christ, there will be a light in the window and a "welcome home" sign on the door.

> *"Blessed are those who wash their robes, that they may have the right to the tree of life and may go through the gates into the city."*

> REVELATION 22:14

Abba's Child (AC), January 17, January 25–27,
February 3–7, March 2, March 9, March 14,
March 17–20, March 25, April 10, April 20,
April 29, May 2, May 9, May 11–14, May 29,
June 7, June 28, September 9–11, September 17,
September 25, October 7, October 14, October
24, November 9, November 26–27, November
29–30, December 28

The Gentle Revolutionaries (GR), January 5–7,
January 13, January 18–19, January 30, February
24–26, March 5, March 13, March 27, April 11,
April 13–17, April 19, May 18–19, June 21, July
3, July 11, July 20, August 4, August 12, August
18, August 24–25, September 1, September 6,
September 12, September 18, September 27,
October 6, October 8, October 13, October 17,
October 19, October 28, November 2–4

Lion and Lamb (LL), January 1–2, January 4,
February 1, March 1, March 29, March 31, April
2–5, April 18, April 23, April 27, May 1, May
21, May 25–26, May 30, June 5–6, June 10–11,
June 14–15, June 18–20, June 24, June 27, June
29, July 5, July 8, July 12–13, July 15, July
18–19, July 22, July 25–26, July 29, August 1–2,
August 5, August 11, August 15, August 20–23,
August 30, September 2, September 13,
September 16, September 19, September 20,
September 26, October 3, October 5, October
10, October 12, October 18, October 21,
October 29, November 5–6, November 22,
November 25, December 1, December 3,
December 5–6, December 8–20, December
22–27, December 29

Prophets and Lovers (PL), January 16, March 12,
March 28, April 7, May 7, June 12, June 17, June
25, June 30, July 7, July 21, July 27–28, August
13, August 27, August 29, August 31, September
4–5, September 8, September 15, September
21–22, September 29, October 11, October 15,
October 20, October 22, October 26–27,
October 30–31, November 7, November 15,
November 18, November 20

The Ragamuffin Gospel (RG), January 28–29,
February 2, February 8–11, March 8, May 15,
May 17, May 31, June 1, June 13, July 17, August
8, November 4, November 11, November 13,
November 28, December 1

The Signature of Jesus (SJ), January 14, January 21,
February 16, February 29, March 4, March
10–11, March 30, April 28, April 30, May 3–
May 5, September 7, December 1, December 30

Souvenirs of Solitude (SOS), January 11, January
20, January 22, January 24, February 19,
February 21–23, March 15, April 9, April
21–22, April 24–25, May 6, May 11, May 24,
May 28, June 2–3, June 9, June 11, June 22, July
4, July 10, July 16, July 23–24, July 31, August 6,
August 10, August 17, August 26, August 28,
September 24, September 30, October 2,
October 9, October 16, November 1, November
19, November 21, November 23, December 4,
December 21

A Stranger to Self-Hatred (SS), January 3, January
January 12, January 15, January 31, February 2,
March 24, April 6, April 12, May 8, May 27,
June 4, June 8, July 1–2, July 6, July 9, July 14,
July 30, August 3, August 7, August 9, August
14, August 19, September 3, September 14,
September 23, September 28, October 1,
October 4, October 23, October 25, November
8, November 10, November 12, November 14,
November 16

Unpublished (U), January 23, February 12–14,
February 20, February 27, March 2, March 6,
March 7, March 21–23, April 1, April 26, May
16, June 23, June 26, August 16, November 17,
November 24

The Wisdom of Accepted Tenderness (WA), February
15, February 17–18, March 16, March 26, May
20, May 22–23

SOURCES BY DAY

10 SOS, Romans 1:4
11 AC, Matthew 28:7
12 AC, Ezekiel 11:19
13 AC, Matthew 6:14
14 AC, Matthew 9:36
15 RG, Romans 8:35
16 U, John 15:15
17 RG, Mark 7:6–7
18 GR, John 16:7
19 GR, 1 Peter 2:24
20 WA, 1 John 4:12
21 LL, Joel 2:13
22 WA, James 2:14–17
23 WA, 1 John 5:1–2
24 SOS, Luke 22:29–30
25 LL, Romans 15:13
26 LL, Exodus 34:6
27 SS, Psalm 112:4
28 SOS, Proverbs 15:15
29 AC, Jonah 2:10
30 LL, John 5:44
31 U, Isaiah 11:11–12

June

1 RG, Psalm 89:1
2 SOS, James 4:i i
3 SOS, Isaiah 53:5
4 SS, Isaiah 64:6
5 LL, Habakkuk 2:4
6 LL, Psalm 123:1
7 AC, Luke 18:14
8 SS, Galatians 3:13
9 SOS, Psalm 114:1–2
10 LL, Psalm 33:3
11 LL, Matthew 11:29
12 PL, Genesis 19:27
13 RG, Romans 12:3
14 LL, 2 Corinthians 5:20–21
15 LL, Psalm 119:10
16 SOS, Luke 6:20
17 PL, Nehemiah 12:46
18 LL, John 11:33
19 LL, Matthew 5:17
20 LL, 2 Corinthians 8:24
21 GR, Psalm 40:10
22 SOS, Revelation 21:1–2
23 U, Nehemiah 6:15–16
24 LL, Matthew 5:39
25 PL, Matthew 5:22
26 U, Genesis 1:27
27 LL, Matthew 8:13

28 AC, Isaiah 41:11
29 LL, Acts, 19:2
30 PL, Mark 2:27

July

1 SS, 1 Corinthians 13:4–5
2 SS, Ephesians 1:5
3 GR, Matthew 25:40
4 SOS, Revelation 1:12–15
5 LL, 1 Timothy 1:5
6 SS, Mark 12:40
7 PL, Psalm 146:1–2
8 LL, Deuteronomy 8:2
9 SS, Job 13:15–16
10 SOS, Philippians 4:4
11 GR, Ephesians 1:17
12 LL, Deuteronomy 4: 24
13 LL, Corinthians 5: 17
14 SS, Galatians 2:20
15 LL, Proverbs, 29:23
16 SOS, Psalm 51:6
17 RG, Acts 26:17–18
18 LL, Jeremiah 29:11
19 LL, Romans 15:12
20 GR, Isaiah 35:8
21 PL, James 2:13
22 LL, Matthew 27:43
23 SOS, Psalm 139:14
24 SOS, Exodus 2:6
25 LL, John 15:16
26 LL, Psalm 37:4
27 PL, Romans 15:6
28 PL, Ezekiel 33:13
29 LL, 2 Corinthians 4:16
30 SS, Proverbs 11:3
31 SOS, Mark 7:29

August

1 LL, Jeremiah 31:20
2 LL, John 11:35–36
3 SS, Zechariah 7:9
4 GR, 2 Timothy 1:14
5 LL, Isaiah 54:5
6 SOS, Philippians 1:21
7 SS, Isaiah 30:18
8 RG, Matthew 9:25
9 SS, Hebrews 10:22
10 SS, Psalm 27:4
11 LL, Jeremiah 20:9
12 GR, Psalm 10:17

13 PL, Acts 13:39
14 SS, Matthew 12:36
15 LL, Psalm 22:24
16 U, 1 Thessalonians 5:6
17 SS, Genesis 1:31
18 GR, Philippians 3:21
19 SS, Psalm 37:5
20 LL, James 1:27
21 LL, Micah 5:4
22 PL, Galatians 6:2
23 PL, Galatians 6:8
24 GR, Job 32:18
25 GR, Isaiah 56:1
26 SOS, Psalm 51:15
27 PL, Matthew 9:28
28 SOS, Luke 6:26
29 PL, 1 Corinthians 12:12
30 LL, Jeremiah 32:40
31 PL, Luke 5:32

September

1 GR, Matthew 3:17
2 LL, Deuteronomy 31:6
3 SS, 1 John 4:7
4 PL, Zechariah 6:15
5 PL, 1 Corinthians 14:26
6 GR, Acts 4:32
7 SJ, Psalm 65:2
8 PL, 1 Kings 8:23
9 AC, 1 Thessalonians 5:23
10 AC, Proverbs 3:5
11 AC, Deuteronomy 13:17–18
12 GR, Revelation 3:12
13 LL, 1 Corinthians 9:19
14 SS, 1 John 4:18
15 PL, Philippians 1:9–10
16 LL, Revelation 3:16
17 AC, 1 Corinthians 13:4–5
18 GR, Revelation 2:2
19 LL, Psalm 23:2
20 LL, Proverbs 16:19
21 PL, Galatians 2:5
22 PL, Luke 6:35–36
23 SS, Psalm 9:14
24 SOS, Proverbs 17:22
25 AC, 1 Corinthians 7:22
26 LL, 1 Peter 3:8
27 GR, Proverbs 3:6
28 SS, Acts 2:42
29 PL, Matthew 9:29
30 SOS, Matthew 18:4–5

October

1 SS, John 21:13
2 SOS, 1 John 2:16
3 LL, Romans 8:18
4 SS, Hebrews 13:6
5 LL, Philippians 3:3
6 GR, Matthew 4:4
7 AC, Galatians 2:6
8 GR, John 4:34
9 SOS, Galatians 6:15
10 LL, John 2:25
11 PL, Isaiah 41:10
12 LL, Psalm 25:6
13 GR, Ephesians 5:3
14 AC, Ephesians 5:15–16
15 PL, James 2:8–9
16 SOS, 2 Corinthians 8:9
17 GR, Romans 5:6–8
18 LL, Luke 19:8
19 SS, Galatians 3:26–27
20 PL, Matthew 6:8
21 LL, Mark 14:7
22 PL, Matthew 24:13
23 SS, Exodus 20:3
24 AC, 2 Samuel 6:14
25 SS, 1 Thessalonians 2:4
26 PL, Romans 8:15
27 SS, John 21:17
28 GR, Romans 5:1–2
29 LL, Psalm 130:7
30 PL, Matthew 7:1–2
31 PL, Psalm 53:2

November

1 SS, Psalm 86:1–2
2 GR, Psalm 69:16
3 GR, Psalm 108:1
4 RG, Isaiah 12:2
5 LL, John 6:26
6 LL, John 9:25
7 PL, Romans 8:14
8 SS, Psalm 116:16
9 AC, 1 John 3:2–3
10 SS, John 11:27
11 RG, 2 Timothy 2:15
12 SS, Matthew 5:4
13 RG, Romans 3:20
14 SS, Ecclesiastes 7:20
15 PL, Luke 19:39–40
16 SS, Mark 14:38
17 U, Matthew 6:3–4
18 PL, Psalm 8:4
19 SOS, Psalm 55:22
20 PL, Ephesians 2:4–5
21 SOS, Isaiah 51:16
22 LL, Matthew 5:45
23 SOS, Philippians 2:5
24 U, John 5:24
25 LL, Lamentations 3:40
26 AC, Lamentations 3:55–58
27 AC, Psalm 15:1–2
28 RG, Deuteronomy 7:13
29 AC, John 16:27
30 AC, Matthew 25:21

December

1 LL, Matthew 1:23
2 SJ, Philippians 2:12
3 LL, James 4:7
4 SOS, Luke 6:23
5 LL, Ephesians 3:19
6 LL, John 16:23
7 PL, Luke 1:68
8 LL, Luke 2:15
9 LL, 2 Corinthians 13:11
10 LL, Psalm 71:5
11 LL, Psalm 126:2
12 LL, Ephesians 3:12
13 LL, Psalm 73:28
14 LL, Psalm 141:2
15 LL, Psalm 107:29
16 LL, Ezekiel 2:4
17 LL, John 16:33
18 LL, John 12:21
19 LL, 1 Peter 1:21
20 LL, Hebrews 5:2
21 SOS, Revelation 21:4
22 LL, 1 Corinthians 1:2
23 LL, Isaiah 45:23
24 LL, 1 John 4:19
25 LL, Luke 2:12
26 LL, Isaiah 40:18
27 LL, John 4:50
28 AC, Philippians 2:9
29 LL, Revelation 3:11
30 SJ, Revelation 19:16
31 RG, Revelation 22:14

INDEX BY TITLE